MW01228585

ABOUT
FACE

*The True Story of an American Couple in China
Entangled in a Web of Intrigue and Crime*

Carole Sumner Krechman

the three
tomatoes
BOOK PUBLISHING

Published January 2023
ISBN: 979-8-9871051-0-8
Library of Congress Control Number: 2022922651

For information address:
The Three Tomatoes Publishing
6 Soundview Rd.
Glen Cove, NY 11542

www.thethreetomatoespublishing.com

Cover design: Simone Matavlo
Interior design: Susan Herbst

Editor: Cheryl Benton

Dedication

To Sheldon...and our adventure of a lifetime.
Now the exciting story is finally told.

Table of Contents

Preface

"The greatest long-term threat to our nation's information and intellectual property, and to our economic vitality, is the counterintelligence and economic espionage threat from China."
~FBI Director Christopher Wray in remarks delivered to the Hudson Institute, Video Event: China's Attempt to Influence U.S. Institutions, Washington, DC, July 7, 2020

"If I could communicate one thing to the American people...it is that the People's Republic of China poses the greatest threat to America today, and the greatest threat to democracy and freedom worldwide since World War II."
~John Ratcliffe, Director of National Intelligence, *The Wall Street Journal* opinion piece, Dec. 3, 2020

"No more turning a blind eye to Chinese spies in our nuclear labs. No more keeping silent about Chinese slave labor camps."
~Steve Forbes, editor-in-chief, *Forbes Magazine*, CEO Forbes Media

THIS BOOK HAS BEEN a long time coming—over thirty-six years. It is a story that many powerful people in corporate and political circles did not want told then, and perhaps even now, despite warnings about China's threat to our country like the above from our top U.S. intelligence people and others, including Steve Forbes.

The 1970s opened the floodgates to trade and diplomatic relations with China. By the early 1980s, everyone wanted to do business in the potentially largest consumer marketplace in the world with an untapped inexpensive labor market. Today, the list of U.S. companies doing business in China is a "who's who" of our most venerable institutions.

In the early 1980s, with the encouragement and mentorship of Dr. Armand Hammer, founder and chairman of Occidental Petroleum Company, my late husband, Sheldon Krechman, and I were presented with the opportunity to expand our U.S. roller rink business into China. We excitedly pursued the opportunity—two innocents abroad in an exotic and unknown land. We eventually abandoned all hope of building a chain of roller rinks, but through a convoluted series of events became involved in a large and complicated joint venture with the Chinese to build a five-star modern office and hotel complex and conference center in downtown Beijing—the first of its kind in China. Juxtaposed against the ancient world of Beijing, it was a towering beacon of light signifying a China that was at long last stepping into the twentieth century.

Over the ensuing years, and amidst a variety of adventures from the time we first entered China to the completion of the hotel and the aftermath, we became ensnared in a web that included the most ruthless of China's security agencies, the FBI, the CIA, and a cast of characters who seemed straight out of a Hollywood spy thriller. In a national discussion of Chinese misdeeds that is sometimes abstract, our story is personal and full of real people. For us, the security and espionage apparatus of the People's Republic of China has a human face. In fact, the multiple meanings of the word "face" make it a useful metaphor for describing the reality of the People's Republic.

In the mid-eighties, after several intrigue-filled years of doing business in China, we told our story to a top literary agent who was certain we would find a major publisher. But as it turned out, no one wanted to touch a story that exposed the truths about doing business in China.

By the late-1990s, many people, like *The New York Times*'s William Safire, started to sound the alarm to the American public that the People's Republic of China had brazenly stolen our technology and exploited the naivete and financial ambition of our politicians and businessmen. In June 1998, the Cox Commission was created by the U.S. House of Representatives to investigate whether technology or information was transferred to the People's Republic of China that may have contributed to the enhancement of the nuclear-armed intercontinental ballistic missiles or to the manufacture of weapons of mass destruction. The controversial report was challenged by many in politics, and people in very high places tried to quash the recommendations.

It was in this new environment that Sheldon and I revisited the idea of a book, and he started putting our story and memories on paper. But as they say, life got in the way, and the book took a back seat. In 2020, during the worldwide COVID pandemic, Sheldon died unexpectedly—not from COVID directly but inadvertently, from being in a hospital overwhelmed with COVID cases. In the weeks and months of grief that followed, my thoughts turned to the incredible life and adventures we had shared, especially our years in China. As I went through his belongings, I came across the draft memories he had written, and that's when I knew that now was the time to tell our story.

Over the years, we came to realize that China would always be a place of mystery and unanswered questions. It is a land of contradictions with many faces. We experienced the best of China, its people, its children, and its rich cultural history, and we also experienced the worst—treachery, subterfuge, and criminal activities. The Chinese have perfected the art of manipulation. We always knew we were being manipulated but often did not know by whom or why. This is our story. While it has been more than thirty years since we left China, our experience is as relevant today as it was then. It's a cautionary tale to anyone doing business in China.

About Face

Who's Who and What's What

Asia Hotel Joint Venture—The compulsory agreement between World China Trade and the Chinese to build the Asia Hotel. All foreign businesses in China must operate under a joint venture agreement.

Denny Barnes—U.S. commercial attache, U.S. Embassy in Beijing; purportedly a CIA operative

Richard Chen—director of Occidental Petroleum's China affairs

Dr. Armand Hammer—chairman of the board and founder of Occidental Petroleum who arranged our first trip to China in 1983

Ford Hart III—head of China desk, department of state, Beijing, China; senior military analyst

Paul Hebner—an executive of Occidental Petroleum, one of the first three employees and confidant of Dr. Hammer

Saul Leonard—advisor and trusted friend; partner in an international accounting firm

James R. Lilly—ambassador to China after Tiananmen Square (1992); former head of the CIA in South Korea

Madam Deng Ling—daughter of Deng Xiaoping, good friend of Mr. Yu Xue Wen, president of World China Trade (our company)

Lawrence Liu—president, Los Angeles Guangzhou Sister City Society

Mayor Yi Long Ki—personal secretary to Chairman Mao; former mayor of Beijing

Winston & Betty Bao Lord—U.S. ambassador to China and his Chinese wife

Zhang Xiao Lu (Ms. Zhang)—senior interpreter for the Chinese government; assistant to Mr. Yu Xue Wen and manager of American affairs for World China Trade

Robert Messemer—special agent, FBI, Los Angeles

Wang Fu Sheng (Mr. Wang)—chairman of the Asia Hotel joint venture, former chief of the Beijing Ministry of Public Security; referred to as "the Mafia Boss of Beijing" by the FBI

World China Trade—the American company formed in China by Sheldon and Carole Krechman

Yu Xue Wen (Mr. Yu)—president of World China Trade (our company); therefore, the first Chinese man to become president of an American company based in China

Charles Wrangham—vice chairman, Standard Chartered Asia Bank (Hong Kong)

Ambassador Ma Yu Zen—counsel general (with ambassador status) to China consul in Los Angeles

Deng Xiaoping—head of the Chinese communist party

The following senators wrote letters on our behalf to the Chinese government. These letters protested the actions of the Chinese regarding our joint venture.

Senator Barbara Boxer—California senator

Senator Dianne Feinstein—California senator

Senator John McCain—Arizona senator

Senator John Glenn—Ohio senator

Let China sleep, for when she wakes,
she will shake the world.
~Napoleon Bonaparte

About Face

~1~

The Dinner

Learning without thought is deceptive;
thought without learning is perilous.
~ Chinese Proverb

IN THE FALL OF 1982, my husband, Sheldon, and I were looking forward to celebrating the opening of our first roller skating rink in an African American enclave near downtown Los Angeles. It was a beautiful, large, modern rink, and, based on the positive community response, we were looking forward to building these skating centers in African American communities around the country. Amid our excitement for this new entrepreneurial venture, we received a dinner invitation from Dr. Armand Hammer, the chairman of Occidental Petroleum (Oxy). We had no idea that this seemingly chance dinner would be the start of a life-altering journey into China.

Our dinner invitation came about from a convoluted, unlikely series of relationships spanning several decades and two generations between my father, B. Allen Sumner, and his accountant, Sam Shapiro. Sam was married to the niece of a colorful, controversial entrepreneur—Armand Hammer. Dr. Hammer was a physician, adventurer, and friend of communists. This New York-born capitalist and international dealmaker had moved west to set up an oil exploration company.

When he arrived in California in 1956, he bought the tiny Occidental Petroleum Company, located in a small office on Melrose Avenue in Los Angeles. When he needed an accountant, he hired his niece's husband. Soon after that, Sam called my parents to invite them to dinner with Dr. Hammer. The dinner was an occasion for Dr. Hammer to promote his fledgling petroleum company, which needed investors. He was a master salesman, and by the time dinner was over, my dad and Sam had agreed to split one share for $25,000 a piece—a great deal of money at the time. There were only nine other investors in the company.

Exploratory drilling commenced a few months later. On their fifth attempt, the fledgling company, with three full-time employees, tapped into the largest natural gas reservoir in the history of the state, the Arbuckle field. One of the three employees, Paul Hebner, remained with Dr. Hammer as his closest confidant and secretary of the corporation and a member of the board of directors until Dr. Hammer's death. My father continued his investments into Occidental, and as the company grew, he kept in touch with Dr. Hammer, but mostly, his relationship, going forward, was with Paul Hebner.

My dad would see Paul at the annual meeting but had not had much of a relationship with him for a long while; so, it was a pleasant surprise when Paul called, inviting him and my mother to a dinner arranged by Dr. Hammer in the dining room at Occidental Petroleum. He also asked how I was doing, and my father told him about our roller skating venture. Paul then suggested that we also come to the dinner and meet Dr. Hammer. I had met him just once when I was a teenager, and we were thrilled to be included.

So, by virtue of this unusual chain of relationships, we arrived at the Occidental building on a beautiful fall evening as guests of the world-famous eccentric octogenarian who, as it turned out, had an interest in China. To say the least, it was an unlikely circumstance—and would lead to an even more unlikely series of events.

Just getting to Armand Hammer's dining room was an event in itself. His office building was part fortress and part museum. It lacked the crenelated towers and portcullis of a medieval castle but certainly had the functional equivalent of a moat full of alligators: alarm systems, security cameras, and poker-faced men with guns. The reason: It was a citadel for art. Dr. Hammer owned a private collection that would be the envy of anyone, anywhere. The tight security protected not only his person but also his possessions. After showing identification and clearing security, we took the elevator to the top floor and walked silently to the dining room, passing walls decorated with original paintings by Rembrandt, Van Gogh, Cezanne, Monet, Picasso, and other great masters.

As we approached the entrance to the dining room, the hushed quiet of the hallway gave way to the cheerful voices of people engaged in conversation. Through the double doors, we could see a large, opulent room furnished with Chippendale antiques, green leather chairs, heavy velvet drapes, and more paintings. Nine tables stood neatly arranged in the center of the room, set with fine China and silver flatware. The windows on the west wall looked out on the Pacific Ocean and the Santa Monica mountains.

People had gathered in small groups around the perimeter of the room, sipping champagne and drinking cocktails served by uniformed waiters. This was a collection of people with long, historic ties to Occidental Petroleum. We looked around until we found my parents, fortified ourselves with champagne, and were taken to meet the Great Man.

Dr. Hammer was an imposing presence but not because of his physical stature. He was a tiny, slight figure, old as Methuselah, and little more than five and a half feet tall with big, coke-bottle glasses, a ready smile, and a commanding demeanor that conveyed a sense of supreme confidence, high intelligence, and personal power. This was the man who had bargained with Lenin, traded with Stalin, served as an intermediary between the U.S. and the USSR, built a hugely successful petroleum company, hobnobbed with heads of state, and inhabited news headlines for a generation.

Much to our surprise, he began to ask us about our roller rink business. We realized Dr. Hammer had more in mind than just polite conversation as the questions continued. Then, after a pause, he told us about all the children in China who would enjoy roller skating, asked us if we had ever traveled there, and suggested it would be a very good idea for us to go to that country and see what business opportunities might present themselves.

We stood there transfixed, saying little, as he continued to persuade us for several more minutes. It was obvious that Dr. Hammer had invited us to this dinner for a reason. This was not a spontaneous conversation; he had an agenda.

We really hadn't thought about expanding our business into China until that moment, but we found the prospect very exciting. But on the way home, my father told us not to get our hopes up that Dr. Hammer would help us in any way. Occidental Petroleum was an energy company, and our roller skating business would be of no interest to him.

That didn't stop us from thinking about what he'd said about China. The next day (Saturday), we called my father at least five times. Maybe Dr. Hammer really was interested in us. During each call, my father repeatedly reminded us how much he loved us—the equivalent of a pat on the head to a naive child—while also reminding us that we were kidding ourselves to think that Dr. Hammer had a genuine interest in roller skating.

We conceded that he was right. There was no rational reason to think that Occidental Petroleum Company would want to promote roller skating in the People's Republic of China. Nevertheless, we spent many hours that weekend dreaming about the possibilities. On Sunday night, as we retired to our bedroom, our thoughts oscillated between our fantasies and the level-headed rationality of my father.

At 9:00 a.m. on Monday morning, we received a telephone call at home from Dr. Hammer's private secretary. She told us to expect a call at 10:00 a.m. from a Mr. Richard Chen, whom she identified as Occidental's director of China affairs. When we asked about the purpose of the call, she told us that Mr. Chen was in charge of all China business for Dr. Hammer and that he had personally spoken to Mr. Chen about our roller skating centers. Dr. Hammer wanted us to talk to Mr. Chen in the hope that we might go to China.

Richard Chen worked as the interpreter for the United States government when China's Chairman Deng Xiao Peng came to the United States for the first time and visited with Jimmy Carter. Several months later, at a dinner party, Richard met Dr. Hammer and subsequently introduced him to Chairman Deng Xiao Peng and the Chinese government. It wasn't long afterward that Dr. Hammer hired Richard as the director of China affairs for Oxy.

After our call with Dr. Hammer's secretary ended, we just looked at each other in stunned disbelief. An hour later, another call came through. This time, it was Richard Chen on the line. He asked if we could join him for lunch at the Occidental building in two hours. Of course, we agreed, but things were happening so fast, we hardly had time to think.

What happened next seemed very strange at the time, and even more so after we had time to reflect on it later. We arrived at the Occidental building and checked in with the guard in the lobby who called upstairs and then directed us to the bank of elevators behind him. But before we could push the button to summon a car, Dr. Hammer appeared, seemingly from nowhere, and motioned for us to follow him to his private elevator. On the way up to the executive floors, he asked us to listen very carefully to Richard Chen and report to him, privately, as much information as we could. He spoke to us in quiet tones as though we were trusted confidants. Strange, since we had only just met him three days before.

The elevator stopped on the fifteenth floor, and Dr. Hammer stepped out. As the doors closed, removing our view of the odd, small man, we just stared ahead silently, questions swirling in our heads. *What was this all about? What information?* It was one of those events that was so bizarre, you had to wonder afterward whether it really happened at all. The elevator rose one more floor, and we emerged into the art-filled hallway and made our way to the now-familiar dining room.

Richard Chen was waiting for us near the door. We introduced ourselves, sat down, and as lunch was served, made small talk.

Richard told us how he came to be hired by Dr. Hammer as his director of China affairs.

According to Chen, Dr. Hammer was interested in doing business in China and had his eyes on a large coal-mining concession. After briefing us on their China involvement, Richard got around to asking about our roller skating business. As we described the workings of our company, he listened with rapt interest and then asked if he could visit our offices the next day.

On Tuesday morning, Chen appeared at our offices and spent nearly the whole day with us. He left in the late afternoon, promising to get back to us shortly.

Three months passed, during which we heard nothing from Dr. Hammer or Chen. It didn't seem surprising. After all, why would he take interest in a roller skating business? Perhaps, if we had shared some kind of friendship or other strong relationship, his interest in helping us would have made more sense. But we had met him only once—twice if you counted the mysterious elevator encounter.

We could only shake our heads. Dr. Hammer, a man with the ambition and financial means to conduct business on a billion-dollar scale, seemed hardly the type to give a moment's notice to a recreational business run by a couple he hardly knew. The unusual request he made of us in the elevator that day receded in our memories, even though, years later, it would explain part of the puzzle. At that time, we had no context for it. Our enthusiasm for China obliterated all rational analysis of the situation. We knew that Dr. Hammer had a reputation for eccentricity and let it go at that.

Then, on a December evening, we received a call at home from Paul Hebner inviting us to attend a dinner at the University of Southern California, hosted by the Guangzhou Sister City Society. Guangzhou, China, is the sister city of Los Angeles. Occidental had purchased a table, and we were to be guests of the company.

On the following Saturday evening, we drove to the USC campus to attend the dinner. Paul was the host at our table; among the guests was a man named Lawrence Liu, the president of the Sister City Association. Paul introduced us to Liu and then said something quite unexpected. "The Krechmans will travel with you to China next March." Our reaction was a mixture of surprise and excitement. Of course, the obvious question still remained: Why? In our enthusiasm, we didn't give it a moment's thought. A free trip to China? Who cared why we were going? Paul Hebner told us that Dr. Hammer would like to see us to discuss the trip.

A week later, we met with Dr. Hammer who told us he had arranged a trip to China for a group of American artists and they would be accompanied by several Los Angeles officials, including city councilman David Cunningham; Bea Lavery, protocol chief for Mayor Tom Bradley; and Warren Thomas, the director of the Los Angeles Zoo. The artists were supposed to meet their counterparts in several cities in China, and Thomas was along for the ride, with two lesser pandas who would be exchanged for two greater pandas in Guangzhou.

That night, in a conspiratorial tone, Dr. Hammer suddenly leaned forward and told us that we were not to disclose to anyone our purpose for going on the trip. That would be easy since we didn't have a clue ourselves. He went on to say that we would meet several Occidental employees who would assist us in anything we might want or need. He told us to keep our eyes open and look for opportunities to forge relationships with Chinese individuals.

We were then shuttled from his office to meet with Lawrence Liu. He told us not to tell David Cunningham, a friend of ours—or anyone else, for that matter—that we would be on the flight until we arrived at the airport.

About Face

~2~

Welcome to the
People's Republic of China

A journey of a thousand miles begins with a single step.
~ Chinese Proverb

A FEW WEEKS LATER, in March 1983, we embarked on our first trip to China. We left LA en route to the Narita Airport outside of Tokyo and then traveled to Hong Kong with a contingent of artists, two politicians, a zoo director, Lawrence Liu, two lesser pandas, and a couple of Occidental employees. Cunningham never asked us why we were part of the entourage, but even if he had, we wouldn't have had an answer for him.

We spent two months traveling the country, meeting a great many people and visiting the Oxy offices in Guangzhou and Beijing. Little did we know that this would be the first of fifty-seven trips we would take to China over the next nine years.

On the flight over, Liu began teaching us all a new game, which he called Chinese poker. The essence of the game was arbitrary and involved a lot of spontaneous rule-making. Whenever there might be a disadvantage to Liu, he would introduce a new rule. Whenever any-one would challenge him—and our friend David Cunningham often did—he would reply that this was Chinese poker, and the rules were different. I eventually nicknamed him "New Rule Liu."

We had no idea at the time, but Liu was teaching us more than a game of cards. The flight and layover in Narita were comfortable for everyone except Warren Thomas who spent the night at the airport, sleeping with the two pandas in quarantine.

After a four-hour flight from Narita, we arrived in the mainland of China in Hong Kong, still a British colony at the time. The old Kai Tak Airport, built on a landfill, projected out into Hong Kong harbor and was infamous territory to many pilots who considered it one of the most difficult approaches in the world. After making a slow, steep low-altitude turn next to a mountain, the pilot leveled out the wings and immediately lined us up with the runway. We were so low, I could see people watching their television sets through the windows of apartment buildings below. *They must all be deaf,* I remember thinking at the time. I breathed a sigh of relief as we touched down.

From Hong Kong, we were scheduled to lay over for one night and take the train into Guangzhou (formerly Canton) the next afternoon. We gathered outside the airport terminal and were bussed to our hotel. The next morning, we boarded the buses again and left for Kowloon's Hung Hom train station to take the non-stop express run into the People's Republic. We were told the trip would take about three hours.

There were two daily non-stops to Guangzhou, and we were scheduled to take the 1:00 p.m. train. Our polymorphous mix of artists, politicians, and pandas boarded without incident. The train was clean, with a combination of wood paneling and painted metal inside, and lace curtains flowed over the windows of the various interior compartments. It looked slightly anachronistic, like an American train car from the 1950s. As soon as we were underway, servers brought out hot tea, and we settled in for the ride.

It took about an hour to pass through the countryside outside Kowloon, an area known to the British as the New Territories, and cross the border into China at Lowu. From there, we entered Guangdong Province, and the country outside our window became increasingly rural. We passed rice fields and vegetable farms, their boundaries defined by a network of small levees. Farm workers labored in the flooded rice fields, and oxen pulled plows through carefully tended vegetable plots. Occasionally, we would see a gaggle of geese or a herd of ducks waddling en masse down a levy road, driven by a man with a long bamboo stick.

We sat enthralled, taking it all in and thinking little about the purpose of our trip. Lunch was cooked in an adjacent car over a wood-burning stove. We made small talk with our fellow guests and shared a meal with several of them. The food was delicious: a chicken soup with dumplings that reminded me of Jewish matzo balls and kreplach.

No one in our entourage seemed curious about our presence. Everyone was so taken by the exotic scenery that the conversation seldom strayed far from the experience of the moment. For the time being, we were awestruck tourists and nothing more.

The filtered sunlight of early spring made the whole landscape seem magical. As we gradually approached Guangzhou, heading roughly northeast, the sun began to inch toward the horizon in the late afternoon, and outside the left windows of the train, we could see the light reflected off the water in the fields. As we reached the outskirts of the city, we passed more and more clusters of housing. Some of the homes looked very old. Small, walled compounds contained what looked like ancient, well-worn houses, drab and gray, with tile roofs.

Soon we passed over the Pearl River and found ourselves within the confines of the city. The view outside our window was no longer pastoral. Houses and buildings, both old and new, were packed together, cheek to jowl, along narrow streets jammed with pedestrians in gray or blue Mao suits, bicycles and tricycles laden with impossible loads, tiny gas-powered jitneys and diesel-powered trucks, and a few horse-drawn carts.

It was an incredible scene. How could so many people and vehicles fit into such narrow streets? It made Manhattan look deserted by comparison. Finally, passing across the eastern edge of the city, gawking all the way, we pulled into the Guangzhou Station. It was a little after four in the afternoon.

On the platform was a large delegation of Chinese officials, artists, and a representative from the Guangzhou Zoo. As we stepped off the train, we were overwhelmed. There were hundreds of people on the platform, with food stands everywhere and people selling everything from lotus leaves filled with rice and various meats to fresh fruit.

The welcoming party greeted each of us, one by one, and we gave and received a business card at each introduction. We had been told that it was impolite to receive a business card and not take at least ten to twenty seconds to study it. The smell of the place was very different from anything we had experienced before—exotic and pungent.

After a short welcome speech, Mr. Shi, the deputy mayor of Guangzhou, invited us all to a banquet to be held that evening. He was dressed in a blue Mao suit that I had only seen before in magazines and films. In this context, I realized it was more than a symbol of proletarian modesty, it was actually a very comfortable and practical way to dress. Loose-fitting, it had lots of large pockets, and its cotton fabric was perfect for the hot and humid climate.

A moment later, as if on cue, everyone began shaking hands. The whole group of Chinese nodded and said, "nee-how" to each of us. We quickly learned that this meant "hello," and reciprocated. We all shook hands, smiled, and then boarded a large van they had brought for us. Three other smaller vans had also arrived for the welcoming delegation. All the vans were of Japanese manufacture, well-worn and several years old. As far as we could tell, everything in China seemed well-worn.

The streets were teeming with people and bicycles; it reminded me of an ant farm. As we drove through the streets, the sea of people would open in front of our vans and close again behind us. After a short ride to the Dong Fang Hotel, we parked, got out, and shook hands with everyone all over again. We were learning quickly that the Chinese have many protocol rituals that seem redundant and tedious to most Westerners.

≈≈≈≈≈

Our room at the Dong Fang Hotel was very plain, with drab walls. It was sparsely furnished, with double beds; a small, wooden console mounted between them; two chairs; a small, low table; and a wardrobe. The console between the beds was replete with several mysterious switches and was built in a style reminiscent of bad American furniture from the fifties. The bathroom had a tile floor that had not been scrubbed in a long while, a bathtub with a hose attached to the water tap, and no shower.

For some reason, that console attracted Sheldon's attention. Some of the switches were unlabeled while others had Chinese captions. Sheldon had an inquisitive nature, especially when it came to electronics or small electrical appliances, and he tried them all. He decided to look at the wiring inside and determine the function of the various switches. He took out his small leather bag with a set of miniature tools, and after about fifteen minutes of removing multiple screws from the console, he found a very sophisticated, miniature microphone.

He was familiar with these types of devices. Years before, he had been in the electronics business and had sold similar devices to the FBI. Our first reaction was to laugh at the audacity of it, but we weren't totally surprised. We looked at each other silently, knowing that it would be a mistake to disturb any of the electronics. Sheldon reassembled everything, and then we went out into the hallway to talk.

We decided to try a little test to see if the microphone was working. We wanted to be as subtle as possible, but we wanted to make sure. In 1983, it was virtually impossible to get Western over-the-counter medicines in China. We went back into the room, and Sheldon said to me with great emphasis, "Sweetheart, I am really sorry. For some reason, I forgot to bring the *Tylenol*. I know you need it for your *back pain*. Maybe we can find some." After his little performance, we made small talk as we changed clothes and prepared for the banquet.

≈≈≈≈≈

The next morning, we met with our group and Lawrence Liu and then were taken to an artists' studio. We met with several of the Chinese artists, and our group exchanged art with them. It was very interesting. The artists got along very well; both sides were very eager because ours was the first group of American artists to visit China. We actually met China's favorite artist, Liu Hi Sui. He was ninety years old and quite honored and respected throughout China.

That afternoon, a ceremony was held at the Guangzhou Zoo where we officially exchanged the lesser pandas we had brought from the United States for the pandas that were going to be shipped back to Los Angeles.

After the visit to the zoo and the panda exchange, the vans reappeared, and we found ourselves in a caravan again, driving from place to place until we arrived at an adult recreation center. Sheldon found the center decidedly uninteresting. We had been told that we were not to go anywhere without a guide, but I wasn't surprised to see him slip out the door. I just hoped he would find his way back.

More than an hour passed, and I was relieved when Sheldon returned. Our Chinese guide was a bit perturbed and instructed him not to go out again on his own.

When we got back to the van, he quietly told me he had walked for several blocks, looking in shop windows, fascinated by everything he saw. After a few minutes, he came to a Chinese apothecary, where, to his surprise, one of the clerks spoke a bit of English. He asked him about purchasing some Motrin and was told there were many Chinese herbal medicines that would have a better effect. He said the only Western analgesic available was aspirin, and even that was rare. He had never heard of Tylenol.

Later that night, we were taken to another banquet. As we stood in the foyer of the immense restaurant, Sheldon asked our guide if he could tell us where we might purchase a pain reliever for me. He smiled and said that it was just a coincidence, but he happened to have something with him. With a little flourish, he pulled a large bottle of Tylenol out of his pocket like a rabbit out of a hat.

≈≈≈≈

Before we were seated for dinner, we had a brief time socializing and met a number of people. One of them was Keith Anderson, the manager of the Guangzhou office for Occidental Petroleum. Keith wasn't hard to find. He was a big man with red hair, a ruddy complexion, and freckles. In a sea of small, dark-haired Chinese, he stood out like a beacon. He told us that he had received a communique from the Oxy office in Los Angeles that we would be arriving and offered to help us in any way he could. He then asked us to meet him for lunch the next day.

Our Chinese hosts had arranged the dinner seating assignments to alternate between Americans and Chinese. The tables were set with China (what else!), chopsticks (forks for the wimps), and three glasses: one for beer, a second for a sweet red wine, and a third—a small liqueur glass filled with a clear liquid.

The small one, as Sheldon would soon learn, was for a Chinese version of Kentucky white lightning called Moutai, not to be confused with Mai Tai. If you put one of those little Mai Tai cocktail umbrellas in a glass of Moutai, the wood would probably dissolve. What a difference a vowel can make.

Moutai, made from sorghum, tastes to the uninitiated like gasoline. It was famously used to welcome President Nixon on his historic trip to China in 1972.

Soon after we were seated, a Chinese official proposed a toast of friendship. He was holding the little glass of Moutai and indicated that we should all do the same. He made the toast, downed the glass in one gulp, and said loudly, "Ganbei!"

Fortunately, women are not expected to participate in this male display of machismo. I glanced over at Sheldon, who did not normally drink alcoholic beverages, and saw he had emptied his glass so as not to insult our hosts. He started to cough, and the Chinese official next to him just smiled and waved his hand, and his glass was filled again.

The food at our banquet was incredible. There were twenty-one separate courses, the first of which was molded or assembled into various shapes like edible sculptures.

There were various meats, vegetables, fish, crustaceans, and dishes that involved creatures I had never seen before. Every time a new dish was served, the Chinese person next to me would pick out the choicest morsel and put it on my plate. Somewhere around the fifteenth course, I thought I could eat no more. Up to that point, I had tasted everything offered, even the delicacies of indeterminate origin. Sometimes it was just best not to know.

Unfortunately, the next course was considered by our hosts to be particularly special, a highlight of the banquet. It appeared to be an immense slug, the size of a sausage. For a moment, I thought the slimy-looking thing might still be alive. I was told it was a delicacy only served at very special banquets since it was very expensive. They assured me it had been cooked. What an honor, I thought, as I contemplated putting a piece of the oversized gastropod in my mouth. I took a bite. It tasted just as it looked. I couldn't get it down. My host thought I was a bit demented when it came to food. Who wouldn't delight in such a delicacy?

By the end of the banquet, we were stuffed with rich food, and I realized Sheldon was drunk from the Moutai. Not wanting to insult our hosts, he had slammed two more shots, and the combination of potent alcohol and jet lag had left him woozy. We were ready to be taken right back to our hotel and just fall into bed. This turned out to be wishful thinking.

As we walked—slowly—back to the restaurant's foyer, we were diverted from the rest of the group. Before dinner, we had been briefly introduced to the city architect of Guangzhou and the deputy mayor. Now, both men stood in the foyer, waiting for us. Through a translator, it was explained that they had planned an after-dinner tour of the city for us so that we could look at potential sites for a roller rink. I looked at Sheldon and knew he was trying his best to look grateful for the gesture.

They took us all through the city, pointing out sites they thought suitable for roller skating complexes. After about an hour of driving, Sheldon was really woozy and having a hard time concentrating, but we knew it would be insulting to complain. Finally, we drove to the White Swan Hotel, the newest hotel in Guangzhou and located on the river.

The architect who accompanied us had designed the White Swan Hotel and proudly wanted to show it off. We were ushered into a private lounge with couches and started talking about the hotel. I took an interest in the design and construction, owing to my degree in architecture. I didn't realize then that Sheldon was really feeling the effects of the Moutai until he got up to go to the bathroom and looked quite unsteady on his feet. I was relieved when one of the Chinese men went with him to make sure he didn't fall along the way and could find his way back.

When he returned, it was obvious he was in distress. Finally, one of the officials acknowledged this, and through the interpreter, indicated that he had something to relieve my husband's dizziness. Reaching into his pocket, he pulled out a bottle of Tylenol.

We never found out whether the Chinese realized that we had set up a test for them or whether that was their way of signaling that they knew exactly what was being said between us in our private conversations. The more time we spent in China, however, the more respect we gained for the Chinese and their talent for surveillance.

The next day, Sheldon woke up determined not to repeat the experience of the night before. He had to learn how to survive a banquet, perform the customary toasts, and retain the use of enough brain cells to function socially. He later learned the Chinese trick of replacing Moutai (a clear beverage) with water and pouring the real stuff out on the floor. Over the ensuing years, he became quite an experienced Moutai drinker and could gulp down nine or ten shots in a sitting. He eventually got to the point where he could engage in a Moutai drinking contest with our Chinese hosts.

But the morning after the banquet, he had cotton mouth and a dull headache as we left the hotel in the late morning for the Guangzhou office of Occidental Petroleum to see the Great Redhead, Keith Anderson.

≈≈≈≈≈

If the night before had seemed disorienting because of all the alcohol imbibed, the day after would prove equally disorienting, only for different reasons. It wasn't clear to us why we were meeting with Anderson. We had vague instructions from Dr. Hammer to keep our eyes open and report back to him, but what were we looking for? When we arrived, Anderson asked us a series of questions. What was our relationship with Occidental? With Dr. Hammer? We told him as little as possible, which was easy, of course, because we knew next to nothing.

At one point in our conversation, he pointed to the light fixture on the ceiling above us. When Occidental rented the office, the Chinese had installed the tenant improvements. When the construction was finished, and Anderson took possession of the keys, he dropped by one Friday evening with another Oxy employee, an American. No one was in the building. While they were standing under the light fixture, Anderson commented that the paint color on the walls was not what they had selected. Monday morning, when they returned, the office had been repainted.

"Welcome to the People's Republic of China," he said pointedly. We smiled at each other but didn't mention the Tylenol incident. Then, lowering his voice, he looked right at us and informed us that we were being used, both by Occidental Petroleum and the Chinese government. Anderson then told us that Occidental and China were embroiled in a difficult negotiation regarding a joint venture to build and operate a large, open-pit coal mine in Shaanxi Province. Our presence in China, he said, was somehow related to this negotiation. We responded to this revelation with blank stares. Though we had no idea what he was talking about, we were beginning to realize that we might be pawns in a very big game.

The Oxy office, built on the top floor of the Dong Fang Hotel, was, by Chinese standards, very opulent. In those days, every foreign company with offices in China was required to hire Chinese citizens, and the Chinese would always put in one or more informants whose duty was to report to the Ministry of Public Security.

As we were leaving the office that day, one of Oxy's Chinese employees followed us into the hallway and said in English, "The journey of a thousand miles begins with the first step—and you both have taken the first step." It was just another inscrutable message on a trip that was, for the most part, inexplicable.

We left the Oxy offices in deep thought, but we were still so enthralled to be in China that we figured that no matter what happened, the experience would still be invaluable.

About Face

~3~

Balloons, Balloons, Balloons

But the true voyagers are only those who leave.
Just to be leaving; hearts light, like balloons...
~Charles Baudelaire

B EFORE WE LEFT ON our trip, we had decided that we would bring
something to China that would make a good impression; something surprising and out of the ordinary. Since we were in a business that catered to children, we decided to bring balloons. We had
packed two thousand of them, all imprinted with our logo, "World on
Wheels."

In the United States, if you went for a walk and approached a
strange child with a balloon, people might think you were a child mo-
lester. Not so in China. The children there were not conditioned to
fear strangers. We walked out into the streets of Guangzhou with a
camera and a bag full of balloons and sought out every child we could
find. The result was an unexpected joy.

We noticed children romping around in a small park near the
Oxy office. We picked out a nearby group and approached a little
China doll—a girl about five or six years old. She was chubby with
long pigtails and wore pants that were split up the middle in back. As
we learned, Chinese children at that age have the back of their pants

29

slit so they can urinate in the gutters if necessary. She looked up at us with wonder in her eyes, and her mother, aunt, uncle, and all her friends looked on also. We were unlike anyone she had ever seen.

Sheldon blew up a red balloon, and I squatted down and handed it to her. Her eyes went wide. Putting her hands to her mouth, she squealed with absolute joy. She had never seen a balloon before. Suddenly, a mob of children surrounded us, squealing and laughing. I tied the balloon with a long piece of string, and the little girl went running through the park, balloon in tow, a throng of children behind her. I felt like the Pied Piper. We spent a joyous afternoon blowing up balloons to the delight of children and adults alike and then retired to our hotel, exhausted.

≈ ≈ ≈ ≈ ≈

The next day, we asked Lawrence Liu if he could take us on a private driving tour of the city. We wanted to see it in the daylight—and Sheldon was curious as to how it looked sober. He arranged a car and driver for the three of us. As we moved slowly down a one-way street, Sheldon spotted a crudely drawn sign, the only one we had seen in English, which said, "Computers." He asked Lawrence to stop the car so we could visit the store. Sheldon was something of a computer expert and was curious to see what they were selling. The car came to a stop, and Sheldon asked if we could have fifteen minutes to look. Liu laughed and said, of course—we could have all the time we wanted.

We expected the car to wait, but after we got out, it became clear that Liu planned to leave. Sheldon looked at him through the open window and told him we didn't know where we were, much less how to get back to our hotel. Liu just smiled enigmatically and said, "I'm sure you won't have any trouble." At that, the car drove away, and a swarm of people closed the gap behind it. We were left standing in the middle of the street.

We had already been told that foreigners were required to always have a guide with them and were forbidden to go out alone. Sheldon had already been reprimanded. As we would later learn, the guides served a dual purpose—they protected state security and kept tourists from being swallowed up in the confusing complexity of the city.

Without such a guide, we felt free but vulnerable. There were no cabs, no comprehensible public transportation, no street signs in English, we had no map, and no one spoke our language. After pondering this for a moment, we walked over to the computer store.

The computer sign was very crude, handwritten on a large, thick sheet of rice paper and tacked to the facade of the store. The store itself was tiny and staffed by three adults and two small children. Inside, a couple of personal computers of unknown provenance—probably Hong Kong—and a few miscellaneous components were on display. The store owners gestured for us to sit down and offered us a cup of tea. We heard the word "qweilo" (round-eyed barbarian) mentioned a few times, but mostly, they just stared silently at us.

We sat there uncomfortably for a few minutes. The children were playing quietly in one corner, so we blew up two balloons and gave one to each child. This simple gesture changed the whole attitude of everyone in the store. We were instantly given the status of visiting relatives.

One of the shopkeepers, it turned out, spoke a bit of English after all, but went out to get a friend who was more proficient. He not only brought his friend but some fresh Chinese pastry for us too. The new person was a retired pharmacist who had taken English courses, and we were able to communicate fairly well. Meanwhile, about fifteen kids had poured into that tiny store, all wanting balloons.

One of the Chinese clerks asked us to take off our shoes. We then followed him into a side room, where we met six people busy translating English computer books into Chinese. They could not speak English yet were laboriously working through operating manuals and reference books with the help of well-thumbed English to Chinese dictionaries spread out on the table. They were writing out the translations by hand.

If you have ever read the instructions for a Chinese consumer product or toy manufactured in the eighties, you can guess what the quality of the translation was like. Only, in this case, it was a bad Chinese approximation of good English syntax. The process was clearly excruciatingly slow, letter by letter, word by word. As we would learn, however, the Chinese are a patient people.

We eventually made our goodbyes and left. Out on the street once again, we wondered how we would get back to our hotel. We stopped passersby on the sidewalk and pronounced the name of our hotel. People would respond by taking us out into the street and pointing—unfortunately, in different directions—so we chose a course arbitrarily and began walking.

After a few minutes, we passed a large, old building and heard music. It was a waltz. Curious, we went inside. To our surprise, we found ourselves in a roller skating rink, full of kids skating on an old terrazzo floor. The skates were antiques, some with bamboo bindings, but they were functional, and everyone was having a fun time. People smiled at us and were exceedingly polite, but no one spoke English. We took some photographs, waved politely, and left.

We were enjoying ourselves and temporarily forgot our anxiety. We stopped at shops up and down the street, looking at things both exotic and mundane. As we continued to wander, we noticed it was starting to get dark. A sense of apprehension returned, with the realization that we were strangers in China and could walk all night and not find our hotel. We didn't know that, in fact, we were safe from crime as no Chinese at that time would have dared harm a foreigner. But coming from Los Angeles, we were concerned about being out alone in a strange city at night.

As we stood on the sidewalk, considering our options, a large, black, Chinese-made car suddenly pulled up next to us. A burly Chinese man emerged wearing a black leather jacket. He smiled at us and, in broken English, told us to get in. The man didn't threaten us but looked determined. We stood there frozen for a moment, wondering what to do. Were we in danger? We started to question him. We asked who he was and what he wanted. He just kept repeating in broken English, "Please, get in car."

Finally, we decided that we had little choice. Further, this man seemed to know who we were. Maybe it was less risky to go with him than be stuck in the middle of a strange city after dark. We reluctantly got in the back seat. The man in the leather coat sat in the front with the driver, and off we went.

At first, we drove in silence. But after a couple of minutes, Sheldon couldn't stand it anymore and leaned over the seat to ask them, again, who they were. As he did so, he noticed they had a tape recorder turned on, ready to record everything we said. We were really surprised but later found out that this was common practice when dealing with important businesspeople. After all, we were there on behalf of Armand Hammer, a man with whom the Chinese intended to do serious business.

In a few minutes, the driver pulled in front of the Dong Fang Hotel, and we got out. The man in the black leather jacket smiled silently and shook our hands. The car then drove away with the leather-jacketed man sitting impassively in the front seat. We stood there for a moment, contemplating what had just happened. Had we been followed? How did he know where to find us? Admittedly, we stood out in a crowd, but it was a big crowd.

Turning around to face the hotel entrance, we could see Lawrence Liu waiting in the lobby with a wry grin. He motioned us to come inside. "I wondered when you would return," he said, but his words didn't ring true. If he had truly wondered where we were, how had he come to be standing in the lobby at that precise moment? He asked us to follow him to a nearby room for a meeting with some unnamed Guangzhou officials—who also just happened to be waiting for us. It was all too convenient.

≈≈≈≈≈

Liu led us to a group of expectant officials gathered in a large room, the perimeter of which was lined with heavy chairs upholstered in a variety of fabric patterns, none of which matched. There, we were seated, side by side, in what appeared to be a giant living room arranged by a really bad decorator and served green tea in beautiful porcelain cups.

He introduced us to the delegation, and according to the custom we had recently learned, everyone stood and exchanged business cards, scrutinized them for the obligatory twenty seconds, and then sat down. He then asked us to introduce ourselves to the delegation and tell them our purpose for coming to China. Although "our purpose" in their country still seemed somewhat unclear, Sheldon gave a short, extemporaneous explanation.

As he began to speak, with Liu translating, an elderly woman suddenly came into the room with an envelope and gave it to one of the Chinese officials. He opened the envelope, pulled out what looked to be color photographs, and passed them around the room for everyone to see. Everyone, that is, except Sheldon and me.

We ignored the small commotion, and Sheldon continued his little speech, telling the group how happy and excited we were to be there in China and that our business in the United States was a healthy form of recreation for children of all ages. We were interested in expanding our business into the People's Republic of China.

Everyone smiled as Sheldon spoke and returned the photos to the man who had distributed them. He put them back in an envelope, and a discussion ensued. It was entirely in Chinese. Liu, apparently, would explain something, the officials would respond, and the cycle would be repeated. We had no idea what the topic was, much less what was said.

At intervals, the Chinese officials would look at us and smile again, then Liu would look at us, and the conversation would continue. It was bizarre. We sat there politely like two mannequins. This went on for a couple of hours until some understanding seemed to be reached, and everyone suddenly stood up, shook hands, and left.

Liu announced to us that we had made a good impression, and if we kept up the good work, we would have a great future in China. We asked him what the pictures were about, and he pulled one out of his pocket. It was a photo of us blowing up balloons and giving them to Chinese children. He was evasive and vague when we asked the purpose of the meeting that had just adjourned.

A bit perturbed by all this secrecy, Sheldon asked him why he had left us alone—and who was that man in the leather jacket? He replied, "The journey of a thousand miles begins with the first step," and then he looked at us and said, "You have just taken your first step." This was the second time that day we had heard that famous Chairman Mao idiom. The Chinese, it seemed, were masters of the indirect reply.

≈≈≈≈≈

During our two-month stay in China, we traveled to many cities, and the balloons became an unexpected source of joy and a wonderful way to connect with the people of China. They also served as an excellent public relations tool for us and Dr. Hammer's business goals in China.

When we arrived in Beijing, we decided that we would experiment by walking over to Tiananmen Square to see if we could interest anyone in a balloon. Tiananmen Square, large enough to hold over one million people at once, was brimming with kids and their families that day. Just as we had done in Guangzhou, we walked up to a family, which usually consisted of a mother, father, aunt uncle, grandparents, and one child. Sheldon blew up a red balloon, then I tied it with a long ribbon and handed it to the little girl. The wonder that came into her little face would have made anyone's heart burst with joy. Before we knew what was happening, a multitude of people converged on us, many of whom were children, all reaching toward us with anticipation. We stayed for over three hours and must have blown up a hundred balloons or more. We were exhausted, but the joy of that memory lasted for many years.

At one point, we realized that we were being watched as we spent those three hours in the Square. We walked over to the Monument of People's Heroes. As we stood on it, giving out the balloons, a red guard came over, shook his finger, and directed us off the monument. Years later, in April of 1989, we saw the first inkling of what was to come in Tiananmen Square with the vision of dozens of youths clothed in black swarming over this monument.

Another time, as we were driving through the country with our group of Western artists, we passed through a village about fifty miles from Shanghai where all the houses were made from mud. It seemed like we had stepped back five hundred years in time. We asked our guide if we could stop, and, of course, at first, he refused; but in China, if you were persistent but subtle, using logic and face and dignity with whomever you dealt with, you could prevail...sometimes.

The Chinese mind is very complex, their thought processes different than those of Westerners. The guide alone could not make that decision because the bus driver, although he had no official capacity in the matter, belonged to the People's Republic of China. After fifteen minutes of discussion and negotiation, the guide and the bus driver finally agreed to stop. We were not allowed to purchase anything with our FECs (foreign exchange certificates) and were instructed to stay with the guide and not wander off by ourselves. If we saw some food that we wanted, the guide would pay for it, and it would be charged back to us later in some way.

We got off the bus, and Sheldon and I (not for the first time) wandered away from the group. We found some children and started blowing up balloons. Soon enough, over one hundred people surrounded us, not all of whom were children. I got a bit apprehensive as the mob closed in around us, but their faces were friendly. Everyone wanted a balloon; you would have thought I was a genie who just came out of a bottle. Their hands started stretching out to touch me, and our guide who had come looking for us became alarmed as he stood at the edge of the crowd and could not get in.

Finally, after many people gently put their hands all over us, the crowd parted like the red sea, and an old man with a long beard and bare feet came through. It was obvious he was an elder and very respected. It felt like we had taken a time machine to another century. He was smoking a pipe, and everyone got very quiet. He pointed to the yellow balloon that Sheldon had just blown up and motioned that he should trade the balloon for a drag on his pipe.

Sheldon got a bit concerned as he was not sure what was in that pipe, but he also did not want to offend him. So, he bit the bullet, gave him the balloon, and took a deep drag on the pipe as he lit a match over the pipe bowl. Everyone cheered, and it wasn't long before Sheldon realized he had just smoked some opium. We continued to give out balloons, with Sheldon in a dreamy haze, to shouts of joy and wonder.

After we returned to the bus, Sheldon told the English-speaking guide that he was sure he had smoked opium. In a very somber way, the guide informed us that opium was illegal in China and that no Chinese citizen would smoke it. Sheldon apologized and said he must have been mistaken—that it had to have only been tobacco he had inhaled. The guide saved face, and we continued on.

By the time we got back to Beijing, news of these strange foreigners handing out balloons to the children all over the countryside of China preceded us, and we were invited to the Ministry of Culture for a discussion with the minister and his assistants. We entered a very nice room, which had several couches, and were served tea. The minister, through his interpreter, told us that they had received reports of our activities and were pleased with our efforts. He said that most foreigners who visit China have business activities they are involved in and spend only as much time as necessary or are tourists who only get involved with programmed activities.

We explained to him that our business dealt with children, and we felt we had a special responsibility toward their welfare. He invited us to a banquet that same night. They served twenty courses of exotically prepared dishes and then had us blow up balloons for each of the twenty people who attended the banquet.

The next day, the *China Daily* (the propaganda daily party paper) ran a picture of us giving balloons to the kids and an article regarding our activities.

In one dramatic balloon encounter, we traveled to a small city in Northern China and were blowing up and handing out balloons to a group of about thirty adults and children. All of a sudden, a young man of about twenty-five came running past me, suddenly grabbed the balloon out of my hand, and continued to run down the lane. Four middle-aged women from the group ran after him, caught him, and started beating him with sticks and their hands and yelling at him in Chinese. He fell to the ground covering his head, and one of the women took the balloon and brought it back to me.

Through a person who spoke a little English, she apologized for the young man's bad manners and told me that he was mentally backward and that we should not think that the people of the city were not very appreciative of our efforts.

Distributing balloons was one of our most pleasurable experiences in China. It also worked out very well for Dr. Hammer and Occidental Petroleum as they were in the midst of a very difficult and impossible negotiation with the Chinese government to open the largest open-pit coal mine in the world, located in Shanxi Province. Since we were partners with Dr. Hammer, our efforts toward trying to bring about the modernization of their roller skating centers were considered a benefit to the children, whom the Chinese realize is their most important asset. It was a show of goodwill for Dr. Hammer.

≈≈≈≈≈

After two months in China, we left for home. The trip had been a feast for the senses, a daily banquet of sights, sounds, and smells. Yet, there was a subtext. Something was going on below the surface that we could neither see nor understand. It was clear that we were along for the ride not just as tourists but also as pawns in someone else's game.

~4~

The Adventure Begins

The ox moves slow, but the earth is patient.
~Chinese Proverb

Soon after we returned to the United States, Dr. Hammer called us late one night at home to ask how our trip went. He inquired as to our experiences with the various Chinese officials we had met and how we liked the country. After a few minutes of small talk, the conversation turned to the Occidental employees we had met. Dr. Hammer wanted to know what we thought of each of them, whom he mentioned by name. We gave him our opinions and did our best to answer his questions, but our knowledge of these people was superficial at best.

Of all the people we had come to know, we were best acquainted with Lawrence Liu, simply because we had spent the most time with him. But that was not saying much. Liu was a cipher to us, as elusive as the wind. As for the others, we knew even less. Keith Anderson and the other expatriates seemed more curious about us and why we were in China than we did about them. They suspected something. But we were truly innocent, only there to have a good time and perhaps lay the groundwork for a future business. Our report to Dr. Hammer seemed like a small price to pay for such a grand adventure, and if we were being used in some mysterious way, so be it. We spoke for about an hour, then Dr. Hammer thanked us and said goodnight.

Two weeks later, we received a call from Richard Chen who told us that Occidental had received a letter from the Ministry of Sports in Shanghai. The letter said that Shanghai wanted to modernize its roller skating rinks and invited us to return and discuss a joint venture. To help expedite this matter, Chen suggested we meet with Mr. Yu Xue Wen, a Chinese national who had recently been hired by Occidental to manage its Beijing office. Mr. Yu happened to be in Los Angeles for a visit.

We arranged a meeting with Mr. Yu for later that day. He was about five foot three inches and appeared to be in his early forties. He spoke heavily accented but understandable English. At the time, he had the title of manager of Chinese affairs for Occidental Petroleum in Beijing and was responsible for the coordination of meetings between Oxy executives and Chinese officials. He was especially proud of the fact that he had personally arranged meetings between Dr. Hammer and the Premier of the People's Republic Chairman Deng.

At our first meeting together, Mr. Yu was dressed in a polo shirt and jeans and was trying very hard to look like a hip Angeleno. Richard Chen, who sat in on the meeting, was more formally dressed in a suit and tie. The two of them had distinctively different styles, not only in their dress but in their personalities. Mr. Yu was outgoing and assertive. Mr. Chen was quiet and impassive.

As the meeting progressed, Mr. Chen said little but seemed to communicate an unspoken secret with Mr. Yu. He would smile knowingly at him, and Mr. Yu would smile back. Mr. Yu told me that there were many business opportunities in China and that he was looking for partners who could develop those opportunities. He said that since we were old, trusted friends of Dr. Hammer, he would like to know if I had an interest in pursuing a business venture.

Mr. Yu carefully explained that as long as any potential venture did not conflict with Occidental Petroleum's principal activity, which was energy development, he was authorized to pursue any opportunity he wanted. "I have the full consent of both Dr. Hammer and the Chinese government," he said. Richard Chen nodded in silent assent to Mr. Yu's statement.

He was gracious, and we seemed to get along well. We agreed to work together and immediately started to plan our second trip to China.

≈≈≈≈≈

The next evening, Dr. Hammer called us at home again and asked if we could come over to his Beverly Hills estate right away, and afterward, tell no one that we had met. In particular, he did not want Richard Chen to know.

We pulled into the circular driveway of his Wallace Neff-designed Beverly Hills home and were surprised to be greeted at the door by Dr. Hammer himself. He ushered us into the French-inspired home and to his mahogany-paneled den.

As soon as we sat down, he launched into a story, telling us how he had started his trading business with the Russians, about his friendships with Lenin and Stalin, and his regret that now, at his age, it was unlikely he could do the same with the Chinese. He quoted Napoleon, who said that "when she [China] wakes, she will shake the world."

He was nostalgic that night. "I wish I was forty again." But he offered to put his resources at our disposal. In return, he asked that we report to him in secret what we saw and experienced in China.

We left his home with the same question that had plagued us since the beginning. Why us? At this point, there were two possible explanations for Dr. Hammer's interest in two roller skate rink owners from America:

Perhaps he needed someone to create goodwill for Occidental Petroleum. Negotiations on the Oxy-China coal-mining venture had been bogged down for months. In theory, we could be here to create a chain of roller rinks for Occidental, demonstrating Oxy's commitment to the children of China. Perhaps all of this was, in fact, just an expensive public relations gesture.

The other explanation we had come up with was something a bit more covert. Perhaps we were to be Dr. Hammer's trusted eyes and ears in China. On the face of it, this seemed logical as he had asked us to fill this role. But we were hardly the kind of moles one reads about in spy novels. We knew nothing, were never briefed, had no specific assignment, and no experience in industrial espionage—in fact, no one could accuse us of even being naturally suspicious.

The truth would turn out to be far more complicated. Slowly, incrementally, we would be drawn into a complex web of relationships that included Occidental Petroleum, the Chinese ministries of state and public security, the FBI, Chinese organized crime, and a whole cast of unlikely characters. It would be a wonderful, painful, exhilarating, exhausting experience—as complex as China itself.

This was the beginning of the adventure.

≈ ≈ ≈ ≈ ≈

On our second trip to China in June of 1982, we were hosted by the Ministry of Sports. The Oxy people had told them that we were interested in building modern roller skating rinks for the children.

When we arrived in Beijing, Mr. Yu and Ms. Zhang (a senior interpreter for the Chinese government) arranged a meeting with officials from the sports ministry in Beijing. We met and talked for about three hours and were invited to lunch. It was the usual banquet, and when the meal was finished, the sports minister told us that they had an immediate project.

We were taken to the Capital Gymnasium, which was next to the Temple of Heaven on one of the main streets in Beijing. The Capital Gymnasium was the largest in Beijing, with several floors encompassing a sports complex. They took us up to the third floor, a space of about 35,000 square feet, overlooking the Temple of Heaven. They said that we could have that space for our business and that they were willing to partner with us in a joint venture to develop it. We were overwhelmed. It was the equivalent of being offered space on Wilshire Boulevard in Beverly Hills.

They requested we create a letter of intent acceptable to both parties and sign it at a formal ceremony in the Great Hall of the People. We were beyond excited and immediately started to put together a document that briefly stated what our responsibilities would be and what our Chinese counterparts' responsibilities would be. It started with the phrase, "This letter of intent is entered into in the spirit of goodwill and mutual trust between the parties." Ms. Zhang translated the document into Chinese, and it was sent to the Ministry of Sports.

Shortly afterward, Mr. Yu told us that he had received a call from the Ministry of Sports in Shanghai. We had visited with them on our inaugural trip to China, and they wanted us to do the project there first, requesting we come as soon as possible. Mr. Yu told us we should go, then assured us he would take care of the Beijing sports people. We could sign the letter of intent when we returned to Beijing.

So, off we went to Shanghai, where we were met by officials of the Ministry of Sports. We discovered they had already reserved rooms for us at the Jiang Jang Hotel and had prepared an itinerary for the day. They took us to scout out several potential locations; we were amazed—each one seemed more promising than the last. We had what seemed to be our pick of places to build our first rink. They also took us to tour a number of the forty-five rinks already in Shanghai. The largest was in the People's Park, where an average of five thousand people skated every day. The largest grossing rink in the United States topped out at five thousand skaters a week.

We chose an existing community center with an outdoor rink located in the city center that we could renovate. We met with the center's manager and an architect from the Shanghai architectural society to lay out some preliminary plans.

Shanghai fascinated my husband and me. It was far more crowded than Beijing, the food was different, and they spoke a different dialect, Shanghainese.

We were visiting the Ministry of Sports complex when Sheldon noticed an empty room filled with snooker tables. He picked up a cue and shot some balls. He was soon joined by a jovial Chinese man who picked up a cue and started playing with him. Sheldon was not a great snooker player, and it seemed, neither was his opponent. They played two games, evenly matched in both.

They were about to start the third game when we were called to meet with some sports officials. The young Chinese man smiled at us and then cleaned every ball on the table with expert shots. He didn't miss one. Yes, we had been snookered, and not for the last time.

We finally sat down with the sports ministry people and negotiated the letter of intent—identical to the one we had created for Beijing. We all agreed on the details, which meant that now, we had two projects to work on in the two major cities in China in conjunction with the Ministry of Sports, Beijing, and Shanghai branches. Our future was secured. We were elated.

A banquet was arranged for the signing ceremony that night. We went off to the telex office to message the sports ministry in Beijing that we would return in a few days and were very enthusiastic about signing a letter of intent to do a joint venture at the Capital Gymnasium.

About three hours before the banquet, we returned to the telex office to see if we had received a reply back from Beijing.

It read as follows: "Dear Mr. and Mrs. Krechman, we have received your telex and wish to inform you that we no longer have any interest in doing a joint venture with you in Beijing. Please do not contact us any further. Signed the Ministry of Sports."

As you can well imagine, we were dumbfounded. We immediately assumed that if the Ministry of Sports in Beijing wanted nothing more to do with us, their branch in Shanghai would feel the same way. We sat in our hotel room for three hours waiting for the message we believed would come, that the banquet was canceled, and our arrangement with the Shanghai Ministry of Sports had ended.

At about 6:30, there was a knock on our door—it was the driver from the sports ministry. He was there to take us to the banquet. All our fears were groundless. We arrived at the banquet with about twenty-five people. We drank Moutai, toasted everyone, and with video cameras recording the moment, we all signed the letter of intent.

≈ ≈ ≈ ≈ ≈

It was suggested that we visit the city of Hangzhou, so the next day, we boarded a train from Shanghai for the twelve-hour trip—one of our many excursions exploring China over the years.

The City of Hangzhou boasts one of the largest man-made lakes in the world, West Lake. Centuries ago, an empress who lived in Beijing at the Forbidden City decided to build a lake there. She also wanted to travel to that lake by water. Since it's about 2,500 miles from Beijing to Hangzhou, over the course of many years, she built a waterway called the Grand Canal, which flows from Beijing to Hangzhou and empties into West Lake. It's been said that the only two things you can see from space are the Great Wall of China and the Grand Canal.

When we arrived in Hangzhou, we were greeted by our guide, a young man from the foreign ministry. When the guide told us that Hangzhou had started to build a computer center and that there were already Chinese companies producing computer products, Sheldon asked if we could visit one of the factories. Our guide just nodded.

We were taken to the West Lake Hotel, one of the original hotels built on the lake, and were given a lakeside room. While sitting at the desk in the room looking out over the picturesque lake, I started to write a letter, just as a cockroach walked slowly across the top of the desk and across the paper. I couldn't help wondering if the empress had ever seen a cockroach on her visits.

Our guide took us to lunch at one of the local restaurants. Hangzhou is famous for its eels; so, we had eel stew. As strange as the meal might have sounded, it was delicious, and we soon acquired a taste for eel.

We walked for miles. We visited the zoo, a very primitive establishment compared to our zoos in the United States. Still, it was large, and they had two giant pandas, which, for us, was a very unusual sight. We also caught sight of some dogs wandering outside the zoo of the German Shepherd variety. This was the first city in China where we had spotted any dogs. In Beijing, dogs were eaten as a delicacy, and the Chinese are too concerned with their own survival to take care of large animals unless they have a productive use.

Our guide came to collect us again that afternoon, this time escorting us to the Yi Ling Temple, a very famous tourist attraction. The temple grounds were quite large, and as usual in China, packed with people. It was like being in an amusement park, except instead of rides and games, temples with incense and huge statues of Buddha, in a variety of poses, colors, shapes, and sizes, were the main attractions. Monks in white robes were a common sight there, as were hot food stands offering fresh food. On one side of the temple grounds stood a mountain with large foothills where, carved out of the stone in several places, gigantic statues of Buddha loomed. It was like being in South Dakota and looking up at Mount Rushmore. We were completely awed by the temple and its grounds. There are wonders like this all over China.

The next stop was the tea plantations. Hangzhou is known for its long, green tea leaves and the production of silk. Tea in China is like wine in the United States. There are countless varieties, and they all seem to have some medicinal value. The long, green Hangzhou tea is known as long-life tea.

The silkworm production was fascinating to watch and seemed a very unusual process. By the time we finished our private tour, it was late, and we all were hungry. Our guide took us back to our hotel, and Sheldon asked again if we could visit a computer factory. He just smiled and said goodnight.

That evening was lovely. We walked through the center of town and dined at a local restaurant, always a unique and interesting experience for us because no one else spoke English, and we were the only "round eyes" in the place. We had to point to what we wanted, but everyone was very friendly, and the meal was fine.

The next morning, our guide called. He would be at our hotel in fifteen minutes to take us to a computer factory. Sheldon was so excited. We dressed quickly and met him out front. To our surprise, he was accompanied by two Chinese-made automobiles and three people we'd never seen before—two were drivers, and one was a representative from the computer factory, located on the outskirts of Hangzhou.

When we arrived, we were escorted to the second floor and met by two women who looked like laboratory workers in white coats, hats, and shoes. We were then taken into a very clean room and asked to put on white coats, nylon gloves, white hats, and special shoes. We were told that this was a clean area and that anyone walking through the factory should shed as little dust as possible.

The factory consisted of a line made up of mostly women assembling personal computers at a long table under the glare of fluorescent overhead lights. The line was hardly mechanized, and everything was being done by hand, including the soldering of certain parts. Everyone was very friendly, and after touring the factory, we were invited into their conference room for some tea and conversation.

Once inside the room, we headed toward a long table that sat about twenty people—and all the chairs were full. Our guides told us through an interpreter that we were the first foreigners to visit this factory, which was only about two years old. It was the first of its kind to be constructed there, though they said that Hangzhou would someday be a computer center mecca like Northern California. Sheldon told them of his long history in the electronics business and that he was looking for some opportunities in China.

We spoke for about one hour, and just as we thought the meeting was over, the doors to the conference room opened, and several people came rushing in with microphones, TV cameras, and cables. It looked like we were about to go on network news.

Everyone jumped up—besides us—and started talking at once while people gave directions to other people. The table was moved and chairs were rearranged as we just sat there watching everything unfold around us. Finally, the interpreter came over and told us that what was going on was very unexpected. It seemed the local TV station had picked that very day and time to do an hour-long special on the computer factory, and it was just a coincidence that we were there. They said they knew it was an imposition but asked if we would mind joining in the program with them.

So, we all sat down at the table after it had been re-arranged by the TV people—and would you believe it? We were the stars. Of course, we realized it was a setup and later found out the event was for propaganda purposes.

They started with a monologue that we didn't understand and no one interpreted for us. Then they asked us questions, which were translated into English for our benefit. The questions were innocuous enough and in the vein of: "How long have you been in China?" "What cities have you been to?" "What do you think of Hangzhou?" "What do you think of the computer factory?" "Have the local people been friendly and cooperative?" "What do the American people think of the Chinese people?" "Were we concerned about the violence in the United States?"

This went on for a while, and then after a bit, they ended the video and started to pack up their equipment. We asked if we could have a copy of the video. No one said a word—they just kept on packing up. We finally asked our guide if he could get us a copy. He just looked at us and didn't answer. He drove us back to our hotel, where we asked him again. He just smiled.

The next morning, our guide picked us up to take us to the train. We thanked him for the tour, and when we arrived at the station, he handed Sheldon a large envelope with the videotape inside.

When we came out of China to Hong Kong, we had the tape converted from PAL to the U.S. standard right away. We were very curious to see it. When we finally played it, the video was great, but they had cut out all the audio. We were later told that they had aired the tape on TV stations all the way to Shanghai.

≈ ≈ ≈ ≈ ≈

We headed back to Shanghai, and as we were getting off the train, Sheldon accidentally knocked me in the neck and shoulder with a suitcase he had pulled off the luggage rack. My neck was twisted, causing me to be in a great deal of pain and discomfort. Since we were guests of the Ministry of Sports, they sent over a sports medicine individual who massaged my neck and shoulder, but to no avail.

Fortunately, one of the local people instructed to look after us happened to be the wife of an Oxy executive who was working in their

Carole Sumner Krechman

LA office but whose family was still in Shanghai. His mother was a doctor. I called his wife; after explaining how much pain I was in, she immediately had her mother-in-law come to our hotel room. The doctor had me remove my blouse. Then, with what looked like a small hammer with sharp points at the end, she lightly hit several places along my neck and shoulders—hard enough for those points to slightly break the skin. She then took some small glass jars, lit a match in the jar to remove the oxygen, and then tightly attached each jar to my neck and shoulders where she had broken the skin, creating a suction effect. Next, she inserted several acupuncture pins in my flesh over the course of the next hour while I sat quietly. At the end, when she removed the glass jars and the pins, I realized the pain was completely gone. It was a miraculous cure and our first, but not last, experience with Chinese medicine.

≈≈≈≈≈

Armed with our letter of intent, we traveled back to Beijing in high spirits, though still resolved to find out just what had happened at the Beijing sports ministry. We gave Mr. Yu a copy of the letter of intent and asked him for an explanation. He told us that both organizations were part of the same ministry and that he had no idea why the Beijing sports ministry had changed its mind. When we asked him to please inquire about it, he said it was unnecessary and that we should forget the entire matter and concentrate on doing business in Shanghai.

And then, surprisingly, the sports ministry in Beijing invited us to a meeting. They said they were very interested in the modernization of their roller skating centers and wanted to introduce us to a bank in Hong Kong that might finance our ventures. These were the same people who had taken us to the Capital Gymnasium and sent us the unexpected telex in Shanghai. Not a word was spoken about our previous meetings. It was like it had simply never happened.

China was always a place of mystery and unanswered questions. Wheels within wheels within wheels.

We traveled to Hong Kong and met with Mr. Nelson Chao, chairman of the Sin Hua Trust. Unbeknownst to us at the time, the Sin

49

Hua Trust was a Hong Kong front for the Bank of China. We were ushered into a large conference room with a table so wide, if you wanted to push any papers over to the other side, you had to lean over the table and stretch out your arms as far as you could to reach them. Mr. Chao asked us to sit opposite him so he could look into our eyes. The first thing he asked us was where we were from. When we replied, "Beverly Hills, California," he looked at us, smiled, and said, "Nice place to live."

We had an hour-long conversation, during which my husband and I realized that he was sizing us up, and, of course, his secretary was taking notes on everything we said. At the end of the conversation, we asked him what the possibility was that he might fund our ventures. His response was "The ox moves slow, but the earth is patient." He then ushered us out, thanked us for coming, and said goodbye.

After several false starts, months of negotiations, and dozens of adventures, we abandoned all hope of building a chain of roller skating rinks in China. Instead, through a convoluted series of events, we became involved in a large and complicated joint venture with the Chinese to build an office and hotel complex in downtown Beijing. We called our company World China Trade.

~5~

Chinese Medical Miracles

Nature, time and patience are the three great physicians.
~Chinese Proverb

W E SPENT OVER 1,500 days in the People's Republic of China. We saw every season there and set foot in that country at least once during every month of the year. The only health precaution we took for the first ten trips was gamma globulin shots. After that, we came and went as if we were going to Santa Barbara.

We drank the water from the taps and ate food from stands along the streets and roads throughout China. Except for the first trip, where Sheldon and I both got a very bad bronchial cough and flu-type symptoms, we never got sick—with the exception of a few unusual incidents.

At that time, before you entered China from the United States, you would receive a pamphlet that would advise foreign travelers on many things. Under the area of health, the pamphlet explained that should a traveler get sick for any reason whatsoever, they should make arrangements to leave China immediately and travel to Hong Kong where proper medical treatment was available.

It explained that China was a third-world country and that their medical treatments were antiquated, and the traveler would be taking their lives in their hands if they received medical treatment in the PRC. They also warned the reader about taking any offered Chinese medicine or herbs because they had not been tested or approved by the American Medical Association.

I first experienced the wonders of Chinese medicine when I injured my neck and had my first acupuncture experience in Shanghai, which completely relieved the excruciating pain. On a subsequent trip, it was Sheldon's turn to experience the Chinese practice of medicine.

We had met a Chinese family in Shanghai with whom we became friends. Zev was the manager of an electronics plant that produced radios. It was very similar to the business run by Sheldon's father, a pioneer of radio and TV manufacture in the United States. For Sheldon, it was like old times, and he and Zeb had a lot in common.

Zev, his pregnant wife, and the rest of his family lived in a very small apartment. Nevertheless, they graciously invited us for dinner. It was not the usual practice for a Chinese citizen to invite a foreigner to dinner at his house because typically, other people were expected to be at the event, who would then report to the party leaders about any strange occurrences happening within their purview. A foreigner coming to dinner was a strange occurrence. Everybody reports on everybody. That's the way a communist country keeps control of the people.

Mr. Yu had suggested that since electronics was the future, we should visit Zev's factory and see if we could work out a joint venture-type relationship. Zev was very receptive to the idea, and Sheldon was excited about touring a radio manufacturing plant.

It was January and very cold in Shanghai. We all dressed warmly and arrived at our appointment on time. The factory was not just one building but a series of them set within a complex surrounded by a twelve-foot chain link fence. At the entrance sat a guard in a small cubicle attached to a gate that he would open if you were approved to enter the complex.

Zev greeted us with a group of four other factory officials, and they all took us on a tour of most of the complex. It was very familiar to Sheldon since it looked like one of his father's radio factories from the early 1950s. There were long benches with seats on either side and an assembly line of hundreds of people, all busy wiring and soldering by hand and assembling radios.

We noticed a more modern building among these other ones, but when we asked to tour it, we were told that it was unavailable for a tour at that time. (Zev later told Sheldon, in a weak and trusting moment, that radios were not the only product that was manufactured at the factory. They also built items of a military nature, which he could not discuss.)

We spent about two hours walking through the complex and really enjoyed the tour. The factory, however, had little or no heat, and the buildings were not well-insulated. It was drafty and cold. Outside, snow had just started to fall. The Chinese were all bundled up with layers of clothes, and all had on heavy, long underwear. You could almost see your breath inside the building. We were grateful when we were ushered into a large conference room, which was, as usual, filled with couches where we all sat and were served some tea. The conference room was heated, which I think was probably done just for our benefit.

We started, as always, with both sides saying positive things about each other's country and then discussing each other's experiences. Sheldon had a lot in common with them, and they were very pleased with his knowledge of electronics and the manufacture of radios. We really appreciated the tea. It was hot and delicious, a special, red, very strong and robust tea drunk in the winter in that country.

After drinking two or three cups, Sheldon had to go to the bathroom. Zev, concerned, told him that they did not have any facilities for guests, and the only men's bathroom was the one used by all the employees. Sheldon told him he had grown up in old factories and not to worry. Just point him in the right direction.

Several minutes later, Sheldon returned to the conference room. We all gasped. His face was white, and blood was pouring from his finger. He was in shock. Zev jumped into action. He took off his belt, then wrapped it around Sheldon's wrist and pulled it tight to act as a tourniquet. He and another official from the meeting took him by the arms, and I followed them down a flight of steel stairs to the factory infirmary.

I eventually learned that when Sheldon entered the men's room, there were four toilet cubicles. The door to each cubicle was metal, with a sharp edge and rusty hinges. A hole had been cut into the window, and the cold air was coming through, making the cubicle doors rattle. As he stood there doing his thing, he put his right hand on the door jamb. Suddenly, a heavy gust of wind caused the metal cubicle door to slam shut on his index finger, crushing it.

As we entered the infirmary, I remembered a story told to us at the U.S. Embassy in Shanghai about a woman who had her hand caught in a car door. She was taken to a Chinese hospital and given treatment. Her hand got much worse, became infected, and by the time she got back to Hong Kong, part of her hand had to be amputated. (That's the story they tell you to make sure you don't receive any treatment in China). Needless to say, I was really scared and worried.

We were met in the infirmary by a woman in a white outfit who immediately sat Sheldon down and examined his finger, which by now was beginning to throb and hurt and looked just awful. She washed it off with some disinfectant and took down a large bottle of Chinese medicine from a shelf. She spread some of the bottle's contents—a white substance with a paste-like consistency—thickly over his injured finger and then wrapped it in a thick layer of gauze.

She then put about eight acupuncture needles in various parts of his body, gave him a spoonful of black, thick liquid, and had him lie down on a cot in the infirmary. She suggested we let him rest for a while, and we went back up the stairs to continue the meeting.

About half an hour later, to my utter amazement, Sheldon returned to the conference room. He said he felt a little lightheaded, and his finger was throbbing but less than before; he felt okay to continue the meeting. By the time we got back to the hotel, the throbbing and pain were gone, and he had just a slight sensation in his finger.

For the next few days, I made sure that Sheldon did exactly what the woman had told us, including taking a spoonful of the black liquid (she had given him a small bottle of it) every morning and night. His finger felt tender, but he had very little if any pain. At the end of seven days, he took off the gauze and, with the exception of a very thin scar, his finger was completely healed.

≈≈≈≈≈

For several years, before we came to China, Sheldon had suffered from a recurring problem with his wisdom teeth. He had never had them removed, and it seemed once a year, he would develop an infection in the lower right or left wisdom tooth. It would start slowly and build up, and within a very short period, he would have massive swelling on one side of his jaw and very intense pain. It would incapacitate him to such an extent that it became impossible for him to work. He would suffer through a week of agony until the infection subsided.

One day in Beijing, during the construction of our hotel project, the right side of his jaw started to hurt. I was concerned when he told me because I knew what was going to happen, but this time, we were in China, without the benefit of our dentist. I asked Mr. Yu if he would take us to the Capital Hospital near the Beijing Hotel. When I told him the situation, he said that he also had a tooth problem that he had been neglecting—a pain in one of his left molars.

He told us that we could not go to the Capital Hospital because we were not Chinese citizens and that I would have to take Sheldon to the expatriate foreign infirmary for treatment. The reputation of that place was terrible, including the fact that they did not have any dentists. I kept insisting that Mr. Yu arrange for me to take Sheldon to the Capital Hospital, but he kept telling me that it was impossible. I informed him that my experience in China had left me with the feeling that nothing was impossible if you had the right guanxi (a Chinese term that loosely means you know people who owe you favors).

Finally, after three days of arguing and Mr. Yu making whatever calls necessary, he told me it had all been arranged. By that time, Sheldon's jaw was swollen, and he was in considerable pain. Mr. Yu also had a swollen jaw, and I could see that he was also in pain, though he refused to admit it.

Lily, Mr. Yu's wife, came to the office and drove the three of us to Capital Hospital. It was a very large complex; when we entered, I saw several patients in striped outfits, similar to the way prisoners used to dress in the United States. We entered a building and walked up the stairs, stepping onto a long hallway with at least fifty women and children waiting their turn for dental work. The main room was very large, with about fifty dental chairs almost side by side. Each chair had a patient (lots of kids), and the dental technicians were mostly young women.

At the end of the large room was an alcove, where a dental chair and an older man with a white outfit worked. We walked directly to the alcove and saw seven people on a bench and a woman in the dental chair. She took off the sheet protecting her and stepped down. Sheldon was then motioned to sit in the chair. Mr. Yu told me that he was the first foreigner ever to be admitted into the Capital Hospital.

Sheldon laid back on the dental chair. Mr. Yu told me the older man was one of the most respected dentists in Beijing and the dentist for the top leaders in China. He smiled at Sheldon and had his assistant bring him a tray of dental tools that had just come out of the sterilizer. He probed very gently and looked into his mouth, and then, one by one, each of the seven people sitting on the bench got up and looked into his mouth also.

Then he took out a small bottle of very dark, thick, liquid-like paste, and with the help of his dental utensils, took a thick, white piece of cotton-like string and, along with the paste, gently packed it down between his gum and the infected wisdom tooth. He then smiled and through an interpreter told Sheldon to keep it in until 6:00 p.m. that night.

Then Mr. Yu nervously got into the chair. The dentist had him open his mouth, and the routine repeated: Each of the seven people on the bench got up and looked into Mr. Yu's mouth. Finally, they all started to discuss Mr. Yu's condition—at least, that's what we think they were discussing. Finally, everybody nodded their agreement. Mr. Yu was not consulted. The dentist put several acupuncture pins in Mr. Yu's face and in a few other places on his body. Attached to the pins was a series of small wires, leading from a box that generated a slight electrical pulsing DC current.

Mr. Yu had to have two root canals, and the dentist worked on him for about an hour. Mr. Yu looked relaxed, and except for having to keep his mouth open (not an unusual action for the man), he did not look uncomfortable at all. When he was finished, he told us that he had felt no pain through the procedure, and, except for a slight tingly sensation afterward, he was okay.

The dentist gave Sheldon three bottles of different liquids and told him that after 6:00 p.m., he could take out the absorbent string. He was instructed to wash his mouth out three times a day for thirty days with the three different liquids—one for the morning, one for the afternoon, and one before bedtime—and not to wash his mouth out with water after using the liquid for at least one hour. We were also told that since we were foreigners, we would have to pay foreign rates for the treatment and the bottles of mouth medicine. The total sum was the equivalent of $3.50 U.S.

As instructed, at 6:00 p.m., Sheldon took out the string and used the mouth medicine, and by the next morning, the swelling was completely gone. He used the mouth medicine for the next thirty days as the dentist directed.

In all the years that followed, Sheldon never had another incident with his wisdom teeth. It's hard to argue with a culture that has been practicing medicine for thousands of years.

~6~

Guanxi

Guanxi: an individual's social network of mutually beneficial personal and business relationships.

THE TRANSITION FROM ROLLER rink entrepreneurs to big-time real estate developers was accomplished over time through a Byzantine process of manipulation, incentive, and behind-the-scenes transactions. Through a series of introductions and inducements, we were linked up with some of China's most powerful players and positioned, unknowingly, to serve the interests of various state agencies. The catalyst for all of this was the inimitable Mr. Yu.

By our third trip to China in 1983, we had formed a California corporation and called it World China Trade. Richard Chen would receive stock and become a director along with Dean Lee, another Oxy employee in Beijing. Dean was an American citizen whose family lived in Orange County, California, but who worked in Beijing under the direction of Richard Chen. We agreed to pay Mr. Yu a salary and cover necessary expenses such as rent, a car, and a driver.

We raised start-up funds from a group of investors, mostly friends, and filed the corporation papers. Sheldon was listed as chairman of the board, I was vice chairman, and Mr. Yu was the designated president. This made Mr. Yu the very first Chinese citizen to be an officer of an American corporation—something that gave him great status in China.

Now that we had a company, we needed offices. In the 1980s, all foreign companies in China had their offices in hotels, the most prestigious of which was the Beijing Hotel. It was located on the corner of Chauhan and Was Fu Jing, which, at that time, was the Chinese equivalent of Rodeo Drive in Beverly Hills, with its high-end stores and food shops.

Oxy's original offices had been located in the Beijing Hotel, spread out over three interconnected rooms. When the Chinese government constructed the first office building in Beijing, not far from the Beijing Hotel, Oxy moved its offices there. Mr. Yu arranged for us to take over Oxy's former space in the Beijing Hotel.

Along with Oxy's former office, we inherited Ms. Zhang, a former Oxy employee and now Mr. Yu's assistant. We gave her the title of manager of American affairs. She spoke excellent English and had been one of the top interpreters for high officials of the Chinese government.

Our funds were limited, so when we moved in, we decided to purchase our office furniture at a modest local store rather than import it from Hong Kong. Mr. Yu and Ms. Zhang had a place in mind, so we all piled into our little company car, a vintage Datsun, and headed out. Finally, after about an hour, we stopped in front of what looked like a second-hand thrift shop.

Inside the shop, a jumble of chairs, desks, and various types of cabinets was piled up in stacks. There seemed no particular order to be found in any aspect of the shop; every piece was different from the others. It was a far cry from the typical American furniture store, with its carefully arranged merchandise.

I have a good eye to go along with my architectural degree, so I went through the store, carefully examined each piece, and picked out the best furnishings for our use. Outside the little establishment, a large group of people had gathered, staring at us and gesticulating and laughing. Shameless gawking is socially acceptable in China. We smiled at them, and they all waved at us.

After I had picked out the furniture, Mr. Yu and Ms. Zhang started the bargaining process. We could not understand the words, but the gestures told the story. The negotiation started out calmly but gradually became heated. The crowd outside had something to say about the transaction too. At one point, Mr. Yu and Ms. Zhang started to wave their hands, and the level of everyone's voices rose considerably. This went on for about twenty minutes.

Finally, an angry-looking Mr. Yu stalked out of the store and motioned for us to follow. Outside the store, Mr. Yu told us in a very calm voice that the manager was being very unreasonable about the price of the furniture. We later found out that a lot of that negotiation was just a show for us. We waited outside for a few minutes, and then we followed Mr. Yu back into the store.

Meanwhile, it seemed that the crowd outside had become very involved in the negotiation, and everyone had a different opinion, including our driver. After another twenty minutes, everyone started to smile, and Ms. Zhang took out a wad of bills from her purse and paid the store manager. We were told the total amount of the purchase was between $150 and $200. The purchase included several desks, chairs, and file cabinets.

That afternoon, the furniture was delivered by two Chinese men in their seventies. These two septuagenarians looked exceptionally fit, with lean, muscular arms and trim physiques. We were curious to see how they brought in the furniture, so we followed them down to the street. There by the front door were two tricycles with wooden platforms attached at the back, each piled high with furniture that had been tied down with hemp rope. These two old men had pedaled those huge loads clear across town and were now preparing to carry everything up to our offices.

The rooms were on the corner of the fourteenth floor and had an impressive view of both a main boulevard, Chauhan Avenue, and a secondary road, Was Fu Jing Street. This was a prime location, near the center of the city and Tiananmen Square. It wasn't fancy—nothing much was fancy in Beijing in the eighties—but we were very pleased.

Our new furniture was quite utilitarian, even though the style and finish quality were far inferior to anything available in the United States. As the last piece was brought in, two young men appeared. A few furnishings had been left over from the Oxy offices. The two men carried it away.

Later that afternoon, a man from the hotel management came to our offices and was introduced to us as an assistant manager. Mr. Yu got into a long discussion with him but did not stop to interpret. After he left, Mr. Yu told us that there would be an additional charge for our rooms. It seems that since the young men had removed the leftover furniture (which apparently belonged to the hotel) and taken it to the basement, we would be charged for storage. We would also be charged extra for the "space" our new furniture was taking up. The whole situation seemed ridiculous, but Mr. Yu simply said, "This is China." It would turn out to be his all-purpose answer for every inexplicable circumstance.

Mr. Yu had procured our furniture, but we were responsible for securing a copy machine, typewriter, computer, and assorted office supplies. None of these items were available in Beijing at the time and would have to be purchased in Hong Kong.

Unfortunately, there was an import duty of 200 percent of the original purchase price on any office equipment brought in from outside China. We told Mr. Yu that since our funds were low, it was not possible to purchase these items and pay the import duty too.

Mr. Yu told us not to worry. He said we should purchase them anyway, bring them through Chinese customs, and declare nothing. He told us his "guanxi" was strong enough to deal with any customs problem. We might have been neophytes in that country, but we were already beginning to learn the importance of guanxi, which translates roughly as "favor." Guanxi is the lubricant that keeps the wheels of the Chinese system turning. In the U.S., it would be called a kickback or bribe. We had already become the beneficiaries and the victims of guanxi.

All foreign corporations in China are required to hire local Chinese employees to work in their offices. This has the dual purpose of helping the local economy as well as, more importantly, guarantee-ing the Chinese government inside access to every foreign business. When you hire a Chinese employee, the government sets the rate, which, in most cases, is slightly below U.S. standards.

The salary is paid not to the employee, however, but to the Chinese government. In 1984, the salary range was between $500 and $1,000 per month, depending on the skill level and responsibility of the employee. The government would keep most of the salary and then pay your employee the average local rate, which ranged between $25 and $100 per month. In this way, you paid the government a handsome sum to spy on you.

Because the salaries those employees actually received were so low, foreign companies like ours were expected to supplement wages by dispensing guanxi in the form of gifts, trips to Hong Kong, and foreign exchange certificates. This was strictly illegal, of course, but routinely done. The amount of guanxi a person received was a quanti-tative measure of that person's social status and financial worth. The entire country was run by means of these under-the-table payoffs.

Mr. Yu, we soon learned, was a master of guanxi. Yu handed out favors that garnered him immense power. For example, one of the scarcest commodities in Beijing was housing. There was a chronic shortage, and housing construction could be seen everywhere you went. Despite the shortage, however, if you could get an apartment, it was cheap. The law of supply and demand didn't operate in China.

If you had the guanxi to get a new apartment in a high-rise, the cost was five dollars per month. They were considered luxury apart-ments, although, by U.S. standards, they were downright primitive. A typical new apartment complex was ten or twelve stories high, had intermittent steam heat controlled by some state bureaucracy, and elevators that stopped at every third floor. The Chinese government assumed that people could easily walk up or down two flights of stairs and therefore saved money by skipping the extra openings and doors.

Apartments in Beijing averaged six hundred square feet divided into three rooms. The rooms consisted of bare cement floors, walls, and ceilings, with one lightbulb per room that dangled from the

ceiling on a cord. Each unit had a tiny kitchen area with two unregu-
lated gas burners (i.e., on or off), a cold-water tap, a small toilet area
with a flush hole but no fixture, and a floor drain where you could
stand and pour water over yourself that you had heated on the stove.
Guanxi determined who got these apartments and on which floor. If
you had good guanxi, you might get an apartment on a floor that the
elevator served.

Mr. Yu was powerful enough to arrange apartments for people
he favored. He lived in a new building himself and had two apartments across from each other. This took considerable guanxi. One of
the apartments was unusually large and had two bedrooms, a den,
and a living room. He had silk rugs, a real toilet fixture, a refrigerator
(which was quite rare), and an electric water heater (a tremendous
luxury).

How Mr. Yu acquired such guanxi we didn't know, though his
ability to import smuggled goods would be a major test of just how
much he had. We agreed to go to Hong Kong and purchase the office
equipment. The rest would be up to Mr. Yu. He instructed us to wrap
the cartons as though they were gifts and cross the border, passing
through the green flag line at customs designated for people who had
nothing to declare.

We purchased the equipment in Hong Kong, including a water
heater for Mr. Yu's other apartment. We returned to Beijing with
stacks of cartons wrapped like birthday presents, with paper, ribbons,
and lots of tape. They were all piled on a big luggage cart that groaned
under the weight.

As we approached customs, we looked for Mr. Yu, but he was
nowhere to be seen. Nevertheless, we headed for the green flag line as
instructed, pushing the cart. The customs official looked at the pile of
cartons and asked Sheldon what was in them. He told him the cartons
contained used toys for the children of Beijing.

It was a ridiculous lie, and I thought for sure we would be arrested on the spot. The officer made a gesture and was soon joined by re-
inforcements who began picking at the packages. Through a few small
holes, they could clearly read the labels on the cartons. They asked us

to wait a moment and walked away to conduct a small conference.

Soon, a customs official came over to talk to us. By this time, a small crowd of curious onlookers had gathered. The official asked Sheldon to open the cartons. With a queasy feeling in his stomach, he told him he'd rather not—they were so full of toys, and they'd be difficult to repack. He asked Sheldon to follow him. I watched in panic as they took Sheldon into a small room, where he repeated his lie to two more officials. They made a call, had a long conversation with someone, and then lectured him on the illegality of bringing in equipment and not declaring it. They said the penalty was very severe. By now, Sheldon was in a near panic too.

After what seemed like an eternity, Sheldon returned to the customs counter. I was still standing by the cart and worried sick as one of the officers followed behind Sheldon and spoke to the counter agent in Chinese. The agent then turned to us and said in English that everyone had agreed it would be too inconvenient to unpack the boxes and, gesturing with his hand, waved us through.

We were both weak-kneed, perspiring, and thinking evil thoughts about Mr. Yu, but we were relieved. Yu was waiting outside in a van. "I told you not to worry," he said. He had let us suffer, of course, so that we would appreciate the power of his guanxi.

≈≈≈≈≈

Our office was all set. We had several Chinese ministries interested in business with the United States and were talking to several U.S. companies wanting to do business in China. We thought we were all set, and then we found out about sponsors.

A few days later, we were visiting the law offices of Graham and James, a large international law firm with a branch in Beijing. Their resident lawyer, named Sally Harpole, spoke fluent Chinese and was an old China hand. We told her about our new offices, and she asked us many questions—what our business was, who we were dealing with, and most importantly, who was Mr. Yu Xue Wen? We explained to Sally that we were a new business and had taken over the old Oxy offices in the Beijing Hotel. Our purpose, we told her, was to develop businesses between the United States and the People's Republic of China, an exquisitely vague but true statement.

She was amazed that Mr. Yu was the president of our corporation. Sally had been in China for years and said it was unheard of for a Chinese citizen to leave the employ of the government and become an officer in a U.S. corporation. She was also very surprised to hear about our new offices. She told us that there were many U.S. companies waiting for months to find office space. The hotel rooms at the Beijing Hotel were especially coveted. When we told her the rent we were paying, she just laughed and said it must be a mistake—it was a fraction of what other companies were charged.

When we stood up to leave, I gave Sally our private phone number. She immediately sank into her chair, her face revealing her utter amazement and concern. It seemed that we had only one of two private lines in the entire Beijing Hotel. She asked us to sit down. Some very sage advice followed.

She said we were novices and should keep our eyes and ears open; that things would change, and what appeared to be reality would shift again and again until we were totally confused. The Chinese agenda—and we could be sure they had one—would proceed with or without our knowledge or consent. Then she asked us an important question: Who was our Chinese sponsor?

Sponsor? We didn't know what she was talking about. Sally then proceeded to explain that every foreign company doing business in China was required by law to have a sponsor. Ordinarily, it was impossible to even rent an office without an official, government-approved sponsor.

One of her functions as an attorney in Beijing was to take foreign companies through the approval process. It usually took anywhere from six to eighteen months to complete, and at considerable cost. Sally was in the process of obtaining approvals for three companies, each with gross revenues in excess of 100 million dollars per year. Our company was brand-new, had not even conducted any business, and yet we were already installed in a premier office space in Beijing with our own private telephone line.

Sally explained that getting a sponsor was no easy task, and the more important your sponsor, the more influence or guanxi one had. We asked her who the best sponsor for us would be, and she said the Ministry of Foreign Trade. She also added that getting this ministry as a sponsor would be out of the question. They only sponsored companies such as General Motors or Boeing. We would have to settle for a sponsor much lower in the hierarchy, and she would be pleased to offer her services for that purpose.

She added that because of Mr. Yu and his guanxi, this task might be easier but not by much. The cost to get a minor sponsor would be around $20,000, plus whatever additional guanxi payments might have to be made to the various ministries. She also said that even with Mr. Yu's guanxi, it would take four to six months to accomplish. Her advice was to start the process immediately as the Chinese government could swoop down at any time, close our office, and order us to leave the country.

We thanked Sally for her time and told her that we would speak to Mr. Yu and get back to her regarding her services. We explained that Mr. Yu was supposed to be taking care of all our bureaucratic necessities, and perhaps he had already acquired a sponsor for us but had neglected to tell us. We left, determined to confront Mr. Yu about who our sponsor was the moment we got back to the office.

When we returned, Sheldon walked directly over to Mr. Yu's desk, where he was comfortably ensconced in his enormous chair, and asked him if we had a sponsor. He asked what sponsor we wanted. Sheldon took this to mean "no" and replied that he wanted the Ministry of Foreign Trade, who could help us the most. Mr. Yu responded that the Ministry of Foreign Economics and Trade—known by the acronym MOFERT—would be the logical choice, but they only sponsored very large companies.

When Sheldon further prodded him over how it was possible that we could have such a coveted office and conduct business in China without a sponsor, he looked utterly unconcerned. Then Sheldon said we should go through the process or hire Graham and James to help us.

Sally Harpole had raised our anxiety. We were worried that we wouldn't be able to conduct business properly until we had a sponsor. The wasted time, we knew, could be costly to our business. Mr. Yu said that if it was important to us, he would arrange everything. He then picked up the phone, placed a call, and carried on a short conversation in Chinese.

An hour later, two Chinese men showed up, sat down with Mr. Yu, and had a fifteen-minute conversation. When they had finished talking, Mr. Yu asked us to join them. He introduced us and explained that the men were officials from MOFERT. At that, one of the men stood up and produced a single piece of paper, handed it to me, and asked if I could fill it out on the typewriter. It was an official form, written in Chinese and English. It required a minimum of information.

I filled in our name and address and the purpose of our business. We then signed it, as did Mr. Yu, and handed it to the official. The man from MOFERT then took out his seal and stamped the document. Immediately, the two men stood up, shook our hands, said something in Chinese, and left.

After they had gone, we asked what the next step was. Mr. Yu said all was finished, and furthermore, there would be a banquet that night to celebrate. We just stood there, amazed.

That same evening, we were honored by MOFERT with an extraordinary banquet. There were twenty-five courses, lots of speeches, and much drinking. The room was full of important people, all of whom came despite only being given a few hours' notice of the celebration. We were seated next to the former mayor of Beijing, Yi Long Ki. Yi had been Chairman Mao's personal secretary on the Long March and was a man of immense prestige. Sheldon was asked to speak to the group, and after several drinks of Moutai, he was more than ready. He made a long speech about how very happy we were to be in China, how we loved the Chinese children, and how much respect we had for the Chinese people. Mayor Yi rose, picked Sheldon up, and hugged him. Everyone was drinking except Mr. Yu, who never drank.

Mr. Yu had very strong guanxi indeed. In China, guanxi is more important than any law or regulation. It is a true measure of personal power. The foreign corporation that fails to understand this will not survive for long. To give and receive guanxi is a delicate transaction, one that requires an intimate knowledge of the subtleties of Chinese power-brokering.

The next day, we went to see Sally and showed her a copy of our sponsor agreement. She was absolutely speechless but told us, after a while, to be very careful. She was convinced the Chinese had some secret agenda for us and our company. She was right.

About Face

~7~

Americans in China

I hear and I forget, I see and I remember.
I do and I understand.
~Chinese Proverb

ONE OF THE GOALS of our company, World China Trade, was to connect American businesspeople with their Chinese counterparts. We made several successful connections, but there were also mishaps with U.S. citizens who personified the derogatory term, "ugly Americans." Here are three stories that run the gamut between the good, the ugly, and the embarrassing.

In the early days of our company, we met an impressive young man, Strauss Zelnick, at a party in Beverly Hills. He was a rising star at Bertelsmann Music Group, which, at that time, was a division of Bertelsmann, the huge German media conglomerate. He and Sheldon hit it off right away. That didn't surprise me since Sheldon had been a music manager before I met him and had handled such diverse talents as Herbie Hancock; Iron Butterfly, an early heavy metal rock group; and Black Oak Arkansas, a southern rock group whose members were friends with Bill Clinton. When we told Strauss we had just started a company in China, he asked us what kind of music was played over there. I flippantly said, "It's Chinese to me." We laughed, but then he said he was really interested in learning what the music scene was like in the People's Republic and mentioned that he wanted to join us on our next trip.

He was an adventurous young man and convinced his company to buy him a ticket enabling him to join us on our next trip to Beijing. The fascinating thing was that he had done some research about underground music under Mao and regarding the current trends in the music world in China. He took us to two places outside our normal haunts, one of which was a small music festival where Strauss knew the musicians hung out to jam. We decided to follow along. He and Sheldon were thrilled to listen to new music created by young Chinese musicians.

Later, Strauss and some of these musicians escorted us to an underground art museum in a bombed-out building that still sported bullet holes in the walls from the "Cultural Revolution," when free thinking and creating did not exist in China under Mao. But the reality is that we humans are all the same, and we bonded over food and music eight thousand miles from home.

It was eye-opening and very cool to witness this underground world of musicians and artists, an experience we would never have had if we hadn't met the young, ambitious Strauss Zelnick. It was no surprise to Sheldon and me that he went on to become a vice president at Columbia Pictures, then president of 20th Century Fox, and then wound up back at Bertelsmann as CEO of BMG Entertainment. Today, he has his own media company.

≈≈≈≈≈

We looked at many industries we thought might be advantageous for connections between American and Chinese businesses. One of those was the silk industry, and, as it happened, Mr. Yu had connections with the silk ministry in China.

Through Bob, an old friend and customer of Sheldon's who was in the printing business in Los Angeles, we met with a large garment company that purchased silk and other materials throughout the world. The company was owned and operated by two brothers, Burt and Arnold. Burt had a very aggressive personality and a large ego, since he and his brother had built a sizable business and had made a great deal of money. Arnold was much more laid back and handled more of the technical part of the business, whereas Burt was the outgoing sales type.

After several meetings, during which we convinced them that we had influence in China and could connect them to the proper factories, they agreed on an arrangement for us to bring them to China and make introductions. The deal was they would pay us $10,000 as an advance fee, and then we would get a sizable commission on any silk goods they purchased from China. Bob also decided to travel with us. He, too, had paid us an introduction fee to connect him to printers in China and had become an investor in World China Trade.

Going to China in the early 1980s was not as simple as having a U.S. passport and hopping on a plane. You first had to get a Chinese visa. The visa office was located at the Chinese consul in Los Angeles, and obtaining a visa through them was a laborious task. You had to go in person, then wait—usually for an inordinate amount of time—to receive an application, which you had to fill out and have approved. The application asked all kinds of questions, and approval usually took six weeks or more.

Sheldon and I had been given multiple entry and exit visas, and therefore did not have to obtain a new visa every time we went back and forth to the PRC. But we should have realized that we might have some difficulties when we brought Burt, Arnold, and Bob to the Chinese consul. It was not very modern, and most of the Chinese spoke with a broken accent and usually took care of the Chinese people before the foreigners.

When we arrived, there were several people in front of us, and Burt got very irritated. He started to complain in a very loud and boisterous manner that he was not used to being treated this way. He insisted that we try and pull some strings to hurry the process along. We were mortified when he was very rude to one Chinese official whom he mistook for an errand boy, who was, in fact, the secretary to the vice-consul.

Sheldon took Burt outside the building and tried to explain that his attitude would create problems for us and that they could refuse his visa application. He responded that they should know who he was, an influential businessman, and that they were just ignorant people from a third-world country. Sheldon managed to calm him down by reminding him that if we could arrange for him to purchase silk directly from China and not through his old Hong Kong sources, where there was a big commission, he would save a great deal of money, and that even though this was a tedious process, it was well worth it.

He continued to be unreasonable, so Sheldon left him outside and came back inside the consul. We asked to meet with the vice-consul, who was a friend. He told us that China was not interested in dealing with rude barbarians and that Burt's actions had created a negative impression. We told him that business was business and that Burt could be a major importer of silk. We asked if he could let his brother Arnold take care of the visas for both of them. He invited Arnold into his office.

Arnold apologized for his brother's actions and told the vice-consul that they were very sincere about doing business with China and that he would personally make sure that his brother behaved himself in the future. The vice-consul agreed to let Arnold apply for both visas. The applications were processed, but we noticed that Burt's had a special Chinese notation that we did not understand.

In preparation for our trip, we explained to Burt, Bob, and Arnold that China was not modern and that they should bring items like toilet paper, hand wipes, and any medicine or over-the-counter drugs they might require, since many such items were not available in Beijing. Burt had a lot to say about that, but we ignored most of it. We were hopeful that once we arrived, he would be overwhelmed and act accordingly. Luckily, he and his brother traveled first class, and we traveled business class.

We arrived in Beijing and started to go through customs. Unlike U.S. customs, Beijing was much more laid back, and the attitude of the Chinese customs inspectors was genial and friendly. Not so with

Burt. Their attitude changed rapidly, and they inspected everything he had in a very somber fashion. He, of course, was, as usual, loud and rude, and after his customs inspection, he was taken to a private room and questioned for about half an hour. He came back subdued, and we felt that the Chinese had, in their own way, accomplished what we could not.

We had red flag limousines used for dignitaries waiting for us at the airport. These Chinese-made autos had red flags above each headlight and taillight, hence the name. We were whisked away to the Beijing hotel, where we met with Mr. Yu and our Chinese office staff and had a grand dinner in the Chinese restaurant in the hotel. We were shown to our rooms, and soon, the trouble started again.

Burt said his room was not acceptable, and he rambled off a litany of complaints. It was dirty, there was no shower (just a bathtub with a hose), the TV had only Chinese programs, the food was lousy, and he wanted his money back because we had cheated him. His brother finally prevailed on him to calm down, and we all went to sleep.

The next day, we met in our office and attempted to lay out our plans for the day, which included a trip for Burt and Arnold to visit large silk factories and a trip to the printing plants for Bob. Burt stormed in, livid. He went on a tirade on how he hated this country and its ignorant people, that he should never have come here in the first place, and that we had taken advantage of him. He insisted on leaving the country immediately. In deference to Burt, I must say that he was not the first who went off a bit after arriving in China. We had another occasion where we brought two partners from the largest accounting firm in the world, and they ended up having a fistfight in the lobby of the Beijing hotel over potential power one or the other could wield (more on that later). So, we tried to calm things down with Burt.

Mr. Yu retired to his office with the darkest look I had ever seen. He was so angry, I thought that Burt might be in personal physical danger. Sheldon went in and tried to explain to Mr. Yu, who had lost considerable face over this issue, that Burt was irrational and that he should not take it personally. Mr. Yu told Sheldon that he was always being personally monitored, that he could be severely criticized for

Burt's errant behavior, and that before Yu would allow himself to be humiliated, he would take whatever drastic steps necessary to resolve this situation with this arrogant and stupid foreigner. He added that they would not let Burt leave the country, and if he continued on, he would have the Public Security people restrain him.

Sheldon and I were at our wits' end. We decided to have a talk with Burt and Arnold. Without mincing words, we told them the facts and warned Burt that his actions could not only hurt him but also the rest of us. We explained that this was a communist country, and the people we were dealing with could eliminate him in a variety of ways, and there would be nothing we could do about it. We also told him that he could not leave the country until permission was given. We left and his brother, Arnold, spent over an hour with him. Finally, they came back to the office and Burt apologized to Mr. Yu and said they were ready to visit the silk factory. By that time, none of us wanted to go with him, but I reluctantly agreed to the task, and off I went with Burt and Arnold.

Sheldon had the easier assignment and went with Bob to tour one of the printing factories. But it wasn't without drama. The factory manager was very cordial, and they were served lunch in the factory dining room. Bob was gracious and very knowledgeable in the printing business. He gave the Chinese several ideas, for which they were grateful. Bob had an interesting sense of humor and throughout the visit would make comments that unfortunately the Chinese could not comprehend.

Near the end of the day, all the factory employees were ushered into a room. The manager introduced Sheldon and Bob as honored guests and asked Bob to make a few comments. He didn't want to criticize, since the factory was old, with ancient equipment and few modern methods, so he decided to lighten up the conversation with some humor. He told the group that he had enjoyed the tour, but somehow, he had gotten printing ink on his pants. He knew that as a printer, it was impossible to tour a print plant without at some point getting ink on yourself.

It was meant as a statement that would bring him together as one of the group. The room got very silent. There was no laughter, no smiles, just somber faces. What happened was they felt he was complaining and that they had made a serious error in allowing him to get his pants dirty. They felt responsible, and the manager was concerned that he could be criticized.

They offered to buy him new pants, clean his pants, or whatever else they could do to remedy the situation. Bob had unwittingly made a serious gaffe, and trying to explain it was just a joke only made it worse. When they arrived back at the office, Mr. Yu informed them that the manager had called and was sending a written apology, and they insisted on buying Bob a new pair of pants.

When I returned with Burt and Arnold, to everyone's amazement, Burt was a totally different person. He was full of smiles, and he went around shaking hands with everyone. He was very impressed with the silk factories. They had treated him with cordiality and respect, but most of all, he was offered high-quality goods at very reasonable prices. All he could talk about was how terrific everything was and what a long and prosperous future he would have with China. He told everyone what a magnificent job I had done, and it seemed that what had started out as very negative was turning into a positive.

But the Chinese have long memories, and Burt had insulted them. The remainder of the week went very well, with lots of banquets and several meetings with silk factories. The day before Burt and Arnold were leaving, there was a farewell banquet, hosted by the silk ministry. Burt made a speech, had several samples to take back to the United States, and was well-satisfied with the trip in general. All the unpleasantness seemed to have been forgotten.

Sheldon and I, along with Mr. Yu, decided to go to the airport to say goodbye. The flight Burt and Arnold were taking was CAAC (Chinese airlines) to Hong Kong, where they would board a United flight back to the United States. We said our goodbyes, and they boarded the airplane. Mr. Yu suggested that we wait until the flight took off before we returned to our office.

About fifteen minutes went by, and we saw Burt being escorted off the airplane by a Ministry of Public Security official. Arnold was told to stay on the airplane, and it took off without Burt. We were very concerned because we saw on Mr. Yu's face that he was aware of what was going on.

Burt was taken to the Ministry of Public Security, and his belongings were searched. They found several antique Chinese coins, which were illegal to take out of China, and some photographs that were taken in an area that the Chinese had strictly forbidden. They allowed us to see Burt, who was very shaken up. His old bravado and arrogance were gone—he was plain scared.

We asked Mr. Yu to take care of this and have Burt released, but Mr. Yu said there was nothing he could do. We were sure he was in on the whole thing. Burt denied having anything to do with the coins and the photos. Meanwhile, the Chinese told him that he would have to stand trial and perhaps go to a Chinese jail. He was frantic when they would not allow him any phone calls. Finally, after two days, they told him they were dropping the charges and put him on a flight back to Hong Kong. Mr. Yu had a satisfied smile on his face, still claiming he knew nothing about it.

≈ ≈ ≈ ≈ ≈

It was January, and we had been in Beijing for a few days with another friend and client, Saul Leonard, a partner in the international accounting firm of Laventhol and Horwath and the partner in charge of the hotel division. His purpose for the trip was to investigate the possibility of building a China business for his firm. Saul was always a polite, courteous, and respectful businessman wherever he went. This time, our cringeworthy moment was due to an Oxy employee.

One morning, Mr. Yu told us that we all had to go to Benxi the next day. He explained it was in Liaoning Province, located in northern Manchuria, not far from the North Korean border. He added that Dean Lee from Oxy would accompany us on the trip to investigate business opportunities. The mayor of Benxi was a friend of Mr. Yu and Dean Lee. The city also had what they considered a natural wonder, the Benxi Water Cave. We were excited as was our client.

It was about twenty degrees in Beijing, and Mr. Yu told us that it would be still colder in Benxi. We had an 8 a.m. train to catch. Mr. Yu hustled us into the car, and we raced to the station. One million people per day go through the main train station in Beijing. It is a vast complex of trains, tracks, buildings, and immense fresh food stands selling everything from vegetables, fruits (the fruit in Northern China is very meager), nuts, rice, and more items.

It was extremely confusing and mobbed with people and animals who were sitting, standing, and sleeping. Dean Lee told us that at any one time, day or night, more than 300,000 people would be packed into the station. We ran for the train, holding onto each other so as not to get lost in this mass of Chinese humanity. We arrived at a train and started to board when Mr. Yu frantically shouted, "Get off. It's the wrong train." We all jumped off, and Mr. Yu sent his assistant racing away toward the right train, which unfortunately happened to be on the other side of the station while we ran after him.

We got to the proper train, all out of breath, and we realized that Mr. Yu's assistant had gotten the train to wait for us (guanxi).

This train looked like something out of an old Russian movie. I felt like were on the Trans-Siberian Railway, which, as it turned out, it actually was. We had a private compartment as did Saul. It was very modest but comfortable, with down feather pillows and mattresses. The dining car was also very modest, with a coal-burning stove in the middle of the car. Lunch was a hot soup made of snake and chicken, with vegetables and noodles. The train had stopped at a small station, and the dining car cook purchased rice and vegetables wrapped in lotus leaves from an open stand, which he also served to us.

The bathrooms on the train were another matter. They were dark, cold, and grimy. The odor was very bad, and I used Handi Wipes over my nose and mouth whenever I went in, which was as little as possible.

At 8:00 p.m., through a speaker in our compartment, a dialogue started and lasted for about thirty minutes. It was in Chinese, but Mr. Yu had told us they broadcasted the same party line with Chinese propaganda every morning and evening.

We arrived in Benxi at 5:00 a.m. the next day. When we stepped off the train, it was twenty degrees below zero. We were all glad Mr. Yu had prepared us, and we had dressed in our warmest gear. Waiting to greet us was the mayor and three other city officials. Benxi is a small industrial city of about 1.5 million people. One of their main industries was the manufacture of steel.

We drove through the city. It was snowing, but because of the industrial setting, it was bleak and grimy. We arrived at the City Hall complex, and as we got out of the car, Sheldon and I noticed an outdoor roller skating rink opposite the complex. About a hundred teenagers were roller skating outside in below-zero temperatures, smiling, laughing, and having a wonderful time. It was a delight to see them.

We went into the City Hall and were ushered into a large conference room. We sat at long tables, where several Chinese were sitting opposite us. Each one would get up and come to the table, sit in front of us, and then tell us, with the help of an interpreter, what industry he was in, facts about that particular factory, and what he had to offer in a joint venture or sale of a product. It ranged from pottery to steel to the distribution of beer, wine, and clothing. They kept coming in a seemingly never-ending stream. They were all very cordial and polite, and no one spoke any English.

The room had no heat. You could see your breath, and there was frost on the table legs. They were dressed in a much more rural manner than the people in Beijing. They all had on long woolen underwear and several layers of clothes under their blue or gray Mao outfits.

We were all dressed warmly with layers of clothes, and it was the first time I could remember wearing gloves inside a room. As the temperature changed, you either added or took off a layer of clothes. This procession of managers or directors from different industries went on for about three hours, and then it was time for lunch.

We moved to a large dining room and saw several tables filled with people invited to our lunch. We sat at the head table with the mayor and other city officials. We started toasting with Moutai almost at once. Benxi made their own Moutai, and it was like mountain brew. The Moutai had a slightly yellow color to it and proved much stronger than the type we drank in Beijing. Everybody was toasting, and it was so cold that the Moutai felt good going down my throat and hitting my stomach.

They served at least twenty courses. The food kept coming—vegetables, meat, poultry, fish, noodles, rice, soup—and each dish was more delicious than the previous one. We drank wine, beer, Moutai, tea...the list just went on and on. Everybody was finally getting a bit woozy and happy. They started to sing and laugh, and we all had a very good time.

After lunch, we were shown to our room for a rest. It was so hot, we had to take off most of our clothes. The heat was hardly ever used except in very extreme circumstances, but as we were honored guests, they turned it on full blast in our room. We had to open a window to get the room moderately cool.

The bathroom was very interesting. The hot water was only available two hours per day from 7:00 a.m. to 8:00 a.m. and 8:00 p.m. to 9:00 p.m. When you first turned on the faucet, the water came out like a black lagoon. When you wanted to drain the bathtub, you had to pull a cork plug out of the side of the tub, and the water would run across the floor of the bathroom to a drain on the floor near the door.

We had a very nice nap, which helped us sleep off some of the alcohol we had been drinking at lunch, and then we were ready for the afternoon session. We sat in a much smaller room with only seven or eight other people present. The city manager and the city's chief architect also attended the meeting. They brought out a large model of a hotel project and a set of plans and specifications. They had worked very hard to develop the model and plans. Their goal was to develop a hotel complex for tourists to come to Benxi and visit the Caves of Benxi. I was excited and spent a long time reviewing the plans and giving advice as to how to modernize them. But we all realized that building a twenty-million-dollar hotel for foreign tourists in a city without an airport was not very realistic.

After spending the afternoon reviewing and discussing the potential development, they took us to a local live theater. It was terrific and very entertaining. The theater was filled with locals, and the entrance price was the U.S. dollar equivalent of thirty-five cents. The first act consisted of a group of acrobats—ten in all. At the end of their act, they stacked themselves five or six high in a pyramid, all carrying burning torches. Then came a group of roller skaters who skated on a tabletop. After them, magicians took the stage. It just went on and on for three hours. We received a lot of stares. Most of these people, if not all, had never seen a gweilo (round-eyed barbarian) before.

The dinner that night was like our earlier lunch—a great amount of food and lots more drinking and carrying on. Dean Lee seemed to take a fancy to the mayor's daughter and was dancing with her. I was a bit concerned as I didn't want any unforeseen difficulties to arise. We finally all retired to bed and were told that we were going to visit the Benxi Water Cave the next morning.

A van picked us up, and we drove for about two hours in the countryside, which reminded us of something out of a Korean War movie. It was bleak and cold, and we passed snow-covered hills with little vegetation. Finally, our van stopped at a small building in the middle of some snow-covered mountains. Inside the building, we were given a small brochure and a cup of tea.

We then walked out of the building on a path for about half a mile and came to a large mountain with two huge, steel doors embedded in the foot of the mountain. It reminded me of the movie *Ali Baba and the Forty Thieves*. Two of the people with us each took a large, steel latch and opened the doors.

We walked into an incredible sight. The temperature was about 65 to 70 degrees, which, we were told, was the average temperature inside the cave regardless of the season.

The ceiling must have been at least fifty feet high; colored lights faced up toward the ceiling, where stalactites hung, some extending down ten feet or more. Inside, a crystal-clear lake stretched, with some small boats bobbing gently on its surface. We got into one of the boats, and our guides started to row us deep into the cave. As we rowed, the width of the lake shrunk, and the ceiling became lower. We saw endless stalactites and stalagmites of incredible colors, widths, and dimensions.

The crystal-clear lake had fish of many colors that we were told were blind. You could actually see down to the bottom of the lake floor, where all types of unusual rocks and life forms resided. The only illumination came from a string of colored lights that had been strung with just a few wires along the side of the lake. We rowed for about half an hour, finally arriving at the area where they had stopped excavating to enlarge the lake so that boats could pass through. They said that the lake went on for miles—they were not sure how long it was or where it ended.

It truly was like one of the eight wonders of the world. We were all very impressed and thanked them for taking us into this wondrous cave.

Mr. Yu told us that we were only ten miles from the North Korean border and asked if we wanted to see it. We said we certainly would. The border was just a stretch of land with a small crossing and guard house on either side. Each side had armed soldiers, and everything looked very peaceful. Sheldon asked Mr. Yu if we could go into North Korea. He replied that even though he had a great deal of guanxi, North Korea was another matter, and that once we entered, we may not be able to leave. Sheldon asked if we could talk to the North Korean border guards. Yu said we could try. The guards on both sides knew each other, and one waved to the other. So, we walked across to the North Korean side.

There was a language barrier, but communication was established. The North Korean soldiers gave us some tea, which was very different from the Chinese tea we had been drinking. We were told there was a small town nearby, and we asked if we could visit the area. Mr. Yu said we were pushing our luck. We decided that it was not a good idea and returned to Benxi.

That night, we had another banquet and started drinking and toasting when I saw Dean Lee disappear with the mayor's daughter. Our train was leaving late that night for Beijing, and when we finally found him with the mayor's daughter, it was obvious that both of them had too much to drink. Actually, that was an understatement as he could hardly stand.

On the way to the train station, we had to stop the car so he could throw up. It seemed embarrassing to me, but no one else gave it much thought. The mayor and his group all gathered to say goodbye and invited us to come back to Benxi and visit its fabulous cave anytime.

Before Saul left China, we had viewed many sites for hotel development and had long meetings with potential joint venture partners, including the Beijing Hotel. He felt there was a great deal of potential for hotel development in China.

~8~

From Roller Skating
Entepreneurs to
Real Estate Developers

Good things are produced only through much grinding.
~Chinese Proverb

A FTER SAUL'S TRIP TO China, we decided that instead of attempting to build roller skating rinks, we would develop a hotel project in Beijing, which would be much more lucrative. We had come to realize that because roller rinks would cater only to the Chinese population, who had only Chinese money (RMB) to spend, a currency that could not be converted into foreign exchange certificates (FEC), there would be no way to take the profits out of China except in counter trade. Beijing, however, was ripe for real estate development, and I had an idea.

As far back as the early 1980s, only two modern hotels in Beijing had ever been built by foreigners. One was the Jianguo Hotel, down the street from the venerable Beijing Hotel, and the other was the Sheraton Great Wall Hotel, located midway between downtown and the airport. The Jianguo Hotel was more strategically located but fairly small. It had been developed by Clement Chen, an expatriate Chinese man from San Francisco. Chen brought in the Peninsula Group of Hong Kong to manage it, and the Jianguo was an upscale place beloved by wealthy tourists and corporate executives.

The Sheraton Great Wall Hotel was largely a place for tourists to stay, although it had its share of offices too. Because there were no office buildings to speak of—and those few that did exist were mostly substandard at the time—and because of its location near the center of Beijing's business district, the Jianguo's hotel rooms were used as headquarters by several major foreign corporations and law firms. Both hotels, of course, were joint ventures with government agencies, without which nothing can be accomplished in China.

My architectural background came into good use, and I developed a unique concept for a mixed-use project that included a first-class hotel with several restaurants, apartments for foreign businessmen, and offices for foreign corporations.

We had never developed a hotel project before, but the word "impossible" was not in our vocabulary. We had spent quite a lot of time in the People's Republic by then and had a clear idea of what the marketplace needed. We were told by Mr. Yu, Richard Chen, and Dean Lee that our idea for a hotel project was excellent, and eventually, our little company was guided into the real estate development business by our Chinese hosts.

In a nation in which there is theoretically no private property, securing a piece of land for real estate development inevitably involves negotiations with some arm of the government. And with a bureaucracy as centralized as China's, you might expect some sort of clearing house with a registry of available land and an efficient bureaucracy whose job it is to arrange for land leases. One of the advantages of communism, according to communists, is efficiency in such matters as part of the distribution of state resources. Of course, you might believe that pigs fly too.

There is, in fact, no such agency, and the process of finding available land, as we were soon to find out, is so complex and mysterious that it makes chaos theory look comprehensible by comparison. The acquisition of a land lease is an arduous process in which the goal is to wear down foreign investors. When the Chinese finally present you with the deal they had in mind in the first place, you are so thankful to have a piece of land—any land—that sheer relief overwhelms good judgment. All the hapless foreigner wants to know at that point is where to sign.

We naively assumed that our experience would be different and that our diminutive master of guanxi, Mr. Yu, would be able to arrange everything expeditiously. Mr. Yu started to contact several sources, and we began to meet many government organizations with property that might be suitable for our type of project. This took many months and several trips back and forth from the U.S. to China.

It was a very frustrating experience. Mr. Yu would tell us that he had found an excellent property, and then we would go investigate the site, meet with officials, and spend endless, fruitless hours in discussion and negotiation.

This routine, or something like it, went along for several months. It was like playing horseshoes—you could get really close to the target but still never quite get there. Each time Mr. Yu would bring us a property, we would get very excited, and he would tell us that this time, it would be different. It always was a bit different, but the result was always the same: *no deal*.

We prepared endless letters of intent, attended banquet after banquet, and sat at more meetings. We went from one side of Beijing to the other looking at properties while meeting with multitudes of people. Ultimately, we grew weary and discouraged. It was like being on a roller coaster ride.

On one trip, we traveled to Shen Zhen to look for property. This was a new border city, next to Hong Kong, that the Chinese were building for the future. We traveled to Shanghai as well, all with the same result.

Then, one day, Mr. Yu told us that he had located an excellent property and that we should go look at it. If we liked it, he would arrange for us to meet with the appropriate officials and begin negotiations.

The property turned out to be directly across the street from the Beijing Hotel. We could actually see the land from our office window. There could be no better site in Beijing. It was two blocks from

Tiananmen Square on Beijing's main commercial thoroughfare, within walking distance of the Forbidden City, and adjacent to the hotel that had served as the main meeting place for businessmen and bureaucrats since the country had opened to the West. Not only that, but the parcel was also nearly vacant—bare land was rare in Beijing—and it seemed not to be coveted by any other foreign investor at the time.

It seemed too good to be true—which, of course, it was. The vacant lot was only being used by an old man who, for a few cents, gave donkey rides to children. The symbolism escaped us.

We were very excited. To call the property "prime" would have been an understatement. We began negotiations immediately, and everyone seemed receptive to our proposal. The land was supposedly controlled by a state-owned shipping agency, although it would have been an odd place for a warehouse. Nevertheless, we spent many hours with various officials, sitting quietly while Mr. Yu negotiated in Chinese.

Over a period of several days, we ate together, drank together, and made many speeches. We told everyone that we were thankful to have this opportunity and were honored by the friendship everyone had shown us. All the social exchanges we took part in seemed genuine. Many foreigners remained aloof with their Chinese hosts, but we never did. I assumed that we were making good progress.

Finally, the officials of the shipping agency indicated that we had a deal and suggested that we all celebrate at a banquet that evening. We toasted one another and to the future of the project.

Sheldon was always asked by the ministry to make a speech at these banquets. The speech was from our hearts. He would tell the Chinese how very much we appreciated the opportunity to come to China and be honored by so many people. He would also tell them that we were Jewish and that the Chinese and the Jews had a long history together. A history that went back three thousand years. He would remind them of Kaifeng, a town north of Beijing that had a temple where Judaism was practiced by Chinese people for a thousand years. He told them the thing that the Jews and the Chinese have in common was a merchant mentality.

We had come to China to build something for the children be-cause we believe, as do the Chinese, that children are their most im-portant asset. Sometimes, he would tell them of the ten lost tribes of Israel and that there is a theory in the Torah that one of the tribes went east, and that it's possible that the Chinese are all Jews.

Mr. Yu would always tell Sheldon afterward that he should not bring politics into the discussions. We would tell him that it is not po-litical, it's life. He would tell us that Israel and China do not have any diplomatic relations. We would always remind him of the fact that the only two private aircraft allowed into China were Dr. Hammer's 727 Boeing and the Israeli jet owned by billionaire tycoon Shaul Eisenberg, who had offices on the ground floor of the Beijing Hotel. Mr. Eisenberg had been doing business with China for many years, and he was an Israeli citizen.

We would always end the banquets with new friends. The Chinese really liked us because we loved their children, we ate with them, we laughed with them, and we wanted to be with them, unlike most for-eign business visitors who spent as little time in China as possible, remaining just long enough to conduct business. Most did not mingle with the "common folk" as they say.

We agreed at the banquet that we would meet the next morning to sign the letter of intent and go forward with the project on that prime piece of property. That night, we stayed up until 3:00 a.m. writing and re-writing it. We arrived at the office early to prepare for the meeting and the signing of the letter of intent. Mr. Yu met us and calmly said the meeting was off, the deal was over, and that the piece of property was no longer available.

We were shocked. We asked him why they had changed their minds, and what, if anything, we had done to cause them to back out. He said we did nothing wrong. They had liked us and were very hap-py to meet us at the banquet. He then looked at us and said, "This is China, and the ox moves slow, and the earth is patient."

Mr. Yu liked proverbs, even if they were entirely irrelevant to the situation at hand. Oxen have no strategy and pursue no agen-da. Americans are not patient. We didn't understand. But before we could ask any more questions, Mr. Yu announced that he had another property for us to see.

The second property was even better, he promised, although it was hard to imagine a site superior to the one we had just spent so much energy trying to acquire.

Nevertheless, we dutifully trudged across town to look at it. It wasn't as good as the first site, but it was the only one available—or so we were told—and we began the whole negotiation process all over again. After another round of meetings, dinners, and a second letter of intent, the deal fell through.

This went on for several months. In a carefully choreographed process, we were subjected to a series of negotiations for a succession of properties, and during each transaction, we came incrementally closer to making a deal. Mr. Yu would bring a property to us and assure us that everything would be different "this time," but the deal always fell through. Each negotiation was slightly different, as Mr. Yu said it would be, and each time, we were allowed to achieve certain small victories—just enough to hold our interest and keep us in the game.

We crisscrossed Beijing, looked at twenty or so properties, and as before, attended a score of banquets and prepared endless letters of intent. Our emotional roller coaster ride continued, designed to wear us down. In retrospect, the manipulation was transparent, but at the time, we had little awareness of the psychological strategy to which we were being subjected. The Chinese are masters of the human psyche and know precisely how to keep you on the edge of the knife between despondency and hope.

Mr. Yu came to us once again and said there was another piece of property we should look at. It was located next to the Workers Stadium, on the second ring road, midway between the Sheraton Great Wall Hotel and Beijing Hotel. We were nearly burned out but grudgingly agreed to go look at the site.

It was a large parcel, and none of it was vacant. Most of the land was occupied by an old glass products factory and the rest by a ramshackle collection of tiny, conjoined, ancient-looking houses.

Building on the site would require major demolition work and the re-location of hundreds of people. The location was okay, but the demo and relocation work seemed daunting. The architectural preservation movement, which is so strong in the U.S., has few if any advocates in China. Most Chinese are free of sentimentality about such things. We made note of the site's facilities and location and returned to our room at the Beijing Hotel.

A few minutes after we arrived, Mr. Yu called and told us he want-ed to bring a gentleman to meet us. His name was Wang Fu Shen—the man supposedly in charge of the glass factory property, although we later learned that he was a high-ranking officer in the Ministry of State Security. This group was the most powerful and feared agency in China, more ruthless and clandestine than its sister agency, the Ministry of Public Security. We agreed to see Mr. Wang, and, in a few minutes, Mr. Yu and Ms. Zhang appeared at our door with him.

This was the first time we had met with anyone on such an infor-mal basis. Usually, negotiations began with a series of formal intro-ductions and long, almost ceremonial meetings. Mr. Wang simply sat down and, with no formalities, produced a site plan, unrolled it, and began to describe the various possibilities for developing the parcel. He said rather matter-of-factly that the project had already been ap-proved and a deal was assured, and then launched into a discussion of the dollar equity each side would contribute to the project.

Sheldon and I just looked at each other with a combination of boredom and detachment. We'd heard it all before. Why should this be different? Detecting our mood, Ms. Zhang looked at us and said, "This is real."

Ms. Zhang was right, and suddenly, the pace began to accelerate. Mr. Yu came in the next day and announced that we had a competitor, Donald Nixon, the former president's brother. This was going to take a lot of guanxi, according to Mr. Yu. We had no way of knowing if this was true or not. They were undoubtedly playing Nixon as well as us, and we later came to doubt whether Nixon was a serious contender.

The Chinese wanted us to have this site—for reasons we would not discover until much later. But the drama was played out as though it were a genuine competition. Nixon's group was in town and supposedly had the backing of the central government—whatever that meant—and the mayor of Beijing. We had several meetings, and Mr. Yu claimed to call in many favors.

The guanxi was flowing. As part of the negotiations, we met with the Beijing branch of the Ministry of Public Security, formerly headed by a man named Li Ping. We later met Mr. Li himself, who was introduced to us as the coal minister. Whatever his title, he was enormously powerful, and we subsequently discovered he was closely associated with the Chinese espionage community. He went on to become the premiere of China from 1987 to 1998.

It was a very hectic week of high-level meetings, but by Friday, Mr. Yu came to the office with a big smile and announced that the deal was made. Our offer to put up an initial 3.75 million U.S. dollars had been accepted. As we would eventually learn, we were the hand-picked choice of the Ministry of State Security.

The following Monday, we decided to go back and look at the site we had just agreed to develop. Our letter of intent with the Chinese included a pledge to construct several new apartment buildings to replace housing that would be lost, and we wanted to revisit the residential area.

We walked all around the property that morning and then decided to tour the glass products factory in the afternoon. The factory was still operating, as it had been for many generations, and its equipment looked as though it dated back to the turn of the century. It was a vast, old, brick building, and in one huge room, we came upon a sight I'll never forget. It was the electrical control room and looked like something out of an old black-and-white Frankenstein movie. Huge transformers, ceramic insulators, old analog gauges, and electrical switches were everywhere. The whole room buzzed and crackled with high-voltage electricity.

Near the center of the room was a massive electrical switch shaped like an inverted tuning fork. It was at least five feet tall and painted bright green. Sheldon walked over and stood in front of it, fascinated. And then, in the blink of an eye, he put his hand on the lever and pulled it down. Instantly, everything went dark, and silence enveloped the room. Mr. Yu nearly passed out. I choked back a laugh while Sheldon stood there, looking a bit dazed. Our tour hosts stood nearby, frozen.

Sheldon later told me he didn't know what came over him. He just had an irresistible urge to turn it off. Maybe it was the months of frustrating negotiations; perhaps it was temporary insanity. I laughed when he said one of the electrical workers, who spoke a little English, whispered in his ear, "I've worked here forty years, and I always wanted to do that."

It took two days to restore power, not only to the glass factory but to the surrounding neighborhood. Fortunately, it didn't scuttle the deal. In China, it pays to be a little unpredictable.

~9~

Interlude:
Our Daughter Comes to China

As distance tests a horse's strength, time reveals a person's character.
~Chinese Proverb

OUTSIDE OF OUR BUSINESS dealings in China, we had many memorable occasions and grand adventures. And of course, there was always intrigue. One occasion particularly stands out to me, and it happened to fall during a time when our sixteen-year-old daughter Jolie came to visit us. It was the summer of 1986 (before the hotel project) and a very important milestone year for Dr. Hammer.

Jolie typically stayed with her older brothers and sisters during our trips to China, but at one point, she asked if she could visit us. We arranged for her to fly to Hong Kong, where she would stay with our Chinese Hong Kong friends Eugenia and Ken Wai before joining us in Beijing. We had met Ken and Eugenia during one of our earlier trips to China. Eugenia worked as an interior designer, and Ken was a refrigeration engineer educated at Purdue University. Both Ken and Eugenia were from old Hong Kong families and were very well-connected in Hong Kong's social and business upper circles. We got to be very good friends and always visited them during our trips in and out of Hong Kong.

We knew Jolie would be in good hands with them, but we were nervous about a sixteen-year-old year taking a trip to Asia alone. Our nerves really went into overdrive when we heard the news of a typhoon off the coast of Hong Kong just when Jolie was supposed to arrive.

We were relieved that the plane was able to land, and our friends had a Rolls Royce limousine at the airport to pick her up and bring her to their house in Wan Chai. Jolie stayed with them for a whirlwind three days. She was escorted all over Hong Kong in limousines, taken to the best restaurants, and had a wonderful time. They then put her on the plane to Beijing.

We were in the midst of a very important occasion. Dr. Hammer was in Beijing, staying at the state guest house. Finally, after several years of difficult negotiations, his company, Occidental Petroleum, and a Bank of China subsidiary signed a $475-million-dollar loan to finance China's largest coal mine. At that time, it was the largest and most high-profile U.S.-Chinese joint venture aimed at more than doubling China's exports of coal.

The night Jolie was arriving in Beijing, a huge celebration banquet was to be held in the Great Hall of the People, with over 1,500 guests in attendance. Mr. Yu and Ms. Zhang were responsible for all the arrangements. Our office was a beehive of activity.

Many top central and Beijing government officials would be attending, including Den Xiao Ping, a Chinese revolutionary leader, military commander, and statesman who was then the paramount leader of the People's Republic of China. Ping famously said, "to get rich is glorious." He is considered by many to be the most significant political leader of the latter part of the twentieth century, bringing China out of poverty and changing the power of the world economy. Also attending was Li Peng who became the fourth premier of the People's Republic of China in 1987.

To say this was a major celebration would have been a gross understatement. Jolie's plane was to arrive at 2:00 p.m., but it was on CAAC, China's airline—not the most dependable. We arrived at the airport at 1:30, and by 4:30, the plane had still not arrived. Somehow, it got diverted to Tianjin. They took everyone off the plane, which made Jolie very nervous. The passengers finally boarded a different plane and arrived at about 5:30 p.m. Mr. Yu had gone with us and was now very anxious about the banquet he was responsible for, which was starting at 8:30 p.m. He spoke to a few of the airport officials, and they went out to the plane, got Jolie off first, and brought her right to us without going through any customs procedures at all.

We immediately got into our car, and as our driver rushed us back to the hotel, Sheldon told Jolie she would have half an hour to get dressed as we were going to a banquet with Dr. Hammer and the chairman of China, along with 1,500 other people. She would be the only teenager.

Jolie looked shell-shocked. She had flown through a typhoon, had three days of incredible luxury and Asian affluence, boarded a Chinese plane and landed in what looked like a field in outer Mongolia, then boarded another plane, landed in Beijing, and was escorted off the plane by Public Security people. But with a resiliency possessed only by the young, she rallied to the occasion and was ready to leave on time.

We arrived at the banquet and were seated at the first table right in front of the dais, where the top officials and Dr. Hammer sat. There are no turkeys in China, so Dr. Hammer brought 250 of them from overseas for this special occasion. Every table got a turkey. There were many speeches, throughout which Jolie sat rapt, seeming to be taking it all in. Then came the pictures. We all posed, and she had her picture taken with the top Chinese officials in the country. Everyone complimented us about Jolie, and Dr. Hammer was beaming.

In those days, China was very safe for foreigners. Sheldon and I walked the streets all over and mingled with the Chinese on every walk of life, and everyone was always very pleasant to us. We left our hotel room door open and our valuables and money right on the dresser; nothing was ever stolen. We decided that we would get Jolie a room to herself so that she could come and go as she pleased, with access to our car and driver.

We introduced her to our friend Joe Roseman who managed the

Great Wall Sheraton Hotel. Joe's son, Kip, currently lived in Beijing with Joe and his wife, and Jolie struck up a friendship with him that turned into a romance. Kip introduced Jolie to all his expatriate friends, and in just a few days, she had a whole group of chums. She started to learn a bit of Chinese and went everywhere with the other kids. There is no legal drinking age in China, so they imbibed large bottles of beer. She met kids from all over the world whose parents were either government officials or expatriates working for foreign companies doing business in the PRC.

It was actually very easy for Jolie to visit us in China. She hung out with her friends, and we never worried. She would join us for breakfast and sometimes dinner and was having a wonderful time.

About a week after being in Beijing, we decided to take Jolie to Beihai Park, where you can rent rowboats with a rower. The nice, young guy who rowed our boat took a fancy to Jolie. Interestingly, he spoke English, which he said he had taught himself. When we were finished, he invited us to his house for some tea. Jolie wasn't too interested, but we agreed because we thought it would be a good experience for her to see how the people of China live. So, we drove to his home, where he lived with his mother, sister, grandmother, aunt, and uncle.

The home was located in a much older part of the city and had no running water except for a spigot in the central courtyard. The units, as far as we could tell, were made simply of mud and brick, and inside, the floor was old cracked cement. The heat was a peat/coal small stove in the center of the room, but there was a sink with a drain to a bucket and two gas burners. It was as clean as could be expected, and we were graciously invited in.

We were served tea and fresh watermelon, which in the summer, is sold in the streets. Only the young man spoke English, and we spent about half an hour there. Sheldon asked to go to the bathroom and was shown outside to a communal toilet. (The reason the U.S. asks people coming to China to bring Handi Wipes is so that they can cover their noses when necessary.) After spending time in China, we got used to the lavatories, and it became almost natural. But this latrine must have been there for many years, and Sheldon was embarrassed over the fact that he found it just too difficult to use. We left and went back to the hotel, where the lavatory facilities were much different but still not up to the standards Americans enjoy in the United States.

The next day, the young man showed up in our office, and Sheldon asked Mr. Yu if we could find him some employment. Mr. Yu said he would try, but nothing ever came of it, and Jolie was not interested in a continued relationship with this boy. She was involved with her group of friends and was enjoying herself. Sheldon decided to try to help this young man. A few days later, he went back to the park with our driver, who spoke a bit of English, and asked for the boy.

It seemed that no one knew of him, and he did not work at the park. We then drove to his home where we had the tea. The driver went in and soon came out, informing Sheldon that the people who we met with had never seen him before our visit. The young man had told them he was with the government, and we were honoring them with our visit. Sheldon asked Mr. Yu what was going on. As usual, when it was a subject he didn't want to discuss, he just ignored my husband as if he hadn't asked anything. We never saw the young man again.

One day, Jolie came to the office and said that a group of expatriate kids had decided to go to Beidaihe, a town on the ocean, for a holiday. It was about a ten-hour train ride for us, and the United States embassy had a house in the community. At first, we said no dice. She was only sixteen, we had no idea where Beidaihe was, and we were concerned over the idea of a group of teenagers traveling around China alone. Jolie, of course, pleaded and so did Kip. They told us that they would be escorted by U.S. marines from the embassy so we had no cause to worry. Those marines were in their early twenties, and I could well imagine what might happen. I asked Mr. Yu to arrange for the Ministry of Public Security to keep their eye on them and make sure they did not get into any trouble. He laughed and agreed and told me not to worry.

So, Jolie went off to Beihai for four days. We didn't hear anything until Mr. Yu came to us one day and told us there was a slight problem. It seemed that Jolie and her friends, including three marines, went over a wall into a public swimming pool late at night after closing and were swimming around and drinking beer at 2:00 a.m. The city officials became aware of their presence there, most likely through the public security people, and streamed into the building.

The marines' story was that they were there to protect the kids and had followed them, and the reason they were wearing bathing suits was to make sure no one drowned. The kids had little to say. They were lectured by the Chinese and their respective parents, and the incident was forgotten, except by Mr. Yu who had a great laugh at the whole thing.

~10~

Due Diligence

If you want to find out about the road ahead, then ask
about it from those coming back.
~Chinese Proverb

W E SIGNED THE ORIGINAL letter of intent to develop the glass factory property for the hotel development project with Mr. Wang's company, BLIPU (Beijing Industrial Product Union). We would later find out it was a front for the Ministry of Public Security. The letter of intent, however, was just a prelude to the real negotiations, which would lead to a formal joint venture agreement—a very complicated and lengthy document. Our company, World China Trade, was responsible for making the financial arrangements, which included finding a lender to provide construction financing. The Chinese, in turn, were to find an agency that would guarantee the loan.

At the suggestion of friends in Hong Kong, we met with Mr. Charles Wrangham, vice chairman of Standard Asia Charter Bank in Hong Kong, to discuss if they would consider funding the construction loan. Mr. Wang had told us that the project would cost a maximum of twenty-eight million U.S. dollars based on his analysis. The first thing Mr. Wrangham asked for was a detailed budget so that he could determine if it was realistic.

We traveled back to Beijing and told Mr. Wang that the bank needed a written budget. Mr. Wang took out a piece of paper, wrote twenty-eight million dollars on it, then took out his chop and sealed it.

We explained to Mr. Wang that the bank would not accept that document and that a detailed list of the construction costs from start to finish was necessary. Mr. Yu then explained to us that Mr. Wang's word would have to be sufficient.

We traveled back to Hong Kong to meet again with Charles Wrangham. This time, he invited us out for an afternoon on Standard Chartered's yacht. It was a wonderful afternoon, and we met Sophia, Charles' wife, and several other executives from the bank. We sailed through Hong Kong Bay and out to Lantau Island. We were wined and dined in a very elegant way.

We finally got to talk about business, and Mr. Wrangham asked if we had received the budget from Mr. Wang. When Sheldon handed him the piece of paper, he started to laugh and could hardly contain himself, which is very unusual for a staid Englishman. When he regained his composure, he added that the budget, of course, was necessary.

Through our Hong Kong friend Eugenia Wai, who was an interior designer, we had been introduced to Arthur Kwok, owner of Arthur Kwok Architects. I was very impressed with him and their award-winning projects, and we wanted him to work with us on the hotel. Arthur, with his knowledge of architecture and construction in China, was able to put together a proper budget, which the bank accepted.

We brought the budget back to Beijing and showed it to Mr. Wang. He took a fast look, then said it was acceptable, signed it, and put his chop on it. Then Mr. Wrangham asked Mr. Wang to guarantee that if there were any overruns on the construction, the Beijing part of the joint venture would guarantee to provide those funds. Mr. Wang agreed, but later in the life of the joint venture, it came back to haunt him when Standard Chartered Bank asked him to honor that guarantee.

We also arranged to create a feasibility study, which was necessary to prove the financial viability of our project to the bank and its directors. At least, that's what it was supposed to have done.

We were clients of the firm Laventhol and Horwath, an international accounting firm, and asked the managing partner in the Los Angeles office if they were interested. They were indeed very interested because it would be the first study of its kind ever done in China and could position them as experts in financial feasibility studies in the hospitality business in the People's Republic of China.

Laventhol and Horwath had a sister office in Hong Kong and arranged for the United States office and the Hong Kong office to conduct the study together. Mr. Wang and the Chinese side refused to have the American firm involved and insisted that the British offices of Laventhol and Horwath work with the Hong Kong office to perform the study.

We flew to Hong Kong and met Jeff Parkinson from the London office, and then we all met with Sam Wong, the manager of the offices of Horwath in Hong Kong. The Chinese arranged visas for all of us, and we flew together to Beijing to assist the Laventhol and Horwath people with the feasibility study.

When we arrived, the Beijing Accountants Bureau held a banquet for us and told the Horwath people that they had already done a feasibility study on the project and were satisfied that it was financially viable. The Horwath people asked to see the study, and, as usual, the Chinese refused. They said it was an internal Chinese document that foreigners could not view. The Horwath people persisted and said it would be very helpful to see this document as it could provide a base for the one they were preparing. The Chinese said they would like to oblige but could not because of the rules of China pertaining to internal financial documents.

The banquet went on quite late, with a lot of Moutai poured and drank. Jeff Parkinson came close to passing out; we had to carry him to his hotel room.

The next day was the start of the due diligence for the study. Our first stop was the office of British Airways. We had made an appointment with the manager who was expecting us. Jeff had a terrible hangover, was dragging his feet, and vowed never again to get into a drinking contest with the Chinese. He was trying to be a good sport, as the English like to be, and, as he put it, "I overdid it a bit."

We arrived at the offices of British Airways in the Jianguo Hotel. The manager, who looked very haggard, brought us into his private office and told us that his staff, with the exception of his assistant, was all local Chinese. He motioned us to whisper as he pointed toward the ceiling and made gestures with his hand. He then wrote on a piece of paper that his office was bugged with secret microphones and that we should be careful what we speak about.

The accountants asked several questions pertaining to the amount of tourism that came in on the British Airways flights, where they stayed, and what the expectations were for the future. His answers were very positive. We asked him how his relations were with the Chinese. He said they were excellent and that the Chinese were easy to do business with and very straightforward. As he was saying those words, he was shaking his head from side to side and pointing up at the concealed microphones.

We spent about an hour with him, and as he walked us out to our car, he told us he was the fourth manager in four years in the Beijing office. The first two managers were relieved because of psychological reasons, and the last manager had to be taken out in a straitjacket. He was completely paranoid, and obviously, very frightened. He told us we should be very careful and that everything we said and did was written down and filed away to be used against us if necessary.

He actually was correct about everything being written down. In every meeting, wherever you were, there was always one person taking copious notes. In fact, we attended several meetings throughout the life of the joint venture where there was a person whose job was to read facial expressions, and after the meeting, they would sit and discuss the foreigners and just how to manipulate them. What was most interesting was that the more we understood what they were doing, the easier it became to deal with them. The Chinese always expected twists and turns, and we were always perfectly straight and honest with them. It confused them and worked to our advantage.

The next meeting was at the offices of JAL (Japan Airlines). We again met with the office manager. As a Japanese individual, he had a broader understanding of the Chinese than any Western foreigner at the time. In the early 1980s, a deep-seated friction remained between the Chinese and Japanese. It stemmed from the past and the rape of Nanjing during the Japanese invasion of Manchuria. There was anti-Japanese literature all over Beijing, and the Japanese never mingled, outside of business matters, with the Chinese.

During one of our many dinners in the Great Hall of the People, many times we engaged in some discussion regarding Japanese products. As one of the ministers poured a dish of sizzling rice over a large soup bowl, he said, "Bombs over Tokyo." Mr. Yu referred to the Japanese as "little yellow dwarfs."

We sat down in the manager's office and introduced ourselves, and he informed us that business was very good. There were many Japanese who wanted to come to Beijing for business and pleasure, and more would arrive every year. He told us that JAL had made a strong commitment to China, and the future was very bright. Even if fifty more hotels were built, he assured us that they still would not be able to keep up with future demand. He was proven right.

The accountants asked him where his flight attendants stayed when they had to lay over in Beijing and how many room nights they used. He told them that JAL reserved several hundred rooms a year in advance. The Chinese also required that JAL pay for them all a year in advance.

The accountants then remarked that if JAL was pre-paying for the rooms, they must be getting a sizable discount. The manager looked at us, and with a typical inscrutable Asian face, told us that the Chinese insisted they pay a 25 percent premium. Using a logic only the Chinese could understand, they were told that by pre-paying and reserving the rooms a year in advance, the Chinese could not rent the rooms to anyone else; therefore, a premium was necessary. The Japanese paid it without a backward glance. It's obvious why. One only had to look at a map of the world to see that Japan is just a tiny island compared to the giant that is China.

We next visited CAAC. The manager was very cordial. They served us tea and told us that they expected a bright future in tourism and that the Chinese government was negotiating for the purchase of several new jet aircraft from the United States and France. They also said they had conducted a feasibility study with the Beijing Accountancy Bureau and that it had come out financially viable for the next ten years. The accountants asked if they could see it or have a copy. We were told, unsurprisingly, that it was an internal document and not available for foreign perusal.

The accountants stayed for four or five days and visited the three foreign joint venture hotels already developed at that time. They spoke to the managers and hotel personnel, then visited the manager of the Beijing Hotel, where we were staying and where our office was located. The manager told the accountants that the hotel was fully reserved for the next year, and requests for reservations came in daily. They asked to see his reservation records and were told they were internal documents and not available to foreigners.

We expected that the Horwath accountants would be getting frustrated, but both Jeff Parkinson and Sam Wong were familiar with the Chinese. This was China, they realized, and it would be an exercise in futility to try to understand.

The night prior to their leaving, another banquet was hosted courtesy of the Beijing Accountancy Bureau, during which they got Jeff Parkinson involved in another drinking bout. One of the Chinese from the accountancy bureau would get up, make the toast, shout, "Ganbei," and he would down his shot glass full of Moutai in one gulp. Then Jeff would get up and do the same. As he would put his glass down, before you could blink an eye, a waiter would fill it again. After about eight "Ganbei" cheers, Jeff was glassy-eyed, and I only hoped he wouldn't pass out. The Chinese, of course, were enjoying themselves immensely.

After the banquet, we took Jeff back to his hotel room. We then had a meeting with Mr. Yu and Mr. Wang regarding the outcome of the feasibility study. We told them that if the study came out negative, the bank could refuse to loan us the construction financing. We also told them that the Chinese were not being very cooperative and were refusing to share the studies they had done. Mr. Wang told us again that Chinese law prohibited the sharing of the Chinese study with foreigners. We had heard that story before, so we stressed that the most important thing for us would be for the outcome of the study to be positive.

Much later in the joint venture, we found out that Mr. Sam Wong, the Horwath accountant from Hong Kong, was called later that night by either Mr. Wang or another Ministry of Public Security official. He was told he should remember that he was a Hong Kong Chinese and that 1997 was not so far in the future—and that it was important that the study be positive. Another mild form of typical Chinese extortion.

The next day, we drove the accountants to the airport, and as we approached, Mr. Yu gave Sheldon a large, brown envelope, informing him that inside were copies of the Bureau of Accountancy feasibility study. He also said that since Sheldon was a foreigner, he could give it to the accountants without a problem. Jeff Parkinson, bleary-eyed, thanked him, and off they went.

The feasibility study was positive.

About Face

~11~

The Architect, Saving Face, and Games

Even the highest towers begin at the ground.
~Chinese Proverb

BASED ON THE FEASIBILITY study, we agreed to move forward in developing the joint venture agreement, which would be the body of the contract, to build the hotel complex. It was Sheldon's job to develop the draft, a tedious process with constant changes that ended up taking weeks and many sleepless nights. I was in charge of the design and construction of the hotel from the American joint-venture side, so while Sheldon was working on the draft agreement, I focused on selecting the architects.

The Chinese insisted that the Beijing Design Institute be the primary architectural firm on the project. However, I helped them realize that since they had little or no experience in the design of modern hotels, a foreign firm would also be necessary.

I chose Arthur Kwok and Associates. Arthur was from a very well-known Hong Kong family who originally came from Shanghai and had prospered in Hong Kong. They had a hand in several businesses such as banking and department stores. Chinese families in Hong Kong are like U.S. corporations, which often involve many varied business entities, and the Kwok family was one of the most prominent.

Arthur, a well-known architect, had already designed many large-scale projects such as hotels, racetracks, marinas, and office buildings. Like all Hong Kong Chinese, Arthur wanted to do as much business in China as possible. The year 1997, when Britain would hand Hong Kong back to Beijing, was coming, and he felt that his position would be safer and more secure if he could do business at any level in China. Beijing was very important as the top leaders were there.

I visited Arthur's office and several of his projects. I was very impressed with his excellent work and knew his manner would be a plus in dealing with Mainland Chinese.

I proposed to Mr. Wang that Arthur be selected. Mr. Wang refused, adamant that we choose an American architect and not one from Hong Kong. We tried to explain to Mr. Wang that an American architect, who did not speak Chinese nor understood how to deal with the PRC, would be useless. Mr. Wang, as usual, held to his stubborn position and said that he would not deal with any Hong Kong Chinese as they were, as he put it, "running dogs." He told us that he would not even sit at the same table with a Hong Kong Chinese.

Despite his refusal, I knew it was in the best interests of the joint venture to have Arthur Kwok involved in the project, and I was determined to convince Mr. Wang of that fact. I explained the situation to Mr. Yu, who informed us that there was great resentment of the Hong Kong Chinese in the PRC, and it would be very difficult, if not impossible, to change Mr. Wang's mind.

I flew back to Hong Kong and met with Arthur to explain the situation to him. He was not surprised as he knew better than us of the resentment between the Hong Kong Chinese and the PRC.

I asked Arthur to fly to Beijing and told him we would try to set up a meeting with Mr. Wang and Mr. Lu Gong, the architect and representative from the Beijing Design Institute. Arthur agreed and said he would also bring one of the architects from his office who had come from Beijing and had worked at the Beijing Design Institute.

We flew back to Beijing, and I met with Mr. Wang. I told him that we had made no commitment to Arthur Kwok but that he had come to Beijing just to sit down with Mr. Wang to discuss the possibility of his involvement in the project. Mr. Wang refused to see him, reiterated his "running dog" litany, and insisted on us bringing in an American architect.

We asked Mr. Yu to intervene, explaining that it was not polite to ignore Arthur Kwok. He was a respected architect and had flown all the way from Hong Kong to meet and discuss this hotel project. Mr. Yu agreed to try to convince Mr. Wang. This negotiation went on for three days as Arthur waited patiently. He knew China better than us.

Finally, Mr. Yu said that Mr. Wang would meet with Arthur on one condition—Arthur was to sign a document that I was to prepare prior to the meeting. The document would state that in the course of our meeting, the site of the hotel project would be discussed and shown to Arthur. In the event that he was not brought on to the project, he would agree not to go behind our backs and try to steal the project for himself.

This, of course, was ridiculous. Arthur Kwok was a Hong Kong Chinese and always fearful that when he traveled to Mainland China, they could revoke his visa and not let him leave the country, not to mention that Mr. Wang was part of the Ministry of Public Security, the most powerful and feared ministry in the country.

The purpose was purely to embarrass Arthur and make him lose face. It was as if they were calling him a thief and wanted him to acknowledge that by signing the document. They also wanted me to prepare it and have Arthur sign it so that I would fully realize their position.

It's interesting to note the differences in the way Mr. Wang and Arthur Kwok lived. Mr. Wang lived in about 1,000 square feet of space, with some luxuries, such as a TV and refrigeration, and his heat was controlled by the government. In U.S. terms, he lived like a lower-middle-class worker at best.

Arthur Kwok lived in a huge estate on top of a mountain overlooking Hong Kong Bay. He possessed several servants, a Ferrari, a yacht, and limousines and lived like a prince. He was a hard worker but lived in the lap of luxury. He was also very aware that when Hong Kong reverted back to the Chinese, it would be under the total control of the Ministry of Public Security.

Arthur was smarter than most of the Hong Kong Chinese who traveled to Beijing flaunting their expensive clothes, fur coats, and lots of jewelry in the faces of the mainland Chinese people. Arthur came in modest clothes, had a very subdued manner, and was very respectful. Unfortunately, he could not speak Mandarin, only Cantonese, and had to have an interpreter.

We met with Arthur and explained the situation. He told us that this project was very important to him and that he would sacrifice almost anything to be part of it, but the letter was a direct insult and he would not be able to survive the loss of face. Therefore, he could not sign it.

We met again with Mr. Yu, and I explained Arthur Kwok's response to signing the letter and requested that we arrange a dinner, hosted by Arthur with Mr. Wang, Mr. Lu Gong, Mr. Yu, Ms. Zhang, Sheldon, and me.

Mr. Wang's reply: If Arthur Kwok would not sign the letter, he would not even sit in the same room with him. I told Mr. Wang that he was being very unreasonable, that we had put a lot on the line for this project, and that the least he could do was meet on social terms with Arthur Kwok. Mr. Wang finally agreed.

Arthur brought along the architect from his office in Hong Kong, and as usual, no business was spoken of at the dinner. There was a lot of drinking and toasting, and Mr. Wang was very social and political, and Arthur, who lost only a bit of face, was very humble. To our benefit, the architect who came with Arthur knew Mr. Lu Gong, and everyone got along very well. The dinner ended, and the next day we met with Mr. Wang who told me, "This guy Arthur is not such a bad guy at all."

We set Arthur up in the small anteroom next to our offices. I spoke to him at length about my concepts of what the hotel/apartment/office complex should look like and asked him to draw some very preliminary plans. We worked closely for about five days. He submitted his drawings and went back to Hong Kong.

Mr. Wang and his group decided that Arthur Kwok might be suitable as the second architect for the project, the first being the Beijing Design Institute. We agreed that each group should create a model for the project and then both models would be reviewed by our group.

I also attempted to spend some time with Mr. Lu Gong to give him some ideas on hotel architectural development, but he was very standoffish, and unfortunately, did not speak any English. My creative ideas were very modern and commercial and dealt with the flow of people and how the project would operate as a mixed-use development. Mr. Lu Gong said that he fully understood the project, and the Beijing Design Institute would build a model that would reflect what the Chinese considered to be the optimum way to construct it.

Sheldon and I returned to Hong Kong to pursue our negotiations with Standard Chartered Bank, and within one week, Arthur Kwok had completed his model. Mr. Yu had telephoned us and told us that the Beijing Design Institute had also completed their model.

We returned to Beijing with Arthur Kwok's model, which was made out of Styrofoam and had most of what I wanted—one overall structure with different buildings that were all connected.

We met in our office, and Mr. Lu Gong brought the Chinese model. It was built like a battleship and was very well put together with hard plastic and metal screws. Arthur's model was glued and precise but displayed nowhere near the effort put in by the Beijing Design Institute. The Chinese design, unfortunately, was very old and not modern, consisting of three separate buildings not connected; it was not at all functional. Arthur's design was more modern but still did not have what I wanted.

I stood in-between both models and started to verbalize what I was looking for. Since I don't speak Chinese, I started to take pieces out of both models to show what I wanted and felt was best for the project. When I started to take apart the Chinese model, Mr. Lu Gong got very red in the face, and Mr. Wang looked distressed. An argument started, and everyone in the room got very upset. Undeterred, I continued to heatedly argue my point. Mr. Lu Gong was blustering in Chinese, and Mr. Yu was trying to calm down Mr. Wang. Sheldon, realizing the situation was totally out of control, calmly took my hand, and we left the office.

Mr. Yu came out and said the situation was deteriorating rapidly and suggested that we go back to Hong Kong and let things cool down. When we arrived and told Arthur what had happened, he was not surprised.

Before this incident, I had found out that Mr. Lu Gong's idol was Frank Lloyd Wright. While in Hong Kong, I decided to try to find some books about Frank Lloyd Wright to bring back to Mr. Lu Gong in an effort to make peace. I found several and purchased five of them.

When we returned to Beijing, I asked Mr. Yu to arrange a meeting with just me and Mr. Lu Gong, with Ms. Zhang as the interpreter. When I gave Mr. Lu Gong the books and told him that my idol was also Frank Lloyd Wright, the whole atmosphere changed. We became friends and started to work together. Ultimately, Mr. Lu Gong accepted most of my ideas and concepts.

The joint venture agreed to employ Arthur Kwok and, as I suggested, to divide the architectural responsibilities. The Beijing Design Institute would be responsible for the structural elements of the design, and Arthur Kwok and Associates would be responsible for the interior and overall project design. The Chinese decided that the Beijing Design Institute would receive 51 percent of the fee, and Arthur Kwok and Associates would receive 49 percent. (The unfortunate reality was that Arthur never received all of his fee, though he did at least 75 percent of the work.)

I shuffled back and forth between Beijing and Hong Kong, working with both groups, trying to create a functional and well-designed complex. It was an interesting experience. Arthur spoke only Cantonese, Mr. Lu Gong spoke only Mandarin, and I spoke only English. Through patience, determination, and years of experience in design and construction, I was somehow able to keep a balance between the two architects and develop an excellent, practical, and functional design.

≈≈≈≈≈

Sheldon and I spent a great deal of time in Hong Kong, meeting with Arthur Kwok the architect, Charles Wrangham the banker, and the Bovis people who were the construction supervisors on the hotel project. It was our responsibility to negotiate with these three entities, and there was a constant, ongoing discussion on a multitude of issues that had to be dealt with.

We would socialize often with our friends Ken and Eugenia Wai. Ken was doing a major part of his business in Southern China, primarily in Guangzhou, where he had family. He had a great deal of knowledge and down-to-earth insight on how to deal with the mainland Chinese, which proved invaluable to us.

He related a story to us of one of his clients, Beatrice Foods, a large conglomerate out of Chicago, Illinois. In 1985, Beatrice negotiated a joint venture with the Guangzhou Ministry of Trade to modernize an existing ice cream factory. This factory had been in existence for decades, and its methods and machinery were extensively outdated.

Ken's area of expertise was in the machinery, and Beatrice Foods had hired him as a consultant to monitor the project as it was being modernized. The ice cream factory had a staff of existing employees, including the manager of the factory, who had been working there for over thirty-five years. He was very respected by all the employees and the city as the factory had consistently produced a quality product through the years. And the machinery, although old, was always properly maintained and kept in good working order.

Beatrice management decided that this existing manager was too old-fashioned, and the fact that he did not speak English was a liability. Therefore, a new manager from outside of China would be necessary. Ken advised them that they should be careful that the old manager not lose face.

The new manager came from the United States and was versed in the management of a modern ice cream factory. Unfortunately, he was not versed in dealing in the People's Republic of China. He treated the old manager, who was now in a subordinate position, as an illiterate because he didn't speak English. The new manager, however, only spoke a little bit of Cantonese.

The renovation and restoration of the factory were completed, and the new factory opened and started producing ice cream the modern Western way. But at the end of each day, some part of the new equipment would break down, and it would take a day or two to solve the problem so that the factory could resume making ice cream.

This went on for quite some time, and Beatrice sent in several engineers and machinery experts to solve the issue. They could not figure out the problem since each one seemed to be of a different nature and involved a different part of the machinery.

The City of Guangzhou questioned Beatrice management as to why this was happening and relayed the fact that prior to the restoration and modernization, the factory was producing ice cream on a daily basis with a minimum of difficulty.

Finally, the Beatrice people called Ken and hired him to investigate the problem and find a solution. He traveled to Guangzhou and met with the new manager, who told him that he was really frustrated and didn't know what to do. Ken asked him if he had asked the old manager if he could help. He replied that the old manager would be of no use since this was new modern equipment that the old manager was not familiar with.

Ken went to talk to the old manager and took him out for some tea. After some conversation, they realized they had friends in common in Guangzhou, and they spoke about family and China. Ken asked him what he thought of this new equipment, and the old manager said that modernization was fine. When he asked what he thought of the new manager, his reply was "Patience is a virtue" and, "A loss of face can be the beginning of triumph."

Ken traveled back to Hong Kong and spoke with the Beatrice management. He told them he had a solution that would remedy the problem. The solution was a maintenance and repair manual written specifically for the machinery in the Guangzhou factory. They agreed and said they would have the manuals written by professionals, but

Ken suggested that the manual should be written by the old manager. They agreed. With input from the old manager, a manual was written, and he was given all the credit.

The old manager got his job back and was assigned an assistant from outside China with modern experience. The machinery in the factory began to work properly. The output and quality vastly improved, and the joint venture was a success.

Ken told us that the old manager was quietly, subtly, and expertly sabotaging the equipment every night in a different place and in a way that was undetectable because he had lost a great deal of face, and so, in a quiet and patient way, he got his face back.

It was a story we took to heart throughout our dealings with the Chinese.

≈≈≈≈≈

One afternoon, while shopping with Ken in Hong Kong, we wandered into a bookstore. As we were browsing the aisles, Sheldon came upon a game of Monopoly that was in Chinese. The board was identical, and so were the pieces, but everything was printed in Chinese. Sheldon suggested that he buy the game, take it back to Beijing, and play it with Mr. Yu and his family. Ken laughed and said, "You are going to bring in the ultimate capitalist game to a communist country." Then he told Sheldon to be careful.

We brought the game to Beijing, and when Mr. Yu invited us to dinner at his apartment, Sheldon brought it along. Mr. Yu's two sons were very happy that he had brought a game, and with Mr. Yu interpreting, Sheldon explained how to play Monopoly. They played for about three hours, and when Yi Yu, Mr. Yu's nine-year-old lost all his houses, he started to cry. But they had fun, and Mr. Yu asked Sheldon to leave the game with him.

The next night, he invited us to his house again, and this time, three of his friends from the Ministry of Public Security were present. The Public Security people never had business cards and seemed to always wear black leather jackets.

Mr. Yu was a great cook, and we had a wonderful dinner. He then took out the Monopoly game, and they all sat down and started to play with Mr. Yu explaining the rules. It became obvious after a while that this was not just a friendly game as all the players were very serious. Sheldon realized he should be careful and not try to win the game since he had some experience playing Monopoly.

As the game progressed, Sheldon realized he was playing with some sharp and determined players. He reassessed his thinking and tried his best to win. They played well into the night, and it was without a doubt the most serious and determined Monopoly game I had ever witnessed. There was a great deal of negotiation and arguing, but since it was all in Chinese, we would only see the final result. They spent hours playing, and when they finally finished, Sheldon was second to last. We were all exhausted, the men shook hands, and one of the three men took the Monopoly game with him. We never saw it again. This turned out to be only the first of many "disappearing" items we noticed during our adventures.

~12~

The Art of Going Slow

A journey of a thousand miles begins with a single step.
~Chairman Mao

THE LONG AND FRUSTRATING search for the property to build the hotel (which we realized, in retrospect, had been pre-ordained from
the start) and the obstacles and subterfuge during the due diligence
process were merely preludes to the misery that was about to come—
the joint venture agreement.

After several months and many trips to Hong Kong, we managed to convince Standard Chartered to underwrite the joint venture—a difficult process that took many months to accomplish.
Working cross-culturally is never easy, and every step in the loan
process required voluminous documents in Chinese and English and
endless explanations of bank policies that are commonplace in the
West but were almost unknown in China during the eighties. Charles
Wrangham, the bank's managing director, probably had little idea
what he was getting into—and neither did we.

It was our job to draft the joint venture agreement, which would
be the body of the contract. Through their sources, the Chinese had
received copies of the contracts of the first two joint-venture hotel

projects that had been developed in Beijing, and we used them as templates for our agreement. We sat for many days and hours drafting our new agreement. We naively thought that once we negotiated the agreement, the final contract would involve just a brush-up on the grammar and a few items that we had neglected to address. We were dead wrong.

There were very few computers available, and Sheldon typed everything out on an old electric portable typewriter. Then he would review each page with Mr. Wang; the Chinese man from Chongqing; our sponsor, MOFERT (the Ministry of Foreign Trade); officials from the mayor's office of the City of Beijing; and the Beijing Lawyers Guild. This was a long and arduous process, with each item carefully discussed, and because of all the people involved, changes were made constantly.

Every night, Sheldon and I would go over the changes throughout that day. Every time we thought we had reached an agreement on an item, the Chinese would change their mind, and we would have to discuss it again. We began to realize that part of their process was to understand as much as they could in the most basic terms, and the other part of the process was...simply the process itself. We drank tea all day, we ate lunch together, we had dinner together, the cast changed all the time, and we continued to negotiate.

The Chinese did not believe in boilerplate documents. They wanted to understand and agree, at least in principle, to every single detail regarding what they would be responsible for and what the American side would be responsible for. Unlike Western contracts, the Chinese wanted little documentation as to what legal remedies either side would have if either side did not live up to their respective responsibilities. Their philosophy was that when and if a dispute came up, the parties, in good faith, would negotiate, agree, and try to solve them to everyone's mutual satisfaction. At the time, this philosophy seemed to make good sense.

Sheldon typed the agreement sixteen times. Each new draft, after being translated into Chinese, would again be looked over by Mr. Yu and our office staff to ensure that the Chinese and English wording were identical. (We later found out that Mr. Yu lied about this—critical elements in the joint venture contract turned out to be different in the final analysis).

When we finally completed the agreement to everybody's satisfaction, it was reviewed by our sponsor, MOFERT, the most powerful ministry dealing with foreign trade.

A banquet was planned in a special room in the Great Hall of the People to celebrate the completion of the agreement and to have a signing ceremony. Several top Chinese leaders attended, and it was very festive. The food—all twenty-five courses—was outstanding and unique. The Chinese would always alternate seating between the Chinese and foreigners. When the courses were served, the Chinese seated next to a foreigner would always pick out the choicest morsel of food with chopsticks and put it on the plate of the foreigner sitting at his right. That custom, of course, was not practiced by Mr. Wang, who always took the choicest morsel for himself.

After the last course (we had learned to eat sparingly with the beginning courses), one of the Chinese men got up and started to sing. This was not the first time we had experienced this. Joe Spielberg, a managing partner at Leventhal and Horwath, joined us at the banquet. Knowing that the Chinese would often get up and spontaneously perform, he brought along his clarinet, and after the singing ended, he got up and started to play Jewish folk songs. I am absolutely certain this was the first time Jewish music had been played in the Great Hall of the People.

The Chinese really enjoyed it, and, on impulse, I got up, took Mr. Wang by the hand, and before we knew it, we had fifteen to twenty people dancing the Hora around the room. We danced for about an hour; it turned into a really memorable occasion.

≈≈≈≈≈

Now we had to negotiate with Mr. Wang (BLIPU) and the City of Chongqing to finalize the joint venture contract. We had foolishly assumed that after having spent so much time and effort on the agreement—and even going so far as to attend an important banquet and signing ceremony—the finalization of the contract would be easy, needing only a few minor changes and little time to complete.

But the Chinese have mastered the art of going slowly, and after all of that, it was as if we had to start at the beginning again. Each item was carefully examined and, in most cases, after hours of discussion and negotiation, had to be rewritten. Sections of the contract that we had gone over for hours in the agreement stage were changed.

The process took several weeks, with Sheldon typing and re-typing sections and pages of the contract daily. Every morning, he would hope that after the translation into Chinese, his newest draft would be complete, but there were always a few more changes, causing him to have to re-type it all over again.

He was responsible for all the editing, and the final draft would be incorporated into the contract verbatim. And because the electricity was intermittent, power outages would interrupt his typing on the old portable. Often, whatever he was working on disappeared, and he would have to start over.

At one point, we came upon a section that we had all agreed upon and was of a simple nature. Sheldon made the mistake of commenting on that fact and that we could move along to the next section. The Chinese looked at him, smiled at each other, and then spent at least three hours on the section. It was their way of saying that one should never hurry the process. Finally, we came to an agreement in principle about the structure and terms of the loan. The only thing left was to put our final understanding in writing and then review the draft. For all practical purposes, the wording of the contract had already been agreed upon and recorded in the minutes of our meetings. What remained was a straightforward job of transcription and formalization.

Sheldon flew to Hong Kong, where the bank prepared the final contract and had a professional translation service prepare copies in Chinese. He then brought the contracts back to Beijing, where Mr. Wang insisted on having the contracts translated a second time. None of the local translators, unfortunately, had experience in dealing with the nuances of legal contracts.

Charles Wrangham and two of his colleagues flew to Beijing a day later and were met by two lawyers from the China office of the international law firm Graham and James. On a Monday morning, we joined the three bankers, the two lawyers, and our employees Mr. Yu and Ms. Zhang. We all met around a table in our offices at the Beijing Hotel with Mr. Wang and his associate Mr. Li, representing the Chinese side.

Along the perimeter of the room sat several other Chinese officials, two clerks who took notes, and a representative from the Beijing municipal government. Nothing gets done in China except by committee.

We thought the meeting would be uneventful as we had already agreed on every important point. And so did Mr. Wrangham, who opened the discussion with a few pleasantries and then asked the Chinese if they had any questions about the contract now that it had been translated (twice!) and they'd had a chance to study it. We were not prepared for the answer. Mr. Wang calmly replied, "We will start with the first word on the first page."

It was the beginning of an excruciating process that would take ten days. Mr. Wang was not unlike an orthodox Rabbi studying the Torah. Every verb was parsed, each modifier explained and noun defined. But the goal, in this case, was not enlightenment. The process was designed to wear us down. It was like dripping water: word, by word, by word, the hours and days went by until I had a roaring headache.

It took us four days to review the vocabulary of the text, and with a great sense of accomplishment, we finally arrived at the end of the process late one evening. Everything we had agreed upon was in the contract, and the Chinese understood every word. That night, we went home and got a good night's sleep.

The next morning, we reconvened, and Mr. Wrangham, with the relieved demeanor of a man just released from prison, optimistically asked, "Now that you fully understand every word in the document, are there any clauses or issues you would like to discuss?" The question was a mere courtesy as we had already spent months hammering out the particulars of our loan agreement. What could possibly be left to discuss? Mr. Li spoke up and said very quietly, "We will start at the first word on the first page."

≈ ≈ ≈ ≈ ≈

The banking agreement was full of boilerplate clauses, standard legalese that is a part of every banking contract worldwide. Mr. Li and Mr. Wang wanted to jettison all the boilerplate, most of which contained language that protected the bank in case of a default. Mr. Wang considered these protections "superfluous." They were asking, in effect, that the bank agree to lend the money on a handshake without any recourse should things go wrong. Perhaps these protections were only symbolic anyway. China had no independent legal system for litigating civil disputes.

We didn't fully realize at the time how dependent we were on the goodwill of our joint venture partners. If the Chinese, for any reason, decided to default on the loan, there would be little recourse for us. They lived up to their contracts not by force of law or fear of litigation but out of simple pragmatism. The Chinese wanted American businesses to invest in their country—and bring with them dollars, expertise, and technology—and they knew that the price of that investment was a semblance of genuine legal obligation.

As we eventually discovered, Mr. Wang and Mr. Li had more nefarious things in mind for our joint venture than just the hotel development and were fighting for as much ambiguity in the contract as possible in the hope that they could exploit it later. However, in terms of their own rights, they wanted as much specificity as possible. Although this strategy was utterly transparent, they acted as though it was perfectly reasonable. The Jews invented the word "chutzpah," but the Chinese were its living embodiment.

After endless arguing over clauses the bank could never agree to remove, Mr. Wrangham reached his limit. He stood up one afternoon and announced that he was going back to Hong Kong and the deal was over. A silence fell over the room.

With the relaxed demeanor of someone who had real power and

knew it, Mr. Wang began to tell a story. He directed Mr. Wrangham's attention to the days when his bank had an office in Shanghai during the Cultural Revolution. The bank had an English manager and fifteen employees in an office building downtown. They had attempted to leave the country when the city was in turmoil with militant Red Guards marching in the streets. The Ministry of State Security, however, imprisoned the bank employees in their own headquarters and refused to give them exit visas. They were not allowed to leave the building for fifteen months. Mr. Wang had been a powerful figure in the ministry then and still was.

The story was a cautionary tale, a not-so-subtle threat that Mr. Wrangham wouldn't be allowed to leave the country until he capitulated. The chastened banker sat down. Having settled nothing, the conversation turned to the interest rate the bank would charge.

Wrangham had offered the bank's best rate, .75 percent over HIBOR (Hong Kong Interbank Offered Rate, similar to our prime rate). The Chinese wanted .25 percent over HIBOR. A two-day argument ensued. Finally, Mr. Li announced that he had received an offer from the Bank of Tokyo for .25 percent over HIBOR. This was a shock to us as it was the first we'd heard of it. Mr. Wrangham asked if there was a written offer. Mr. Li said it was in his briefcase at that very moment.

It was critical for World China Trade that Standard Chartered get the loan because our investment funds were coming from Union Bank in Los Angeles, which was at that time owned by Standard Chartered, and it was a condition for us to borrow our equity. It certainly put us in the middle, but what else was new?

Mr. Wrangham asked to see the document, and Mr. Li refused. A tense silence fell over the table. He insisted again on seeing it. More silence. At that point, one of the men who had been sitting quietly at the perimeter of the room slowly rose and spoke. He was from the Ministry of State Security. He announced in heavily accented English that it was not necessary for Mr. Wrangham to see the document and that there would be no more discussion at the table regarding that issue. End of conversation.

Mr. Wrangham and his associates and lawyers all got up and left the table. There was nothing more to say. This wasn't negotiation, it was blackmail.

Later that night, we sat with Mr. Wrangham, who said he had never before in his life been in a negotiation like that but that his bosses in London had a long-range view of China business and this just came with the territory. He wondered if the Chinese would really stop him if he tried to leave the country.

≈ ≈ ≈ ≈ ≈

We thought it was all over. Sheldon and I went back to our room and tried to figure out if we had any options left. It seemed to us that the Chinese strategy depended on a certain behavioral consistency on our part.

As far as the Chinese were concerned, all Westerners shared certain traits and tended to react in predictable ways. Americans, in particular, were impatient and easily frustrated. When confronted with negotiations that proceeded at a glacial pace and demands that were patently unreasonable and self-serving, Americans tended to break down and give away many, if not most, of their bargaining points. The prospect of enormous profits in the awakening economy of the world's most populous nation motivated people to make the deal—no matter what.

But what if we weren't predictable? What if we did something entirely unexpected like Sheldon's unexplained impulse to turn off that switch at the glass plant? It shut down a huge factory with hundreds of workers for two days. It was an expensive indulgence, but the Chinese were more bewildered than angry. The Chinese have more impulse control than the strictest Puritan ever had. It was an act so utterly unexpected that it short-circuited the normal system of rewards and punishments. There was no punitive response, not even an official reprimand.

During the whole course of our negotiations, Sheldon and I had shared almost every meal with our Chinese associates. Business was never discussed on these occasions, and sharing food was always an amiable and good-natured social exchange. Mr. Li and Mr. Wang would joke with us, and we would pass food back and forth, serving each other as is the Chinese custom.

It occurred to Sheldon that our meals played an important symbolic role in the ongoing process of cementing our joint venture agreement. To the Chinese, a shared meal is a symbolic act of great importance, a cultural trait they share with the ancient Jews. In spite of the hardball tactics of our formal meetings, the meals had an independent purpose that was unrelated to the content of the negotiations.

Hospitality to guests was a social responsibility deeply rooted in the Chinese psyche. To be inhospitable to an outsider, particularly in the context of forming a partnership with that person, represented a significant loss of "face." And that was when Sheldon had a stroke of genius. "What would happen if I refused to eat with them? What if I went on a hunger strike?"

The next morning, Sheldon arrived at the meeting and announced to Mr. Li and Mr. Wang that he would not eat a single morsel of food until they changed their position. It was like dropping a bomb. They were horrified. Mr. Wang said that he would get sick, and they did not want to be responsible for the damage it might do to his health. Their concern was genuine. Sheldon reiterated that they were behaving unreasonably and that he would not eat until they changed their minds. He said this with a sober face, although I thought the situation was somewhat comical.

That day at lunch, and again at dinner, he sat silently at the table, refusing to eat anything. Everyone passed food around and encouraged him to eat. As a special inducement, they prepared his favorite noodle dish, but he refused it. In the meantime, I was secreting away food in my bag, which I sneaked up to our room. I had no intention of letting Sheldon starve.

This went on for three days, and every day, we would meet with Mr. Wrangham and make no progress. The Chinese were getting increasingly frantic about the supposed hunger strike, which Sheldon played to the hilt, acting faint and having dizzy spells at the negotiating table. Finally, they sent someone from the ministry of health to visit him. The earnest medic tried to explain that his fast could damage his health, and since we were honored guests, it would cause them great embarrassment. Sheldon simply restated his position and refused to eat.

The ninth day of our negotiations and the fourth of his hunger strike rolled around, with no seeming way to break the deadlock. Mr. Wrangham had reached the end of his rope and wanted a resolution. We met in his room and discussed the situation. He said that he would consider anything that would break the impasse, but not to reveal this to the Chinese.

The next day Mr. Wang repeated, verbatim, what Mr. Wrangham had said to us in our private discussion. That night we went to visit him in his room again, and Sheldon pulled out the console between the beds and found a microphone. We explained to Mr. Wrangham that he was in China and should have expected his room to be bugged. We left him looking weary and downcast and headed back to the office.

As we entered, Mr. Wang and two of his Ministry of State Security thugs were waiting for us. Sheldon kept up his act and stumbled as if from weakness. The two thugs took his arms and forcibly sat him down on the couch. Unbelievably, Mr. Wang straddled his legs and sat down on his lap, facing him. He had brought some dumplings, and he proceeded to force-feed Sheldon. I couldn't believe what was happening. Ordinarily, such an assault on my husband would have left me very angry, but the whole situation was so farcical that all I really wanted to do was laugh. I watched as Sheldon dutifully ate the dumplings, and then he started to talk.

Sheldon told Mr. Wang that we would guarantee that the documents would be valid in both English and Chinese—as this had been a sticking point earlier in our discussions. It wasn't a particularly timely or meaningful offer as the negotiations had already moved on to other, more difficult issues. They asked Sheldon what he meant. He was honest and said he didn't know, but if it would end the stalemate, we were willing to do it. He was operating on pure intuition. It seemed like the face-saving concession they needed, although it gained them nothing tangible.

Sheldon's hunch turned out to be right. He had done the one thing they had never expected us to, and it worked.

In short order, the interest rate was settled and the boilerplate clauses were accepted. The last item was the bank's legal fees. It ended with Mr. Wrangham thinking that he would prevail by letting the Chinese decide what the fees should be instead of presenting the bill which, at that time, amounted to over $150,000. Mr. Wrangham stated to the Chinese that he felt they were fair and honorable in their dealings and that they were aware of the bank's legal costs. Therefore, he said he would leave it up to Mr. Li to decide what the joint venture would pay to the bank.

Mr. Li, in his Chinese way, told Mr. Wrangham that he felt that there should be no payment at all because all foreign lawyers were parasites and hindered the business relationship between parties interested in doing business. Everyone finally settled at $15,000 dollars.

The deal was agreed upon. However, our ten days of misery were not yet over.

≈≈≈≈≈

After we had signed our joint venture contract, and the proper entities gave their approval (all one hundred of them), the Chinese side of our joint venture put half of their required equity in RMB (Chinese currency)—equivalent to 1.875 million U.S. dollars—into our account at the Bank of China, Beijing branch. Per our agreement, we were also supposed to put up 1.875 million U.S. dollars. Union Bank in Los Angeles, who agreed to loan us our equity, would not issue any funds until we had secured the financing for the construction of the hotel project, which was being funded by Standard Chartered in Hong Kong. The Chinese would not negotiate for the construction or financing until our money was deposited in the joint venture bank account. It was a classic chicken and egg situation.

When we told the Chinese and Mr. Wang that we did not have the funds and the bank would not release the money, Mr. Wang became very upset. He told us that we had agreed in writing to deposit these funds. All the approvals were in place, the contract was signed, and we were not living up to what we had agreed upon.

We explained to Mr. Wang that our equity was conditioned on Standard Chartered providing the construction financing, and until that was in place, we could not get any funds released. Mr. Wang said that the joint venture's negotiating position with Standard Charted bank was compromised because they knew that unless the joint venture took the loan from them, we would not have our equity infusion.

There was much consternation, and they called a meeting with our joint-venture board members from Chongqing, representatives from the mayor's office, officials from the Ministry of Public Security, and Dean Lee and Richard Chen from Oxy.

It seemed liked much face would be lost over this issue since there were so many agencies and governmental authorities involved in this transaction. The meeting was held in our offices in the Beijing Hotel, and it was one of the few times that very little translation took place; instead, we were treated to a lot of glaring. We got the sense that everyone was on the spot. This joint venture seemed to be very important to many people, and this apparent breach of the agreement was causing a great deal of concern.

After a while, we all went down to dinner. At least fifteen of us, including two children belonging to one of the officials, sat down to eat. It was not uncommon for children to be brought to some of our meetings. Sheldon went to the hotel store, bought two small toy airplanes, and gave them to the children. At dinner, everyone was very cordial, and as usual, no business was discussed.

After dinner, we went back to our offices and continued our discussion. Richard Chen and Dean Lee were on the spot, and both started to sweat as the questions poured out at them. Mr. Yu was more relaxed; it seemed he was not part of this interrogation. At least, that was how we read the situation because they were speaking Chinese, and nothing was being translated.

Finally, Sheldon and I came up with the idea of an escrow account, where the funds would be held and automatically released when the construction contract was finalized. We told Mr. Yu our idea, and he brought it into the conversation.

Since the Chinese had never heard of an escrow account, the whole concept had to be explained to them. A great deal of silence followed this idea, and then they continued in loud voices to interrogate Richard and Dean. It turned out that the concept of escrow, in their minds, equaled mistrust. They resented the idea, but we finally told them there was no other way.

They agreed, but of course, that was just the beginning. The next day, we flew to Hong Kong and met with Charles Wrangham to tell him what had transpired. We explained that if the bank did not accept and place the funds in an escrow account, the joint venture would be canceled, and the Chinese would probably have negative feelings regarding the bank because of mistrust issues.

We got on a three-way conversation with Union Bank in Los Angeles, and they agreed under certain terms and conditions. Standard Chartered said that the funds would have to be placed in their bank in Hong Kong.

We flew back to Beijing and had a meeting with all concerned. The Chinese agreed to accept the escrow, but the funds would have to be placed in the Shenzhen branch of the Bank of China. Shenzhen was a comparatively new mainland Chinese city, right across from the Hong Kong border territories. We called Mr. Wrangham, who said that was not acceptable. The funds had to be placed in Standard Chartered in Hong Kong. So, there we were, in the middle again.

We argued with the Chinese for two days. They insisted they had gone as far as they could by accepting the whole escrow concept but had reached their limit. The funds had to be deposited in the Bank of China, Shenzhen branch, or they would cancel the joint venture.

Once again, we flew back to Hong Kong to inform Wrangham that the Chinese were threatening to cancel the joint venture. He said the bank was already out on a limb and that if the funds went into China, it would be too big a risk for the bankers in Los Angeles.

He invited us out to dinner on the Standard Chartered yacht, and we had a great time. He told us he really wanted to make this deal, but there was only so far he could go. He asked us to go back to Beijing and try again to convince Mr. Wang and the Chinese group. By this time, we were exhausted. We felt like ping pong balls, bouncing back and forth between Hong Kong and Beijing, but agreed to make the effort nonetheless.

We flew back to Beijing for yet another meeting, where nothing was resolved. The Chinese seemed very calm, a huge contrast to Mr. Wrangham's attitude in Hong Kong. We finally got Mr. Yu away from the group and had a heart-to-heart talk. We realized that we had to solve this problem or the joint venture could be terminated. Then Sheldon had an idea. What if the funds were put into the Bank of China in Hong Kong?

Mr. Yu brightened and said he would try to sell the idea to the Chinese. After about a day, they accepted, and we flew back to Hong Kong to meet with Mr. Wrangham again. He said the idea had some merit, and he would try to convince his bank to accept.

Thankfully, the bank agreed, and we flew back to the United States to arrange the transfer of the funds to Standard Chartered, who in turn would make the escrow deposit.

We then flew back to Hong Kong and notified the Chinese and the Bank of China that Mr. Wrangham and Sheldon had decided to personally bring a cashier's check to the Bank of China, Hong Kong Branch.

The next day, with a cashier's check in hand, my husband and Mr. Wrangham walked over to the bank together, where they were met by the manager and high officials of the bank. They first asked to see Sheldon's passport to verify his identity, then asked to see a copy of his visa and a copy of the signed escrow agreement. They then checked Mr. Wrangham's identity and credentials, and after a very tedious hour, informed them that everything had checked out, and they could continue with the transaction.

They presented the cashier's check, and the bank examined it and made some calls to verify its authenticity. That took another hour. The two men were served some tea while they waited.

The bank officials finally said everything was in order, but unfortunately, they could not at that time accept the check and asked them to come back in two days. At that point, we decided that trying to figure out the Chinese psyche could drive anyone crazy. They returned in two days, and the transaction was completed.

The last step was for our board of directors to ratify the contract. What was supposed to be a mere formality would ultimately get us expelled from China.

About Face

~13~

Expulsion from China

"Fuck you, fuck you, fuck you."
~American proverb

T IME PASSED UNTIL WE found ourselves in the middle of summer; it had taken months of long, tedious negotiations to finalize the joint venture contract. Now, all that was left to do was hold a board of directors meeting to ratify what we had agreed upon and then deliver the documents to the Chinese governmental agencies dealing with these matters. The meeting was to take place at our offices in the Beijing Hotel.

At the same time, I had invited several people from the Natural History Museum of Los Angeles, including Craig Black, director of the museum, and his wife, to join us in China. I was on the board of governors and had gotten to know Craig well. His father had been a missionary in China, and he had grown up there, so he was very excited to return—and even more excited since the museum was very interested in being the first in the United States to show treasures from China that nobody had seen. By then, we had been in China for over three years and had developed excellent connections with the right people.

While I was busy hosting our visitors from LA, Sheldon attended the board meeting to ratify the joint venture contract, a "simple" formality. After three weeks of going at it day and night with bankers, lawyers, Chinese officials, and the like, we had agreed on all the issues and had a written agenda for the board meeting. All the key parties were now present, including Richard Chen, who was on our board and working for Dr. Hammer as his vice chairman. The meeting itself was, in effect, just a transcript of what we had previously agreed to for an official record.

The Chinese side was not happy with us at that moment because we had insisted on several checks and balances. The most important was our insistence that checks written on the joint venture account for any amount over $500 had to have agreement and signatures from both sides. The meeting was progressing, and around two hours in, an item was introduced on the agenda that was not previously discussed or disclosed to us.

In our joint venture contract, we had agreed that half of our investment (1.875 million U.S. dollars) would be released from escrow at the start of the project. Six months after this initial contribution, we were to have a board meeting to decide mutually when the next payment would be due. In fact, that was the way we set up our funding with the banks and our investors.

This new item was a bombshell, and the first one ever introduced that had not been disclosed and agreed upon prior to the meeting. Mr. Wang stated through an interpreter that the second installment was due three weeks after the first installment was received. This was not what we had agreed upon and was not stated in the English version of the contract, nor in the Chinese version—at least, so Sheldon thought at that moment.

He questioned Mr. Wang and told him that the item was not on the agenda and, therefore, should not be discussed. He added that the item was mentioned in our contract and that the details were far different. Mr. Wang, through the interpreter, told Sheldon in his inimitable Chinese fashion that it was government law that dictated how foreign investment was to be funded in a joint venture relationship. We had been through this before. When the Chinese wanted to change something, they always used the excuse that it was a law. Unfortunately, these laws were not written down anywhere and seemed to be verbal at best.

Sheldon brought out the contract, and they argued for a while. Then Richard Chen said that it was unnecessary to debate the issue. Since the item was not on the agenda, it would not be stated in the minutes, and therefore was a waste of time to deal with at the board meeting.

They went on to discuss several other items, but the atmosphere was filled with tension. The meeting finally adjourned at about 1:00 a.m., and Sheldon returned to our room. I was still awake when he came in. After he updated me on what had happened, we both fell asleep, exhausted, until the phone woke us at 3:00 a.m.

It was Mr. Yu. He told Sheldon that it was very important that he come back up to our office and sign the minutes of the meeting as the deadline for the consummation of our contract had been reached. Sheldon asked him if the minutes were translated into English. Mr. Yu said no but Sheldon should just sign the Chinese version and then it would be translated into English the following day.

Sheldon explained that he was weary and could not sign the Chinese minutes without understanding what they had to say, so he would wait for the translation. He told Mr. Yu that he was concerned about the item that had come up during the board meeting and that he was not comfortable signing the minutes until he had a chance to thoroughly review them. Mr. Yu insisted that Sheldon come up immediately, that he had no choice and must sign those minutes tonight.

Sheldon became very upset and told him that he was going back to sleep and that we would deal with this in the morning. Mr. Yu said if he didn't come to the office, he would come to us and get those minutes signed. Sheldon became very irritated and told him that if he came down, he could wait outside the door all night, and then he hung up.

About twenty minutes later, the phone rang again. This time, it was an official from the Ministry of Public Security who spoke

English. He informed Sheldon that he was being an obstructionist, and that since the Ministry of Public Security was a partner (this was news to us), Sheldon was ordered to come to the office and sign those minutes.

Sheldon reiterated what he explained to Mr. Yu. He was an American citizen trying to do business in the People's Republic of China, and he would not be intimidated by him or his organization. He had the responsibility of American investors and would not sign those minutes until he had thoroughly reviewed them in English and had an independent Chinese individual verify that the English and Chinese versions were identical.

The ministry official became very angry in a Chinese way, which translates to obtuse threats made without that person raising their voice. He informed Sheldon that our visas could be pulled, our status in the country could be called into question, and that it was to our benefit to sign those papers now. I had to admit, we were very nervous. Here we were, in a Communist country, having an argument with the Chinese KGB. But Sheldon stuck to his guns and refused in as polite a way as possible. It was very important to save face in China—that alone is a long, learning experience.

After a short night with little sleep, we both got up early. I had planned a tour of the Forbidden City with Craig and his wife for a private walk-through of the acres of treasures. As I headed over to meet them, Sheldon went to our office, determined to resolve the impasse.

I spent the day with Craig and his wife selecting what we wanted to bring back to the United States for the first major exhibition of Chinese treasures at the museum. It was a fascinating day. I wish that mobile phones were a common possession at that time because I would have filled mine with pictures of that huge, cavernous space in the Forbidden City with ancient treasures that went back thousands of years.

It was also my birthday, so the Chinese had planned a huge party for me that evening at the Temple of Heaven, a masterpiece of architecture and landscape design built in the fifteenth century. The emperors used to hold their parties at the top of the five staircases, and the views are spectacular. Among the many dignitaries were Dr. Brown, chairman of the Natural History Museum, and his wife.

While I spent a glorious day at the Forbidden City going over treasures and making lists, unbeknownst to me, Sheldon had a knock-down, drag-out fight with Mr. Wang.

When Sheldon arrived at the office, everyone was very quiet and somber. The fact that my birthday party was that evening, and our office and Mr. Yu were helping the museum people to forge a relationship with their Chinese counterpart at the Forbidden City, complicated matters.

Sheldon asked Mr. Yu if the minutes had been translated into English, and he grudgingly informed him they had. Usually, the translated minutes were typed correctly and gone over minutely before presented to us. This time, they were hand-scrawled on some small pieces of paper that were torn and smudged. Sheldon sat down and read through them, and wouldn't you know it, the item that was not on the agenda—and that Richard Chen told him would not be in the minutes—was indeed there, and, according to the minutes, everyone had agreed upon it.

Sheldon told Mr. Yu that he would not sign those minutes and they would have to be changed. Mr. Yu became very upset and said his personal safety and that of his family were at risk if Sheldon didn't sign those minutes. Sheldon explained to him that our deal with the bank called for at least six months before we had to come up with our final payment. In the new minutes, it said the payment was due in three weeks. If we were unable to make the payment, then we could lose our initial payment of $1.875 million, and our investors would skin us alive. Our issues with our American investors seemed to make no difference to Mr. Yu, however.

Sheldon then went to one of our Chinese employees and asked him if that item in our joint venture contract was the same in the Chinese and English versions. He hemmed and hawed, and with a very sheepish grin (Chinese always laugh when they are put into difficult positions) told us they were not and that the Chinese version of the contract was similar to what was on the board agenda.

Sheldon was furious. He confronted Mr. Yu and asked him if he knew there was a difference. He admitted he did and had lied about it. When Sheldon asked him why, he said because he knew we wouldn't agree to it.

At that moment in time, Sheldon didn't trust any of the Chinese, and he knew he had to stand his ground. He asked to have a meeting with Mr. Wang to try to settle this issue.

Mr. Wang and a few of his cohorts showed up. Sheldon started to discuss the issue, but Mr. Wang stubbornly refused to bend in any way. Sheldon told him that if the language could be changed in some way that would give the U.S. side some protection, he would consider it. Sheldon was adamant and forceful. This went on for hours. He tried to call our attorney in Los Angeles but could not reach him. (In those days, you had to reserve a call to the U.S., and it took between three to six hours to get a call through).

The Chinese had several different people come to the office to try to convince him, but it just ended in more arguments. Finally, two large Chinese showed up; it was apparent from their demeanor that they were thugs from the Ministry of Public Security. They took Sheldon into the inner office and tried to intimidate him to sign the documents. They told him he was obstructing the joint venture and that there could be severe penalties and repercussions if he did not comply.

Sheldon explained that he was an American citizen and not subject to Chinese law. We were trying to do business and had been lied to. We had a responsibility to our U.S. investors and certainly would accept and listen to a compromise, but he could not sign the documents the way they were written. They continued to harass Sheldon, and things got very ugly. They sort of forced him into a corner of the room, put their fingers hard on his chest, and said, "You will sign those documents right now with no further hesitation."

At that moment, something inside my husband snapped. Sheldon thought to himself, *I am an American from a free country, and no one has the right to force me to do anything against my will.* He knew if he succumbed to their intimidation and threats, he would be useless in any dealings with the Chinese in the future. He turned to them and, in a very loud voice that was heard by everyone, said, "Fuck you, fuck the Chinese government, and fuck the Ministry of Public Security. I will not sign those minutes the way they are written." He then pushed them aside and stormed out of the office yelling, "Fuck you!" I don't think anyone had ever said that to the Chinese Ministry of Public Security. Sheldon became a legend in the banking circles of Hong Kong.

That night at my birthday party, all the Chinese officials, including Mr. Wang and the two thugs Sheldon had sworn at, were there, along with the entire party from the Natural History Museum and several dignitaries. Except for the extreme tension, it was a wonderful party. The Chinese went through the evening as if almost nothing had happened.

We returned to our room, and again, at 3:00 a.m., we received a call from Mr. Yu telling us to meet in the office first thing in the morning. When we arrived at our office, Mr. Wang and the Ministry of Public Security were waiting for us. They informed us, as they aptly put it, that it would be in our best interest to leave the country immediately. I wanted to stay, but it was obvious we were in a mess.

When we told them we would leave, they asked us where we were going. Sheldon told them to Hong Kong to tell the entire story to Charles Wrangham at Standard Chartered. They told us we could not do that because it would screw up the joint venture. We told them that the bank had read the contract and approved it with the English version, and they had a right to know that the Chinese contract was different, since they were lending the joint venture over $20 million.

After they left, Mr. Yu told us if we didn't leave immediately, there was going to be trouble. And even more ominously, he said if Sheldon came to the border, he'd be shot. He also told us we'd have to designate somebody as our representative to sign the documents the way they were and added that we were no longer welcome in China. We designated our attorney, Joe Brightman. We prepared to leave the next day and left Joe to sign the board meeting notes ratifying the contract.

We had real concerns that the Chinese might not let us leave the country since you cannot leave China without a stamp from the Ministry of Public Security on your passport. But to our great relief, they didn't stop us, and soon we were headed back to LA, wondering if we'd ever see China again.

Photos and Letters

*The signing ceremony making our joint venture with the Chinese
to build the Beijing Asia Hotel official.*

Rendering of the Beijing Asia Hotel

Location:
No.2 Xin Zhong Xi Jei
Gongi North Road
Beijing

Client:
Beiijing Asia Hotel Co Ltd

Contract Value:
US $33 Million

Construction Period:
26 months, September 1986-
End 1988

Consultant:
Bovis (Far East) Limited

Architects:
Arthur CS Kwok of Hong
Kong
Beijing Architectural Design
Institute

A 19-storey hotel block
proving 330 medium
standard hotel guess
rooms and 90 service
apartments and a 4-storey
low rise commercial
complex incorporating
10,881 sq meter of office
space, shopping arcade,
two basement-levels of
parking and hotel supporting
facilities.

The hotel under construction.

New and old China juxtaposed.

OCCIDENTAL PETROLEUM CORPORATION

10889 WILSHIRE BOULEVARD · SUITE 1500

LOS ANGELES, CALIFORNIA 90024

(213) 208-8800

JUN 28 1988

ARMAND HAMMER
CHAIRMAN AND
CHIEF EXECUTIVE OFFICER

June 17, 1988

Mr. and Mrs. Sheldon Krechman
273 So. Almont Drive
Beverly Hills, CA 90211

Dear Mr. and Mrs. Krechman:

I have returned from back-to-back trips and have the
magnificent photo album of Deng Xiao Peng which you
so thoughtfully sent to me. I look forward with great
pleasure to viewing this fine pictorial record of one
of our world's great leaders. Thank you for your warm
birthday greetings.

With best good wishes,

Sincerely,

Armand Hammer

AH:fa

cc: Mr. Paul Hebner
    Mr. Richard Chen

---

*Deng Xiao Peng was the paramount leader of the People's Republic of
China from December 1978 to November 1989. He led China through
a series of far-reaching market-economy reforms earning him the
reputation as the "Architect of Modern China."*

Embassy of the United States of America

April 24, 1991

Beijing, China

The Honorable
Mayor Sun Tongchuan
Chongqing Municipal Government
Chongqing, Sichuan

Dear Mr. Mayor,

It was a pleasure meeting with you on April 4, 1991. Chongqing and America have a long history of cooperation. I believe we can build on this solid foundation and further our cooperation.

I am now writing to introduce Mr. Sheldon Krechman, Chairman of the Board, World China Trade Inc. (WCT). WCT is the American partner in the Ramada Asia Hotel joint venture in Beijing. As you know, Chongqing International Trust and Investment Corporation is one of the Chinese partners.

I hope you can assist WCT in achieving the four basic requirements necessary to make the Ramada a successful joint venture:

(1) Prevent closure of the hotel by arranging an immediate working capital loan;

(2) Extend the term of the joint venture;

(3) Assist WCT in finding a Chinese financial institution to buy the loan held by the Union Bank of Los Angeles and restructure the debt;

(4) Preserve the hotel management contract between Ramada International, Inc. and Asia Hotel Company Ltd.

These problems need to be resolved before the end of April. WCT has 48 individual investors that now face serious personal financial difficulties. Some of their Congressmen and Senators have already contacted the American Embassy. I believe that these problems can be resolved through friendly discussion between the two parties.

Thank you for your personal assistance in solving these problems.

Sincerely,

James R. Lilley
Ambassador

---

*U.S. Ambassador to China, James Lilley, wrote a letter
to the Mayor of Chongqing on our behalf.*

BARBARA BOXER
6TH DISTRICT, CALIFORNIA

COMMITTEE ON THE BUDGET
HUMAN RESOURCES TASK FORCE CHAIRMAN

COMMITTEE ON GOVERNMENT OPERATIONS

SELECT COMMITTEE ON CHILDREN,
YOUTH, AND FAMILIES

COMMITTEE ON ARMED SERVICES
(OR LEAVE)

MILITARY REFORM CAUCUS
CO-CHAIRMAN

WHIP AT LARGE

Congress of the United States
House of Representatives
Washington, DC 20515

307 CANNON BUILDING
WASHINGTON, DC 20515
(202) 225-5161

DISTRICT OFFICES

SAN FRANCISCO
450 GOLDEN GATE AVENUE
SAN FRANCISCO, CA 94102
(415) 070-6943

MARIN
3301 KERNER BLVD.
SAN RAFAEL, CA 94901
(415) 457-7272

VALLEJO
(707) 552-0720

SONOMA
(707) 763-8033

April 1, 1991

Premier Li Peng
Peoples Republic of China
Bejing, China
c/o Ambassador Ma Yu Zhen
Consul General
501 Shatto Place Suite 300
Los Angeles, CA 90020

Dear Premier Peng,

Enclosed is a copy of a letter I have received from World China Trade, Inc., an American corporation doing business with your country. It fully explains problems they state they have been having with the Peoples Republic of China.

I request that you review this matter and that you do all you can to see that they are treated fairly.

Thank you for your attention to this matter.

Sincerely,

BARBARA BOXER
Member of Congress

BB/sc/bjm
Enclosure

In addition to Senator Barbara Boxer, Senator Dianne Feinstein, Senator John McCuin, and Senator John Glenn, wrote letters on our behalf to the Chinese government protesting the actions of the Chinese regarding our joint venture.

~14~

Back In The Game

No words spoken when leave.
~Chinese Proverb

WE RETURNED HOME AND consoled ourselves with the fact that the hotel project would proceed. The land deal had been made, the designs had been semi-approved, and we communicated regularly with Mr. Yu on the progress. We were also sending materials and supplies from the U.S. for the construction. We hadn't told anyone we had been thrown out of China. While we were back in the U.S. protecting ourselves, we stayed busy looking for new projects. Fortunately, Dr. Hammer was always trying to connect us to people who were looking to invest in China.

One day, we got a phone call from Richard Chen who informed us that a couple of guys were interested in investing in the hotel or building something in China, and that Dr. Hammer suggested we meet with them. A couple of days later, the two guys, who happened to be Donald Nixon (Richard Nixon's brother) and John Dean (who, a few years earlier, had served time in Federal prison for his role in Watergate) showed up at our home in Beverly Hills. The investment opportunity for the hotel was closed, but the discussion soon moved toward potential opportunities. We liked John and soon met his wife; the four of us became friends and often socialized.

We were also doing a lot of PR around the hotel and got a call from Jerry Speyer, one of the two founding partners of the New York real estate company Tishman Speyer, which controls Rockefeller Center. We had met him two years earlier when he was trying to build an office tower complex in Shenzhen with American Express' name on the building. Shenzhen was officially made a city in 1979 and was on the verge of becoming a modern metropolis linking Hong Kong to China's mainland. We agreed with Jerry that the office tower was an excellent opportunity, but he was stymied by a lack of progress.

Jerry sent us tickets to meet with him in New York. He was enthusiastic when we told him we had already put together the Asia Hotel project, which was starting construction, and we were available to work on his project.

Sheldon and I figured it was a good thing for us to work on since we were stuck in the United States and had to figure out how we were going to get back into the good graces of the Chinese as Mr. Wang was a very powerful man. We started to put together a proposal in which John Dean was to be one of the investors. Unfortunately, the project never came to fruition. When Tiananmen Square happened a few years later, we were in the middle of the hotel's construction and had to focus on making sure that didn't go down the drain.

About three months into our expulsion, fate stepped in. I got a call from HUD, the Department of Housing and Urban Development: "Mrs. Krechman, we understand you're building a hotel in China, and we're putting together a group of women in construction—developers, architects, and designers—to take to China. We would like you to lead the delegation."

Sheldon was still stinging from our being thrown out when I told him about my invitation. I saw this as a windfall and a chance for us to get back into the game, although he wasn't quite so sure. He did agree, though, that I was unlikely to be thrown out of China while leading a delegation of well-known women from around the globe on behalf of HUD that included the deputy director, plus a representative from the state department and a representative from security. So, I accepted the invitation.

≈≈≈≈≈

On January 20, 1985, six months after we had left China, I headed to LAX for my flight to San Francisco, where I would meet the group, then fly to Tokyo to spend the night before going on to Beijing. I had booked an early flight from LA so that I would have plenty of time before our flight to Tokyo. As it turned out, it was Super Bowl Sunday and the first time that the game was played in San Francisco. Everyone must have booked early flights too. We taxied away from the gate and then sat and sat on the tarmac in a very long queue of planes. We were not moving at all. I was getting really nervous and kept looking at my watch.

Finally, out of desperation, I called over the flight attendant with a strange request. I explained that I was on my way to meet a group of twenty women from HUD in San Francisco to fly to China, and if I missed my flight, it would be a disaster because I was their leader. No one else in the group, not even the deputy secretary of HUD, had any experience in China. I asked if maybe there was a way we could jump ahead of all these planes. I didn't think anything would happen, but the next thing I knew, our plane was moving out of the queue and into the front.

I got to San Francisco barely in time to get to the international terminal to meet my group and board the plane. When we arrived in Tokyo after our eleven-hour flight, all the women collected their luggage. They each had several bags with many changes of clothing. As they gathered their belongings, I was still on the TSA side waiting for my bag. Finally, after waiting in vain for quite some time, we left the airport without my luggage. I figured eventually they'd find it and get it to me.

I was wearing a comfortable jumpsuit, which I had selected for the long flight, some weird designer thing, and I realized I couldn't wear that for the rest of my trip. After spending the night in Tokyo, we had plans to go to a very nice little Japanese town called Narita just to give the group a flavor of Japan. We would spend the night there and then leave for China in the morning. When we arrived in Narita, I bought myself a pair of black tights, a black skirt, a black shirt, a jacket, a T-shirt, some toothpaste, and a little bit of makeup. And that was what I wore the entire ten days of our journey.

I swear to this day that the Chinese orchestrated my "late luggage" issue as a test. I traveled throughout China with these women all dressed to the nines. And then there was me, dressed in my black clothes that I had to wash each night. After visiting many locations in China, we finally arrived in Beijing. It had been six months since I had last been there.

This was our last stop in China. I brought the women to the site of the old glass factory to show them what we were doing. The factory had been demolished; in its wake now stood a two-story office building on the property. We had bought materials in the U.S. for the hotel, which were shipped in containers to China by boat. The work crews unloaded all the materials, then used the containers to build the office. And who was there to greet us? Mr. Wang himself. He was very gracious and excited about meeting these women. And he was very kind to me.

And then, low and behold, that very afternoon, my luggage was delivered to the hotel. In it was my red Chanel suit, just in time for a big banquet hosted for us by Betty Bao Lord, an international best-selling author, and her husband, Winston Lord. At that time, he was the United States ambassador to China. They were very charming and excited to host us for a very special evening.

The group went home, and I stayed on to talk to Mr. Wang. I told him Sheldon had to come back and help get this project done, and we had new things we wanted to do in China. What did we have to do to make this happen? That was when he asked me if I could get him airplanes for the airport he had built on Hainan Island, which, with its tropical climate, beautiful beaches, and forested, mountainous interior, had excellent tourism potential. Yes, he had built an airport despite the fact that he didn't have any planes.

As it turned out, I knew somebody in LA who bought used planes, so I told him we could work on making that happen. A month later, Sheldon was allowed to return to Beijing. Mr. Wang met him at the airport, took him to the hotel and into our office, and then lifted him up in joy. I had stayed in LA to find the airplanes. We were able to buy 747s, 720s, and several smaller planes and shipped them off to the island, which made Mr. Wang very happy.

And that was how we maneuvered our way back into China.

About Face

~15~

Interlude: The Station Wagon

Nothing in China is ever as it seems to be.

THE MONOPOLY GAME THAT disappeared after we had taken it to Mr. Wang's home was child's play compared to the event that became known as "the disappearing station wagon."

In the early 1980s in China, the only transportation was by cab or car and driver. The cars were all small-to-medium Japanese sedans that held four passengers at most—three in the crowded back seat and one in front. The only larger vehicles were vans, which were prohibitively expensive to bring into China, if allowed at all. The going customs rate was 200 percent of the value of the automobile, and, of course, there were few or no parts available for American automobiles.

We were bringing businesspeople to China and were always cramped for space in the automobiles. Back in LA, we had a Mercury station wagon that Sheldon had souped up with a very large four-barrel carburetor and some other modifications, including the elimination of all smog devices (thus increasing its performance.) The car was five or six years old at that time and was loaded with full power, leather seats, a sunroof, and all the amenities. When Mr. Yu came to visit in the United States, we would use this vehicle.

We decided that we would sell it to our company, World China Trade, fill it with all kinds of parts, and then send it off to Beijing. We painted the sides with our company name, World China Trade, and Mr. Yu was responsible for arranging shipment to China.

After a great deal of paperwork and red tape, the Chinese sent a cargo ship to Los Angeles, and the station wagon was put on board to be shipped to Tianjin, the northern seaport. The car arrived close to schedule, and Mr. Yu was supposed to pick the station wagon up from customs and have it driven to Beijing. As always in China, nothing is ever as it seems or simple.

Mr. Yu called us from Beijing and told us the customs bureau would not release the wagon without customs duty, something Mr. Yu neglected to mention. He said the law stated that the duty would be 100 percent of what the car cost at its new value. That amounted to almost $20,000. Sheldon told him that was ridiculous, that we had only charged the company $5,000 for the wagon, and the most we should pay was 10 percent of that value, or $500. Mr. Yu said this was a customs law and there was no negotiation, the same as U.S. customs, which doesn't negotiate. He added that they also wanted customs duty on the parts.

Sheldon told him this was not the U.S., it was China, and everything could be negotiated. Mr. Yu argued and said there was nothing he could do. Sheldon told him to just leave it at customs until they changed their mind. Mr. Yu defiantly said it could just stay there forever and hung up on Sheldon.

About a week later, he phoned us to say he had used all his influence to the highest level and that he had gotten them to accept $15,000, a 25 percent reduction. Sheldon told him that was unacceptable and he should continue to negotiate.

We then received a call from Richard Chen from Oxy, telling us that the Chinese government had called his office in Beijing. Knowing of our relationship, they complained to him that this vehicle was sitting at customs because we refused to pay the duty. The Chinese suggested that since Oxy was involved with World China Trade that they should do it instead.

Mr. Chen politely refused and told us that it was our responsibility and that Oxy should not be involved—they had enough difficulty with China business without this problem. Sheldon explained to Richard that we felt the duty was exorbitant and we could not afford to pay that much. Mr. Chen recited the mantra—it was Chinese law.

After five phone calls and three weeks of negotiation, the Chinese agreed to $5,000 in complete payment for the duties. We told Mr. Yu that was acceptable; however, we did not have the money. Sheldon asked that he request the terms of payment (30, 60, or 90 days) after we took the car.

Mr. Yu almost had a fit of apoplexy. He said that was absolutely impossible. It could not be done, and there was no more discussion to be had about this issue. Customs did not offer open accounts, and it would be impolite for him to ask. Sheldon asked him to call the Oxy office in Beijing and ask them to make the payment for us. We would then pay them back per the payment plan he suggested. After much discussion, the Chinese took Mr. Yu's word, and we were able to make the payments over time.

The next step was to register the station wagon with the Ministry of Public Security as no vehicle could be driven without their permission. This was a long process, and Mr. Yu somehow got permission for the station wagon to be driven to Beijing and parked at the Beijing Hotel. It sat there for three weeks until finally, we received permission for our office driver and personnel to drive the car. The purchase of gasoline was also monitored by the Ministry of Public Security. You could not just drive into a gas station. You had to have prior approval and gasoline certificates before being able to fill the gas tank. Fortunately, we received those approvals.

The wagon was a sensation. Everyone turned and looked at it. It was the first vehicle in Beijing with a sunroof and an alarm. When the alarm went off, which it did often, as our driver somehow could never figure out how to set it properly, the crowds would gather in wonder and delight. At one point, the Great Wall Sheraton Hotel offered us $20,000 for the wagon, but after all the difficulty in getting it into

China and the thought of what we would have to go through to replace it, we turned down the offer.

We loved having the station wagon there and available for our use. Mr. Yu, however, was always reserved about it. He told us that it made too much of a spectacle, and he was concerned.

One morning, we went up to our office and were told that the station wagon had been borrowed and that it was uncertain when it would be returned. When questioned as to who had borrowed it and why, we received a look from Mr. Yu and no explanation. For the next three weeks, we used a small Japanese sedan, and no one mentioned the station wagon. We asked several times, but our questions were never answered or responded to.

Then, one day, we met our driver downstairs at the hotel entrance, and wouldn't you know it, he was driving the station wagon. It was very clean inside and out, and I noticed that the lettering on the sides was a slightly different color and font. It was obvious that it had been repainted. We asked Mr. Yu what was going on. He just looked at us and said that there were certain things that were not necessary to explain.

We had the wagon for a year, and on one of our return trips to Beijing, Mr. Yu told us that the station wagon had broken down and he had to leave it. When he returned, it had disappeared. That was the last we ever saw of the wagon.

~16~

Friendship Stores, Chinese Army, Pigeons

Brainwashing is a Chinese Art Form.

E VERY TRIP BACK TO China was a new adventure. We learned more about the Chinese each time, but we also came to realize it would always be a place of mystery and unanswered questions. I can think of two occasions that took place during the early development of the hotel project that really illustrate that point.

We always stayed at the Beijing Hotel, which had grown and expanded over the years as tourism and business increased in China. Our offices, located on the fourteenth floor with a corner view of the main avenue in Beijing, were some of the nicest in the hotel and had been converted from hotel rooms. This part of the building was solidly constructed with thick cement walls. As the newer additions were built, the Chinese, in a hurry to collect the foreign currency, changed their building standards, and the construction was very different and hastily put up. At that point, the hotel had over one thousand rooms.

We always requested rooms on the same side of the hotel as where our offices lay, but on this trip, no rooms were available on that side due to a convention of Chinese Army high-level officers from all over China. With the hotel fully booked, we were put in a room in the most recent addition to the hotel.

It was a very strange trip; I should have realized that the karma was different as soon as I walked into our office. The Chinese did not use screens on the windows, and the air conditioning mostly did not work. If it did, it just cooled the cockroaches and not much more. Therefore, the windows were left open in the summer.

When we arrived in the office that morning, we were surprised to see two pigeons flying around the rooms. In the U.S., that would have been, needless to say, considered very strange since it not only disrupted the day-to-day office business but pigeon droppings were also left everywhere. When I asked what was going on, Ms. Zhang replied that everything was normal. When I mentioned that having pigeons flying around the office was not what I considered normal, she told us that when a pigeon flies into your office, it's a sign of good luck, and they must not be disturbed.

I decided to take Ms. Zhang out and buy her a gift as she was working very hard, and it would be an opportunity to talk to her about the inappropriateness of having pigeons flying around our heads, especially when important people were scheduled to visit us.

We went to a local friendship store—a type of department store where foreigners could purchase Chinese goods such as clothing, food, appliances, jewelry, luggage, and more. The store we stepped into was not in the mainstream area but toward the northern outskirts of Beijing.

We found a leather coat that she liked, and I paid the clerk in FEC, what foreigners converted their currency into when they came into China. The Chinese used RMB, the Chinese currency, and supposedly were not allowed to use the FECs, but there was a black market for them. We returned to our office with the coat but with no luck in convincing Ms. Zhang to get rid of the pigeons.

Later that afternoon, two security people showed up. They were never uniformed, but you could always tell by their demeanor. After a rapid conversation between Mr. Yu and the security people, Mr. Yu told me that these people wanted to speak to me and that he would interpret. He told me not to be concerned and to tell them whatever they wanted to know. If Mr. Yu felt the questions were inappropriate, he would intervene.

It seemed that when I gave the clerk in the store payment in FECs, he put them in his pocket and put the RMBs in the cash register to cover the payment for the coat. He was seen doing this by another employee, who immediately called the local Ministry of Public Security. When you live in a country that's a police state, there is always a fear you will be turned in. After I explained that I had given payment in FECs, they thanked me and left.

Later, I found out that within two weeks after I gave the clerk the FECs, he was convicted and sent off to a farm (if you could call it that) in outer Mongolia. He shoveled night soil (human feces used for cultivation) for a few years until he was sufficiently "rehabilitated."

The pigeons really started to irritate us as we tried to work, especially Sheldon. One afternoon, he decided to go to our room in the new wing and take a nap. The rooms were much smaller, and the location was not as convenient. The walls were paper-thin, and in the next room, some of the Army contingent must have been having a party. It sounded like the entire army was present, with all the boisterous shouting, laughing, and bouncing around. Since it was late afternoon, he just put some cotton in his ears and tried in vain to get some rest.

At about 7:00 p.m., a somewhat cranky Sheldon joined me in the western dining room. We talked about the pigeons, and that made us laugh as there was not much we could do about it. At about 10:00 p.m., we returned to our room, but the noise was deafening. The party next door did not stop until about 4:00 a.m. By that time, we were fit to be tied and exhausted, so we decided we'd nap until the early afternoon—until, to our disbelief, the partying started up again at about 7:00 a.m.

We gave up, got dressed, and off to our office we went, where we were promptly greeted by two flying pigeons and pigeon shit everywhere. As the day progressed, we began to wonder what we were doing in China in the midst of this apparent insanity. People came and went, telexes were sent, and we had two important meetings with our Chinese sponsor, Mr. Wang. No one seemed to care about the pigeons. In fact, in one of the meetings, someone brought a flat box filled with live little ducklings, and Ms. Zhang ended up with three of them to take home. At one point, we thought those ducks were also going to live with us in the office.

Through all this, we conducted serious business, drank a lot of tea, and ate very well. All our meals were a treat, and lunch always proved to be a very exciting event. No business was spoken at lunch, and Mr. Yu always ordered. There was always a minimum of five or six dishes, all of different varieties, always shared. They had menus available for foreigners, and ordering was always a negotiation between the waiters and Mr. Yu, but the food was always great, and our lunch was filled with laughter and carrying on.

After lunch, Mr. Yu and Mr. Wang would take a forty-five-minute nap, and then we would resume our meeting. We told them that the office was becoming a mess and that we just had to get rid of the pigeons. They all looked at us and said it could not be done. They must stay.

We ate an early dinner in the Hot Pot restaurant in the hotel and returned to our room at about 9:00 p.m. The wild clamoring in the next room was still going on. Between that and the pigeons, our nerves were frayed. Sheldon moaned and groaned and stuffed cotton in his ears. Finally, he'd had enough. He got up, grabbed his shoe, and banged it several times on the wall. Suddenly, the noise stopped, and we finally thought we would get peace and quiet. Then we heard pounding on the other side of the wall, obviously a shoe, and the noise started again louder than before. At that point, we had only one option left.

I put on my bathrobe, went out into the hallway, and knocked on the door. An older Chinese man opened it and looked at me. I told him I had a sick husband in the next room and would appreciate it if they could quiet down a bit. He looked at me and, in broken English, told me he was alone in his room, was asleep when I knocked, and he had no idea what I was talking about. Of course, I could see into his room behind him, where several people roamed about drinking and shouting. He then politely said goodnight and closed the door.

Their party went on all night as usual, and we were very haggard when we got to our office the next morning. The pigeons were still there, the mess was worse, and Sheldon was not in a good mood. He asked Ms. Zhang to please call and find out who the person in the next room was. It turned out that he was a very well-known and respected army general from the south, and the people coming in and out of his room were paying respects to him.

I implored Ms. Zhang to please call and ask him to let us have some peace and quiet. She called. They were on the phone for quite a while, and she was laughing. She got off the phone, smiled at us, and said he was very concerned since we were respected foreigners and he was a very important general in the PRC. He said that last night, he was fast asleep when there was a knock on his door. He opened it to find a foreign lady in a bathrobe, asking him to stop his party and be quiet. Since he was alone in his room and asleep, the only conclusion he could come to was that the foreign lady and her husband must be a bit insane, and he suggested that Ms. Zhang seek help for us.

He also told her to tell us that he would be leaving the following morning. They partied all throughout that night. In the morning, he knocked at our door, shook hands with Sheldon, and said he hoped we would be successful doing business in China. Brainwashing is a Chinese art.

Later that day, Sheldon told Ms. Zhang that if the pigeons were not gone by the following morning, he would personally grab each one, take them down to the kitchen, and cook them for dinner. The next day, they were gone, the place was clean, and when we asked her what she did with them, she looked at us as if to say, "What pigeons?"

≈≈≈≈≈

As the construction of the hotel project was progressing, Mr. Yu and Sheldon and I were constantly looking for new business opportunities. Entrepreneurs from a multitude of Chinese ministries would come to our office after contacting Mr. Yu to review joint-venture opportunities with us to see if we had any interest.

We met with one particular group of Chinese officials involved with the overall management of the largest friendship store in Beijing, on the main street where the Beijing Hotel and the Forbidden City were located. This store was four stories high and busy all the time.

I suggested that a new friendship store be constructed on the site of the existing one. I envisioned a twenty-story building that would encompass the department store, the market, and an entertainment complex, which would include bowling, roller skating, ice skating, and movies. The Chinese side also wanted to have office suites available for rental to Chinese provinces throughout the PRC that wanted to have a presence in Beijing, to sell their services and products.

Everyone thought it was a great idea, and after we did some diligence work, Mr. Yu arranged meetings with the officials we had previously met with, and we negotiated a letter of intent to be the joint venture partner in the project. The estimated cost: just under $100 million.

We returned to the United States and contacted a variety of potential funding sources, including investment bankers, merchant banks, and real estate developers. We assembled a team of professionals to travel back to Beijing with us to attend the letter of intent signing ceremony and banquet, of course, and to view the sites and work with us to come up with a proper business plan.

It was an impressive group that included Sheldon; the managing partner of the Los Angeles office of Arthur Anderson; Ivan, the national partner in charge of a large real estate development; Marvin, a partner in one of Los Angeles' most prestigious architectural firms; Pei, a Chinese architect from Marvin's office; and Bernie, vice president of MCA Entertainment.

We, of course, organized this trip with Mr. Yu, and he arranged our itinerary in Beijing. This was the first time we had traveled to Beijing with so many people, and it was our responsibility to arrange the Chinese visas and take care of the group.

Our first stop was Hong Kong, where we stayed for a few days. Charles Wrangham from Standard Chartered hosted a lunch for us, and we also met with and had dinner with Arthur Kwok, the architect of the hotel project.

The Chinese are great actors. When they wanted to impress a foreign group, they would put on a show that could turn anyone's head and bring certain traits (such as greed) to the surface, changing someone's personality completely. We knew Mr. Yu would organize something very special for our group, but he really outdid himself on this trip.

We were met at the airport with Red Flag limousines. The drivers in these cars ruled the road as all the top leaders were driven in these vehicles. It was a sign of great importance to the average Chinese citizen.

We were whisked to the Beijing Hotel. After everyone was settled, Mr. Yu arranged for us to visit Tiananmen Square and the Beijing Zoo prior to the banquet to be held that night.

We all piled into the limousines and headed for Tiananmen Square. It's important to note that there is absolutely no public parking anywhere near Tiananmen Square, so we usually walked there from the Beijing Hotel, which was only three or four blocks from the square.

Much to our surprise, we drove right onto Tiananmen Square. Sheldon and I had been to China many times, and in all the hours we had spent walking through the huge space of Tiananmen Square, we had never, ever seen an automobile there. Our limousine drove right up to Chairman Mao's tomb, and there, we got out. Two to three hundred people stood in line, waiting to see the tomb. One of the officials with us moved to the front, and, of course, we went in first. Chairman Mao is laid in state in a glass-covered cubicle (he stood over six feet tall), and we filed in and looked at the remains of one of the great leaders of the modern world.

When we returned to the limousines, a heated discussion ensued between our driver and a uniformed Chinese man. It seemed that it was a gross violation to drive on Tiananmen Square. Then Mr. Yu got into the discussion, and it went on for several minutes. Finally, we saw Mr. Yu give the uniformed man some Chinese money.

We asked Mr. Yu what had transpired. He said it certainly was not proper to drive on Tiananmen Square, but because of his guanxi, it was acceptable. We asked why, then, had he passed the uniformed guard some money. He explained that the man was one of the people in charge of keeping order on the square, and if Mr. Yu did not pay a minuscule fine, the uniformed Chinese man would lose face. By charging a fine and having it paid, he saved face.

We then headed to the Beijing Zoo, quite large but certainly not as modern as the Los Angeles Zoo. We arrived at the front entrance, and again, Mr. Yu had the gate opened, and we drove right in. We did not take any roads but drove along walking paths almost too small for the limousines. All the professionals in our group were very impressed, but the best was yet to come.

We drove back to the hotel to rest and then were off to dinner. Mr. Yu had not told us where the banquet would be held. To our surprise, it turned out to be the newest and most plush Chinese hotel in Beijing. We arrived and were ushered into the grand ballroom. Awaiting us in the room were various top Chinese leaders, including Mayor Yi Long Ki, the former mayor of Beijing and previously Chairman Mao's secretary on the historic, long march.

Television cameras, reporters, and red carpets were everywhere. Mayor Yi Long Ki walked up to Sheldon and me and gave us big bear hugs, as did several other Chinese leaders. It was very exciting, and we felt like royalty. The banquet progressed, and speeches were given about how respected our company, World China Trade, was in China; how Sheldon and I were old friends of China; and how liked and respected we were by the Chinese governmental officials.

The banquet was, for us, the most elegant yet. A lot of toasting and drinking to the success of our new project took place. The signing ceremony was filmed by several video and still cameras, and we were treated like celebrities. Our guests from the United States thought that World Trade China had to be the most influential foreign trade company doing business in China, and that was when the trouble started.

For the next few days, we toured the potential site for the new friendship store, and the architects discussed design and construction.

The Arthur Anderson people talked about potential profits, and Bernie from MCA discussed what the entertainment complex would contain and how his company would participate.

Sheldon, from Arthur Anderson, took us aside one evening and said he wanted to have a long talk with us. He said we had struck gold and had no real concept as to how rich the vein was. He said he could bring whatever investment we would require, and he wanted to be a part of it. We listened and told him we would consider his proposition. Then Ivan from Arthur Anderson took us aside and said that he could top whatever Sheldon offered and that he wanted to be part of it.

They got into a fierce argument over who should be our partner and how it should be handled. The fact that they both worked for the same company didn't seem to matter. It was like both men turned into completely different people. Their eyes glazed with greed and power, they got into a fistfight in the Beijing Hotel hallway over the issue.

What no one realized then was the game the Chinese were playing, which intentionally pitted each of us against the other. The dream of power was fleeting, and the Chinese gave and took it away at will.

Everyone was very enthusiastic about the friendship store project; when we all left Beijing and traveled back to Hong Kong, we thought we owned the world.

Then, in April 1989, the protests in Tiananmen Square happened, and everything changed.

~17~

Interludes: The Great Wall of China and U.S. Customs

Not reach great wall, not good man.
~Chinese Proverb

CHINA IS A LAND of contradictions. During our years there, despite becoming ensnared in a tangled web that included the most ruthless of China's security agencies, the FBI, the CIA, and a cast of characters who seemed straight out of a Hollywood spy thriller, we were also fortunate to have many special experiences and cherished adventures.

Mr. Yu knew a great many Chinese government officials and did many favors (guanxi) for them. Before he became president of our company, he served as manager of Occidental Petroleum when it first opened its office in Beijing, where he watched and reported back to the government on its activities in China. He and Ms. Zhang were responsible for all the preparations, dinners, and events when Dr. Hammer came to Beijing. Hammer was welcomed into China as his reputation had already reached far and wide regarding his dealings with the Russians.

One of Mr. Yu's very good friends, Madam Deng Ling, the daughter of Deng Xiao Peng, had a twelve-year-old son named Maza, who was friends with Mr. Yu's oldest son, Yishin.

On Sunday, all offices were closed, and Sheldon and I would spend time with Mr. Yu's family, going to dinner at their house, traveling with them, and seeing some of the sights of Beijing. One Sunday, he had Madam Deng Ling and Maza over, and we all went out for dinner at a local hotel that had an English-style restaurant

Madam Deng Ling was a very simply dressed person; you could not tell her from other Chinese of any class. This, you must remember, was the People's Republic of China, and Ling's lack of obvious stature was evidence of that. Madam Deng Ling spoke a little English; Mr. Yu, though not fluent, certainly could keep up a conversation in English.

While we were seated, Sheldon had a great time with the kids, who included Mr. Yu's youngest son, YiYu. None of the kids spoke English, but we had flown kites together and always brought them presents when we came to China. In fact, Sheldon taught them how to use the computer we smuggled in on Dr. Hammer's private jet.

That night, Sheldon showed them his spoon and fork trick. It involved putting the fork with the handle down and touching a glass on the table, with the tines of the fork facing you. The next step was to take a spoon and lay the handle under the fork, with the spoon's head toward you. Next, one needed to tap the spoon, which, if done properly, would flip the fork in the air and into the glass. Unfortunately, the fork could also land anywhere on the table—or on another restaurant customer's table—if tapped with too much gusto.

The kids loved it, and soon forks were flying everywhere. Mr. Yu and Madam Deng Ling gave Sheldon very dirty looks as the kids kept flipping the forks. It was really fun.

Afterward, Mr. Yu told Sheldon that the game was not proper for a public restaurant and that he should remember that he was with the daughter and grandson of the most powerful leader in China.

Despite his admonishment, we all had such a good time together, we decided that the following Sunday we would take a trip to a section of the Great Wall not open to the Chinese. So, we climbed into a van with Madam Deng Ling, Mr. and Mrs. Yu and the kids, and the former head of the Beijing Ministry of Public Security, his wife, and older children, who were all in their late teens, to begin the two-hour journey to the Great Wall from Beijing.

We first stopped at a small village in one of the new industrial areas, where we were treated to a lunch by the mayor and his retinue. Since so many honored guests were among us, we were wined and dined, and the mayor and several of his colleagues decided to join us. By the time we arrived at this portion of the Great Wall, we had gained another van, and our group ballooned to sixteen people.

The Great Wall of China, originally constructed to keep out the Mongol hordes, stood at about three to four stories high and stretched over 3,500 miles, with a road that ran along the top of the mountains wide enough for a team of eight horses to run along it side by side. It's hard to imagine how it was built, how the materials could have been dragged up to the tops of the mountains, where the labor came from, and how many Chinese who labored to build it must be buried up on top of those mountains.

There are no elevators; you must climb to the top. The workers had just constructed steps on this portion, so our ascent to the top took a while. The kids, of course, were way ahead of us. Since Yishin and Maza were the same age, and poor Yi Yu was younger, they went along without him.

What awaited us at the top was quite spectacular. Workmen were restoring parts of the wall in many places, and our path did not necessarily run entirely on level ground. It went up and down, following the contours of the mountains. We walked at least two miles, awed by this wonder of our world.

Refreshments were brought up by the mayor's people, and he later invited us back to his village for dinner, accompanied by entertainment by a local group from the Peking Opera. After walking the wall for about three hours, Mr. Yu decided we should go down and head back to the village. We rounded everyone up, but somehow, nine-year-old Yi Yu had disappeared. Mr. Yu asked the two twelve-year-olds where the younger boy was, and they both gave him an innocent look—which obviously meant that they were hiding something. They said they had no idea where he was.

We all fanned out and started to call out his name. Mr. Yu was getting very angry. Madam Deng Ling was waiting at the bottom of the wall with Mr. Yu's wife, and we were going to be late for the dinner being prepared in our honor. Finally, Mr. Yu decided it was time to go down. With a very knowing look on his face, he glared at the two twelve-year-old boys for a while. We tried to talk Mr. Yu into staying because we were afraid that something must have happened to Yi Yu. He could have fallen off; there were no guard rails, and that portion of the wall needed repair. Holes, broken pieces of stone, and sheer drops were constant dangers.

Mr. Yu insisted, "Let's go down," in a very authoritative voice. It was a long way down through the paths and stairs that were not finished. Forty-five minutes later, with the sky growing dark, we finally reached the bottom. There was little Yi Yu, standing with his mother. He shouted that the two boys had been mean to him and chased him down. The two twelve-year-old boys then ran to their mothers. Mr. Yu had blood in his eyes. He was really angry.

He started toward the boys, his fists clenched. Mr. Yu had been through the Cultural Revolution and had seen and done things, that we, as foreigners living in the United States, could never conceive of. He was a very tough individual, and as one of the Americans we brought to China once remarked, "I would never want him as an enemy."

As he started toward the boys, Madam Deng Ling stepped in front of him and said in a very quiet voice, "Please leave the children alone. They are just boys." He stopped immediately, unclenched his fists, and just stood there. Madam Deng Ling had a short conversation with all three boys, who then came forward with their heads bowed and formerly apologized to Mr. Yu and then to all of us for their behavior. They said they were ashamed of themselves and promised we would have no further trouble from them.

We got into the vans and headed to the village for dinner. It was wonderful, with local vegetables and a delicious fish we could not identify. We drank wine, Moutai, tea, and beer. The kids were really enjoying themselves, and every once in a while, Mr. Yu would give them very stern looks. Once, just after he looked away, they made a funny face at him. Kids will be kids, which is one of the wondrous parts of our world.

The local Chinese opera was performed by children between the ages of eight and twelve. The music part of it was hard for us as it had a screeching type of sound, but if you could understand the storyline, it was very interesting. The costumes were elaborate and unique, and the makeup was just incredible. The troupe portrayed not only people but also dragons, snakes, and an endless variety of other creatures. Those stories are like soap operas, and there is a great deal of emotion involved. We really enjoyed ourselves.

We arrived back in Beijing at about 10:00 p.m., and Mr. Yu told us that he was going to the house of the former Minister of Public Security of Beijing, the very nice gentleman who accompanied us to the Great Wall. When asked why, he responded that they were going to play Mahjong. I told them I played Mahjong and asked if I could join them. They said, of course, and soon, we arrived at his house. The building waited behind closed gates; you could tell nothing from the outside. The house looked special indeed with three floors and several bedrooms. Obviously, he was a very important person.

Chinese Mahjong is a bit different than U.S. Mahjong, but I fit right in, and we played for two hours. We were later told that we were the first foreigners ever invited into that house.

We embarked on several outings with Madam Deng Ling and Li Peng, who, at that time, was the coal minister. Eventually, he became president of China. Mr. Yu's associates were not from the liberal side of politics.

≈≈≈≈≈

Our custom incidents in China always involved Mr. Yu and were somehow resolved by his guanxi. Interestingly, though, in the fifty-seven times (over nine years) that we returned to the U.S. from the People's Republic of China, we were only hassled by U.S. customs agents twice. The second time that we were stopped, we discovered we had our own form of guanxi.

During our return from our first trip to China, our United Airlines flight stopped in Hawaii. Since it was the first U.S. stop, we were required to go through U.S. customs prior to our departure to Los Angeles.

Not knowing if this would be our only trip to China, we had brought several suitcases, much more than we needed, to bring souvenirs and gifts home for everyone. We were loaded with stuff, and it was difficult to fill out the duty certificate that must be presented to customs, outlining what you have purchased and the amounts.

Usually, customs officials randomly pick out people to examine as there is never enough time to deal with everyone, and we were selected. They examined everything, took apart everything, asked questions regarding everything, and kept us for more than one and a half hours. It was very exacting and irritating, especially since coming back from Asia, you lose twelve hours or so.

Finally, they let us gather our stuff, and we passed through and got on the plane back to Los Angeles. After that experience, we were always very leery and nervous when going through customs.

Fortunately, until the incident in Vancouver many trips later, we were never hassled again. We would go through customs, where they would look at our passports, check our names with some papers they always seemed to have, and just move us on through, regardless of what we were carrying or how much luggage we had.

We started flying Cathay Pacific Airlines to China. It was a great airline, and the service was always incredible. We would purchase business-class tickets to Beijing, and United would fly us in business class to Vancouver, where Cathay Pacific would upgrade us at no charge to first class from Vancouver to Hong Kong and then back to business class to Beijing.

In those days, clothes and many other items were much cheaper in Hong Kong than in the United States. Hong Kong is one big shopping center, a fact we took advantage of at every opportunity.

On this particular trip, I decided I wanted a fur coat and found a Chinese fur shop very close to the Beijing Hotel. I picked out what looked like Chinese ocelot. When we told the shopkeeper we heard it might be on the endangered species list, she said she was not aware of that and that we would have no problem bringing it into the United States. I loved it, and the price was less than a wool coat at home.

We brought it to Hong Kong and settled into our hotel room for the night. At about 2:00 a.m., we awoke to a very strange odor. We searched and found that the odor was coming from the coat. We actually had to hang the coat outside the window because the smell was so pungent. The next day, it really stunk, so we took it to a local Hong Kong furrier. He remarked, "Pretty smelly," and offered to trade the coat for what he said was a Siberian wolf coat. We accepted the offer but later joked that it was probably a German Shepherd coat. I also purchased a very pretty pearl ring for my mother, and Sheldon bought an Omega watch.

We stayed in Hong Kong for about a week. The new coat didn't smell, and the owner of the shop told us that this type of coat was duty-free.

Our last stop before home was Vancouver. U.S. customs has a unit in Vancouver that checks U.S. citizens on the way through to the United States. We had been back and forth so many times that customs was easy for us, and this customs station happened to be small. In our rush to fill out the customs form, we did not declare anything. I was wearing the wolf coat and placed the pearl ring in one of the pockets. Sheldon was wearing his new watch. Most of the people went through, but for some reason, they stopped us.

They asked if we had anything to declare, and we said we did not. They then asked where the coat was purchased. I told them Hong Kong, and we were told, there was no duty on the coat. They asked to see the coat and discovered the ring in the pocket. Yes, I fibbed and told them it was an old piece and that we had brought it to Hong Kong for repair. They flatly told us that they did not believe our story and that we were in a great deal of trouble. Then they noticed Sheldon's watch, and, as the saying goes, the shit hit the fan.

All of a sudden, five or six customs officers appeared. They even had us take off our clothes and told us that they were going to confiscate everything and charge us triple duty. By that time, they were even inspecting the seams of our luggage. Everything was scattered around, and we were being questioned intensely.

Meanwhile, our flight to Los Angeles was close to boarding. When we complained, they said that missing the plane would only be a small inconvenience compared to what we were up against.

I was very upset and argued with the customs agents. At one point, they told me that if I did not calm down, they would put me in a room and restrain me. We knew we were in trouble and were very concerned.

They finally took Sheldon's wallet and pulled out its contents for examination. While searching through his business cards, they noticed that we had an office in Beijing and started to ask questions regarding our business ventures.

One of the customs officials took the business card and disappeared into an inner office. He came back, followed by the senior agent in charge. He asked us several questions, then said he would be back after he made some phone calls.

Meanwhile, the search through our belongings continued, with questions on almost every article we had and more threats about what was going to happen to us.

At last, the senior agent came back, then called all the other agents into a corner and spoke to them for about ten minutes. He then returned and, with a very strange look on his face, told us that we must hurry to catch our flight to Los Angeles. All the customs agents then started to repack our luggage and belongings and were very gracious. In record time, we had everything back together. When we asked how much we owed, the senior agent said nothing—just that we should hurry to our flight.

When we got on the airplane, Sheldon and I wondered who he had called and what had transpired to give us complete clearance. We were never bothered again. Customs would just look us up in a book and pass us right through.

That was when we realized that we had attained our own form of "guanxi."

~18~

Mr. Yu's Other Businesses

He that once deceives is ever suspected.
~Chinese Proverb

Aᴏᴏ ᴛᴏᴇ ꜰᴛᴇʀ ᴛʜᴇ Tɪᴀɴᴀɴᴍᴇɴ Sϙᴜᴀʀᴇ incident, things changed dramatically in Beijing, China. The Chinese maintained that what had transpired in Tiananmen Square was an insurrection and that they tried for days to find peaceful means to end the demonstration, but to no avail. For the safety of the city and the government, the Chinese maintained that they used as little force as possible to curb the insurrection.

Not long after the incident in the square, we returned to Beijing. Mr. Yu had wired us before we left, saying that he had decided to move our offices out of the Beijing Hotel. Naturally, he had not consulted us. The People's Liberation Army had recently built the Capital Hotel, according to the telex, and he had managed to rent us a modest suite of offices in the new development.

Sheldon and I were disappointed because we had come to feel comfortable and at home at the Beijing Hotel, though we'd only had three small rooms there. The place had a unique ambiance and an interesting history. We would miss it. Mr. Yu claimed that the Beijing Hotel had raised its rates and the new offices were much cheaper. We were just starting construction of our development and were strapped for cash, so we were thankful for the savings and expected our new headquarters to be very modest. But we had mixed feelings about it.

By now, we didn't trust Mr. Yu at all and never knew exactly what he was up to. He made decisions unilaterally and seldom explained the reasons. We knew he had considerable guanxi, wielded much more often for his personal benefit than ours. We never knew if the joint venture or some other phantom business was the focus of his attention.

The language barrier was a constant problem. Mr. Yu would conduct transactions right under our noses, speaking Chinese, though it was never made clear to us what he was saying or to whom. We had suspected for quite a while that he was using joint venture funds for his own purposes but could not prove it. We were paying his wages, but he really was an employee in name only. We sent his salary to the state ministry; in the end, he worked for himself.

Our new offices turned out to be quite different than we expected. They were located on the top floor of the hotel in a corner suite, at least four times bigger than our old offices and far more luxurious. Mr. Yu had ensconced himself in a large private office behind a huge mahogany desk and sat in a new leather executive chair that was obviously not made in China.

The scale of his furnishings made him look like a dwarf. A large oil painting of himself hung on the wall behind the desk. The room read like a Freudian satire. Every object was an oversized icon of power. We had to wonder how a culture so sophisticated, so adept at reading every nuance, could produce a man with taste this crass. Mr. Yu's office only reinforced our suspicions. Something was going on.

Ms. Zhang, who had served as Mr. Yu's assistant and as office translator, now resided in the United States. We had arranged for her to enter a special MBA program at the University of Southern California. We had become close to her, knew her parents, and treated her like family. She spoke and wrote English expertly but with a distinct accent. Mr. Yu had hired her replacement while we were gone. Her name was Jingua, but she preferred to go by the English name, Jennie.

Jennie spoke in perfect English. In fact, if she had not been born in China, those she spoke to would have surely thought she was an overseas Chinese woman born and educated in the United States. I asked where she learned to speak English so well, and she told me in school in Beijing. She had never been out of China, she swore to me. We later found out that Jennie attended a special Chinese "spy school."

All new employees had been hired during our absence from the office, including a young man named Mr. Xue. He was very pleasant but distant. When we questioned any of the new employees regarding the comings and goings within the office, they would always give vague answers and direct us to Mr. Yu.

We also noticed a locked door to a small room near the entryway of the office. When we asked Jennie what was in the room and why it was locked, she said she did not know and that they did not have the key. Just then, we heard a sound from the locked room that sounded like a fax coming in. Sheldon called out to Mr. Yu and asked, "What's in that room? I hear a fax." Mr. Yu appeared, put his ear to the door, and said, "Sheldon, I don't hear a thing."

Later that day, I witnessed Jennie head over to a safe in the office and take out a large amount of FECs, which she put into a large paper envelope and then left the office for at least two hours. During the two or three weeks we stayed in the office, I witnessed the same type of thing several times. It was obvious Jennie and Mr. Yu were involved in some type of payoff process.

Sheldon had become friendly with Denny Barnes at the U.S. Embassy. Denny had the title of commercial attaché, but as we subsequently discovered, he was, in fact, with the CIA. Sheldon decided to pay him a visit. He was not aware that Mr. Yu had moved offices. He introduced Sheldon to a state department official, Ford Hart, Jr., who asked if he could visit the new offices. Sheldon arranged lunch, and when Ford arrived at our office, Sheldon introduced him to Mr. Yu, who was very gracious. We had noticed that Mr. Yu was now growing the nail on his right small finger over an inch long, per the custom of the old Chinese mandarins. Ford Hart also noticed this.

Ford was very curious about Mr. Yu and his associates in the Ministry of Public Security. He told us that this was the most unusual Sino-Chinese business arrangement of which he was aware. Then he point-blank asked if we were involved in the buying and selling of armaments. We told him that we had no knowledge of the armament business, except for the fact that at one point at the beginning of our relationship, Mr. Yu asked if we knew anyone in Washington. He said he had strong relations with the ministry involved in the manufacturer of weapons and asked if we were interested. We told him straight out that we and our investors had absolutely no interest in that type of business.

We noticed that most of the activity in the office seemed to have nothing to do with World China Trade business, but since it was conducted in Chinese, we couldn't figure out what was going on. When we went to look at documents, we would find them turned over, and all the drawers in all the desks were kept locked. Mr. Yu seemed to make sure that we were never in his office alone and kept nothing on the top of his desk. Everything stayed in drawers and bookcases that were locked up tight.

We realized before long that the married Mr. Yu had taken up a personal relationship with Jennie, similar to the one he had with Ms. Zhang. We began to get friendly with Mr. Xue, and every time we asked him about it, he would get a sheepish look and not answer.

When we asked Jennie about the Tiananmen Square incident, she gave us the party line. It was not the fault of the government, which was now much more liberal with the students, and everything was roses. Mr. Xue told us a different story. He said the recriminations against the students who had participated were very tough, and he had friends who were jailed and sent away. He said we should be very careful as Sino-China relations were very tense, and he intimated that Jennie reported back to secret government intelligence sources.

Sheldon directly asked Mr. Yu if he was conducting any other business. He said he was not and insisted he was living up to our agreement. The situation frustrated us. At that point, it was obvious what was going on. Jennie was always watching us. When we would pick up a letter or document from a desk, she would run over and grab it before we could see it and make some excuse.

Late one day, while in the lobby of the hotel, we met Mr. Xue who was leaving for the day. He was looking for us and said he had left a paper on his desk at the edge of the ink blotter with the address of a wonderful restaurant, and on our way back up to the office, we should retrieve it and enjoy ourselves.

We immediately went back up to the office. I went over to his desk and started looking for the aforementioned address. I found no piece of paper, but hidden under the edge of the ink blotter was a single key. We looked at the key and wondered. Then Sheldon took it and slid it into the keyhole of the top drawer of the desk. It clicked open, and inside we discovered a variety of items, including a Sino-American flag pin in a small box with the lid opened. Sheldon lifted it; underneath was another key with a small piece of paper on the bottom of the box with one word on it: FAX.

The puzzle was getting very interesting. We took the key and tried it in Mr. Yu's door, Jennie's desk, and then finally, the door to the locked room. Bingo! We opened the door and, sure enough, found ourselves staring right at a new fax machine and a large, locked cabinet filled with folders and papers.

Several faxes rested in the machine's tray. We read them and grew shocked. We had suspected that Mr. Yu was carrying on private business but never to the extent that we discovered. Sheldon looked at the fax machine (electronic equipment always interested him) and thought about the one-word message: FAX. Curiosity got the better of him; he started to look at the machine from all sides, then picked it up and looked underneath. A plate had been screwed into the bottom. It looked like someone had opened it because scratch marks were clearly visible on it. Sheldon decided to unscrew the plate. He always carried a small tool kit with him in China since he was always fixing things. And that was where he found three keys taped underneath the plate: one for the locked cabinet in the room, one for the door to Mr. Yu's office, and one for the locked cabinet in Mr. Yu's office.

Although we were in the office after-hours, we realized that the monitors on the floor would call Mr. Yu who might show up at any time. We discovered documents proving that not only had Mr. Yu created a new company that was doing business but also that his partner was one of our investors and a director of our company. We also found business cards indicating that Mr. Yu was now an agent for the Chinese elevator company that we had purchased elevators from for our hotel project, and he was getting a commission on that sale.

The most damming documentation was that Dr. Hammer's Oxy employees, directors of our company, were conducting an oil and gas business without the knowledge of Oxy and Dr. Hammer. We also found two documents written in Chinese that we later found out had to do with weapons.

I rushed to the copy machine and started copying all the documents we found, which numbered at over fifty. While I was copying, Sheldon decided that he would give Mr. Yu a hard time with the fax machine. He set the fax machine on a setting that would disable it, realizing that if it didn't work, Mr. Yu might ask him to fix it since he knew Sheldon was a technical guy. Then, we assumed, he would have to fess up about the faxes.

True to our suspicions, we had just finished copying all the documents when Mr. Yu showed up at the office. It was after 10:00 p.m. As innocently as we could, we asked why he had come back so late. He countered by asking what we were doing in the office at such a late hour. Sheldon told him he needed to use the computer to write a letter, and I had come along to keep him company. Mr. Yu's excuse was that he had forgotten a small piece of work that he had to accomplish before tomorrow. He walked into his office and closed the door.

We went back to our room paranoid as to what to do with the documents. We knew without a doubt that our room was bugged and were worried we may have left traces of our copying activities in the fax room. Overwhelmed by anger, anxiety, and stress, we worried over what to do. It was our office, and we were paying the expenses, yet we had to sneak around and copy documents in the middle of the night. We taped the large manila envelope under one of the drawers in the dresser and tried to sleep.

We returned to our office the next morning. Throughout that day, Mr. Yu and Jennie clearly seemed to be in a state of anxiety. I even saw him go into the locked room after he thought I had left the office. Nothing was said. Then someone we did not know came into the office. We later discovered that he had tried to repair the fax machine but could not.

The next day, Mr. Yu called Sheldon into his office and, in a very friendly way, told him he had taken his advice and purchased a fax machine. Sheldon replied that he had never suggested that he get a fax machine, although he thought heard one in the locked room. Mr. Yu explained that he had gotten the key to the small room and had the fax machine installed, but, unfortunately, there was a problem. The machine was not operating properly.

He asked Sheldon if he could fix it. It was hard for Sheldon not to laugh at that point, but he solemnly told Mr. Yu that he would do what he could. I watched Sheldon walk into the small room and sort of glance at the fax machine while I tried to keep a straight face. Then he went back to Mr. Yu and told him he thought it was a serious problem and that he should consider replacing it. Mr. Yu looked at him with a sickly sort of smile and told him that this was China, and replacements were not available. Sheldon said he realized that, but at the moment, it was his only suggestion. He asked Sheldon to try again. After a day of delays while letting Mr. Yu sweat it out, Sheldon decided to reset the fax machine, much to Mr. Yu's relief.

We were nervous about our safety this entire trip, concerned that the documents we had copied from Mr. Yu's office would be discovered and that the consequences for us could be dire indeed. We breathed a sigh of relief when we landed back in LA with the documents in hand.

~19~

The Plot Thickens

Fidelity, Bravery, and Integrity
~FBI Motto

W E HAD JUST RETURNED home from Beijing, and one of the first things Sheldon did was check his messages. To his surprise, one had been left by a Mr. Robert Messemer, special agent from the FBI. Sheldon called the number and was told that Mr. Messemer was not available and would return his call as soon as possible. We wondered what the message was about but didn't give it much thought. We had much more pressing matters to deal with, namely, figuring out what those documents we had brought back to LA might uncover about Mr. Yu's businesses.

Mr. Messemer returned Sheldon's call later that day and said that he must see Sheldon alone, *immediately,* to discuss an extremely critical matter of national security to our country. Now we were very concerned. We assumed that our joint venture partner, the Ministry of Public Security, was deeply involved in Chinese politics, but we had always made it very clear that we were only interested in our business relationship and that politics was something we never discussed or got involved with.

I dropped Sheldon off at a local Westwood restaurant to meet Agent Messemer. When I picked him up a short while later, Sheldon looked ashen.

When Sheldon had arrived at the restaurant, he found Agent Messemer already there, waiting for him. At six-foot-six, Messemer was a very imposing presence. They sat down, and the agent immediately informed my husband that Mr. Yu and Ms. Zhang had been under FBI surveillance for several years. They had determined that Mr. Yu was a Chinese spy working for the Ministry of Public Security and that our hotel joint venture was being used as a front for military espionage in the United States. He also informed Sheldon that we were "up to our eyeballs" in this intrigue. It was the FBI's contention that funds were being diverted from the joint venture to pay for this clandestine operation. He told Sheldon, he should be very careful because the Chinese would not hesitate for a moment, as he bluntly put it, "to spill your blood" on the streets of Los Angeles.

FBI Agent Messemer then informed Sheldon that he was going to speak individually to me and our attorney, who was a principal in World China Trade, to determine just what our involvement was and how, if at all, we were connected to the alleged espionage conspiracy. By then, Sheldon had lost his appetite completely, and he left the restaurant with Messemer telling him that he would be contacted again shortly and to keep this conversation in the strictest confidence.

I was flabbergasted when Sheldon told me about this encounter with the FBI agent. How in the world did we get ourselves into this situation? After talking about it further, we decided that we would take an aggressive approach and not be interviewed individually. Sheldon called Agent Messemer and asked to arrange a meeting to include all of us—Sheldon and me, our attorney partner Joe Brightman, and Marty, an independent legal counsel representing us. Sheldon made it clear that we would not meet separately to discuss any aspects of the joint venture or its participants.

A couple of days later, we all met for lunch. Agent Messemer brought an additional agent along with him from the Federal offices in West Los Angeles. He reiterated what he had told Sheldon. We explained to him that although we were partners in the joint venture with the Ministry of Public Security, we had absolutely no knowledge of any doings other than what pertained to the business of the joint venture. We then provided him with the documents we had discovered in Mr. Yu's office. After examining them, he told us that these were indeed valuable to his investigation and cautioned us not to disclose this meeting to anyone.

It reminded us of a conversation we had a few years back with Mr. Yu in our office in Beijing, when we voiced our concern about being involved with the Ministry of Public Security as American citizens. Mr. Yu said we didn't have anything to worry about and that we could always live in China if any political problems arose. We realized at that moment that our relationship would always be on a strictly business and not political basis. Now, here we were years later, and the meaning of Mr. Yu's comments was coming to light.

We assured Agent Messemer that we would cooperate with him, but we were concerned about the joint venture and our investment in China. Messemer assured us that it was not the FBI's intention to create any havoc with the joint venture. However, they fully intended to prosecute, if possible, the individuals involved in the alleged espionage.

From that moment on, and until our interest in the joint venture was sold back to the Chinese government, we cooperated and worked with U.S. government intelligence agencies in several different respects.

~20~

The Chinese and Israeli Ambassadors

A well begun is half done.
~Chinese Proverb

It was very tense returning to Beijing and continuing to work with Mr. Yu. At one point during the construction of the hotel, Sheldon became friends with the Chinese ambassador to the United States, Ma Yu Zen, and on this trip, he introduced us to the Minister of Culture, who arranged a visit to Tianjin that was a welcomed relief. Ambassador Ma was later to play an important role, with our assistance, in forging a relationship between China and Israel.

This trip was not long after the Tiananmen Square incident that was televised to a shocked world, and the Chinese were looking for ways to improve their image. Ambassador Ma suggested that we meet with Ying Ru Chen, who at that time was the Minister of Culture for the People's Republic of China. Mr. Chen was an actor who played Willie Loman in *Death of a Salesman* in China and played the warden in *The Last Emperor.*

The meeting took place in The Forbidden City, which reminded us of *The Last Emperor.* We felt like we had traveled back into the past. Ying Ru Chen was very gracious and spoke excellent English.

After we were served tea, he explained that Ambassador Ma told him we were friends of China and could assist in creating a better image by dealing with the children of China and the local people.

He wanted us to visit Tianjin, the largest seaport in Northern China, to meet with their Minister of Culture. From Beijing, it is about a three-hour train ride, and he had arranged for one of his assistants to take us to the train and provide us with tickets. We thanked him, and he thanked us as well.

The next morning, we were picked up by his assistant, who unfortunately spoke little English, and were taken to the Beijing Train Station. During a normal day, as many as 300,000 people could be packed into that station at one time, and foreigners needed a guide to find the right train. The assistant escorted us to a local train, and we, of course, were the only foreigners aboard. When we stopped at a small-town crossing, we noticed several people purchasing rice and vegetables wrapped in lotus leaves from a vendor cooking right beside the train. We bought some—it was delicious.

When we arrived in Tianjin, we were met by the Minister of Culture, his secretary, and his driver. It's interesting to note that the people of Tianjin are very tall; it's not unusual to see many people over six feet. Our first stop was, of course, a restaurant. In China, the normal greeting people give each other is not, "How are you?" but, "Have you eaten lately?" We were told the restaurant was very famous for its dumplings, called Chaozhou. Joining us were three additional people, all either friends or part of the Ministry of Culture of Tianjin.

The Chaozhou started coming to the table, and we thought it would never stop. Each Chaozhou dumpling—similar to Kreplach, a Jewish form of that food—is filled with something different: meat, poultry, vegetables, fish, or things that would probably make your stomach queasy. They must have set thirty different types of dumplings in front of us, and it would have been an insult to our hosts not to try each one.

Of course, along with the food, they served Moutai and wine. Everyone would down a shot glass of Moutai while shouting, "Ganbei." It was by far our most memorable meal in China. We also noticed the security people, quiet and observing, in the background.

After lunch, our retinue had grown to over ten people and two vehicles. We traveled through the very crowded streets of Tianjin, where, reportedly, ten million bicycles are used, and arrived at a local family adult center. In China, all communities offer centers for adults, teenagers, and small children. These centers are not free but only charge a minimal cost. We were introduced to the director of the center, who gave us a tour. It was old and by U.S. terms dilapidated, but it contained a movie theater with a small projector, snooker tables, and several project rooms where adults could sit and do creative things. We spent about forty-five minutes there and then were off again. By this time, three vehicles and about fifteen people made up our group.

Our next stop was the teenage center, which offered a roller skating rink, basketball, baseball, and other activities. The teenagers were interesting as several wore sunglasses—their way of standing out. As honored guests, we created a lot of excitement, and the teenagers gave a brief performance for us, tumbling and skating.

We moved on to the small children's center. By then, our caravan had grown by leaps and bounds. We made a stop along the way, as we had been invited, it seemed, to a musical recital conducted by a group of six- to eight-year-olds. The recital took place in a building with a dirt floor. I am sure most of the children in attendance and their parents had never seen a qweilo (round-eyed barbarian) before. I took one of the children in the audience and sat her on my lap. She was very nervous, but many pictures were taken. As a side note, we were told that there were more teenagers in China than there are people in the United States.

By this time, we were really overwhelmed and wondered once again what the Chinese agenda really was for us in Tianjin. The Chinese are a very clever people, with plans and purposes designed to carry long-range results not often evident in the present. The next stop at the children's center was a treat. At one point, we sat on the floor with about fifty to sixty little children surrounding us, all jumping around and touching us with wonder.

When we left, with five vehicles in tow and many people aboard them, we noticed thousands of residents watching us as we rolled through the city. The next stop proved a strange one; to this day, I cannot say I understand the purpose behind our visit, except maybe to expose us to a high official in an unofficial location.

We stopped at a large apartment complex similar to many others we had seen that rose several stories high, with elevators that only stopped at every third floor. This saved construction costs, and it was expected that people could walk up and down two flights of stairs. The apartments were very small—about six hundred square feet each—with concrete walls all around. Most had no refrigeration or hot water. A drain had been installed to allow them to heat the water in the kitchen and then use it to wash over the drain. A small area, serving as the apartment's kitchen, contained just two gas burners and no oven. Despite the lack of amenities, these apartments were considered a luxury.

The units' residents had come from homes that were barely more than huts, hundreds of years old. The only heat available was the peat they bought in the streets, and the only water came from a cold-water spigot in the central courtyard outside. The toilet facilities available were not worth mentioning.

Our entourage had expanded to over twenty people by then, and we all entered the apartment of what we were told was a retired army general who had cancer. He was most gracious. We noticed fish tanks in every room of his apartment, housing the greatest variety of fish I had ever seen outside of a public aquarium. As interesting as all this seemed, Sheldon and I still had no idea what we were doing there. Most of the people with us did not speak English.

We finally left; our final stop was also in an apartment complex. We all crowded into the smaller apartment, a big group in a small space, much like the conditions in China everywhere. We learned that this was the home of Mud Family Zhang, who had, for centuries, created mud sculptures. Their technique was handed down from father to son, and we marveled at their creations. The sculptures, though not for sale, were exhibited in museums and had been possessed by emperors and royalty throughout the ages.

We liked to talk about our family; so, Sheldon told everyone present about our niece who was undergoing surgery for her back deformity. The sculptor's ten-year-old son, who was just learning the craft, showed us his sculptures of Snow White's seven dwarfs, which he had made over a long period. Much to our surprise, they gave us one of his dwarfs, and the father presented us with a statue of an old Chinese judge. We told them that these priceless gifts were too much and that we could not take them. But they insisted.We called our niece to thank them for the gift of the dwarf. Since there was only one phone in the entire complex, it was quite an experience.

Somehow, we got to the last train in time to return to Beijing but ended up in a different train station than the one we had left from. We were concerned as we weren't familiar with the southern outskirts of Beijing, and of course, no one spoke English. We wandered around for a bit, but before long, someone tapped Sheldon on the shoulder—an English-speaking gentleman sent to pick us up.

It was a wonderful day; we told many people of our adventure. I'm still not at all sure what the visit was about or if it had any impact on changing the image of China after Tiananmen Square.

≈≈≈≈≈

Sheldon's friendship with Ambassador Ma Yu Zen ultimately led to a very gratifying relationship with China and Israel, a relationship we did, in fact, have an impact on.

From the very beginning of our travels to China, Sheldon never hesitated to tell everyone that we were Jewish and that our heritage and history were as long or longer than the Chinese. In Beijing, we met several Jewish people who had lived in China for many years. The most interesting among them, Israel Epstein, a Polish-born Chinese journalist and author, was one of the few foreign-born Chinese citizens of non-Chinese origin to become a member of the communist party of China. He had lived in China for sixty-five years and became a personal friend of Chairman Mao.

During one of our trips home, Sheldon received a call from

Ambassador Ma Yu Zhen who was in Los Angeles. He invited Sheldon to lunch at the Chinese consul located near downtown Los Angeles. Sheldon was honored by the invitation since Ma was a very important man in Chinese political circles.

He arrived at the Chinese consul and was ushered into a private dining room, where he was greeted by the ambassador and the vice-consul. After an elegant lunch, during which the ambassador asked how our joint venture was proceeding, he mentioned that the Chinese government was very interested in a positive outcome. According to the ambassador, Sheldon and I were very respected in China and had attained a foreign status called lau pengyou (old friends)—a high honor for a foreigner.

After lunch, Sheldon and the others moved into a small conference room with soft couches and Chinese antiques. Tea was served, and Ambassador Ma then told Sheldon that the conversation they were about to have would be confidential and was very important. He explained that he was speaking in an unofficial capacity. China and Israel did not have diplomatic relations; however, the Chinese government was very interested in forging a relationship to their mutual benefit. He asked Sheldon for his help in this endeavor.

Sheldon told him he was very interested because he thought there was great similarity between the Chinese and the Jews, and that he would speak to me, and we would come up with a plan. He also suggested that a good start in opening up lines of communication between the two countries would be for him to make arrangements with the Israeli ambassador for a Chinese representative to come to Tel Aviv and for an Israeli representative to come to Beijing.

Sheldon and I decided that an unofficial dinner at our house between Ambassador Ma and his wife and some prominent Jewish leaders would be a good beginning. We called our friend Harvey Schacter, head of the local office of the Anti-Defamation League (ADL). Harvey suggested that we bring the head of the ADL and some other prominent Jewish leaders to the dinner.

I arranged a typical Jewish dinner, with chicken matzo ball soup, roast chicken, egg bread, and kishke. The people from the ADL questioned Ambassador Ma repeatedly about the human rights issues in China, and Ambassador Ma, being somewhat of a smooth politician, answered every question in a soft manner. The dinner went very well. It was, in fact, the beginning of several more such meals—unofficially, of course—between Ambassador Ma and the Jewish community.

Then one day, Sheldon received a call from the ambassador inviting him to lunch at the Chinese consul again. He told Sheldon he had arranged with the Israeli ambassador to have the Chinese open a tourist office in Tel Aviv, and the Israelis would open a science office in Beijing. He thanked Sheldon for his suggestion and help and said it was still unofficial but a first step toward relations. He suggested that on our return to Beijing, we meet with the Minister of Foreign affairs for North Africa, whose area encompassed Israel. The minister was a friend of his, and he would arrange the meeting.

Sheldon went to visit the Israeli consul in Los Angeles. He also met with the vice-consul and asked him for the address in Beijing where the Israeli office was being opened and the name of the representative. He told the vice-consul that he would visit the office, meet the representative, and try to open some doors for him in Beijing. The vice-consul replied that he was not aware of any relations between Israel and China and had no knowledge of any Israel office opening in Beijing. Sheldon suggested that he meet the vice-consul from the Chinese Embassy in an informal way, and he arranged a lunch in Chinatown with the three of them.

The lunch went very well, and when the Israeli vice-consul asked the Chinese vice-consul if he was aware of the Chinese opening an office in Tel Aviv, he said he was not but that it certainly sounded like a good idea. Sheldon was certain both vice-consuls knew of the arrangement, but it was not politically correct to admit it at that time.

Sheldon asked the Israeli vice-consul if he could communicate with the proper officials in Israel and tell him where the office was in Beijing. He sent several communications, and they all came back, saying that they had no knowledge of any office. He then called Ambassador Ma and asked him where the Israeli office was in Beijing, and he said that unofficially, it had already opened, but he did not know the location.

When we returned to Beijing the next month, Sheldon told Mr. Yu that he wanted to meet with the Minister of Foreign Affairs for North Africa. He wanted to know what reason Sheldon had for requesting this meeting and if it pertained to our business and not politics. Sheldon explained to him that our being in China was more than just doing business and that the more relationships one made, the more opportunities would come.

The next day, Mr. Yu arranged the meeting between Sheldon and the minister. Sheldon's driver waited for him after he went inside the Ministry of Foreign Affairs, a huge complex with gates in the front and a guard. He was escorted into a typical Chinese conference room with couches and antiques. While the minister and Sheldon sat side by side, the minister told Sheldon that China would like to have diplomatic relations with Israel but that they also had friends in several of the Arab countries who had embassies in Beijing and diplomatic relations with China.

He said China wanted to have relations with all countries and not get involved in the internal politics of each country. A relationship with Israel was very important for China. The Chinese could learn many things from the Israelis, as could the Israelis from the Chinese. China and the Jews have had thousands of years of history between them, and Jews had dwelled in the court of Kubla Kahn. In his opinion, the thinking processes between the two peoples were very similar.

Sheldon asked if he was aware of the Israeli office in Beijing. The minister replied that had heard something about it and was pleased as it was a good step forward. When Sheldon asked for the address, the minister replied that he had no idea where it was located. Sheldon thanked him for his time and gave him a personal letter that Ambassador Ma had asked him to deliver to the minister.

Very frustrated at this point, Sheldon told Ms. Zhang that he wanted to find the mysterious Israeli office in Beijing that no one seemed to know the location of. Her response was, if the Minister of Foreign Affairs didn't know where it was, how was she to find out? Sheldon patiently explained that he knew she had the ability and enough guanxi to locate it. She laughed, and fifteen minutes later, Sheldon had the address. The office happened to be in the Jinguo hotel, the same place as the JAL office and other foreign offices.

Sheldon approached the hotel's front desk and inquired as to which floor the Israeli office was on. The Chinese clerk said no Israeli office was in that hotel. Sheldon then wandered back to the ground floor where the offices were located and found a closed door with no markings. He opened the door and saw an Israeli calendar on the wall and one Chinese man sitting at a small reception desk. Sheldon asked him if this was the Israeli science office and was told he had been assigned there by the government. When Sheldon asked who was in charge, the man said, "Yoel Guillat." Sheldon asked to meet him, and within moments, Mr. Guillat came out of the office and greeted him warmly. The office had been open for a month. Sheldon was their first visitor.

The Chinese had opened a tourist office in Tel Aviv and staffed it with five Chinese men, but Yoel was the only person sent from Israel. He brought a gift for the Chinese, a software program, that converted Pin Yin (Chinese into English, and vice versa.) His goal was to meet with as many Chinese as he could, but he was having a problem— so far, all his attempts had been rebuffed with a polite no. He asked Sheldon for some assistance. That night, Sheldon and I had dinner with our new friend Yoel, and we really enjoyed ourselves.

The next day, Sheldon asked Mr. Yu for some assistance in inviting some of his friends in the different ministries to meet with Mr. Guillat. Mr. Yu said he could ask but that none of the ministers or other officials were willing to meet with the Israeli because the office was just an experiment. If it went badly for whatever reason, they would not want the visit on their record.

Sheldon then asked Ms. Zhang to come with him to try to convince some of them to visit the office or at least invite Mr. Guillat to visit them. Ms. Zhang obliged. Everyone was very polite and said they understood but still refused. Mr. Guillat was very disappointed but continued doing what he could. Sheldon finally convinced a friend of his to meet Guillat. This friend happened to be an official at the ministry that specialized in high-tech devices and computers. He had been trained at a school in London and was interested in the software brought over by the Israelis.

Sheldon arranged for the three of them to eat lunch together in one of the dining rooms at the Jinguo hotel. His friend was very nervous and feared he could be criticized for attending this lunch, but his interest exceeded his anxiety. Mr. Guillat gifted his Chinese friend with a software product designed in Israel that could automatically fix hard disk errors in a DOS-based system—a valuable tool for any person who dealt with PCs. Then they decided to visit the Beijing computer economic zone.

This zone, which consisted of five street blocks, was lined on both sides of the street with nothing but computer stores. When the three men arrived, trucks were pulling in and out filled with American and Japanese computers and products. They discussed the future of computer products and computers and spent most of the day together. Sheldon's Chinese friend was very impressed, and Sheldon asked for his assistance in getting other Chinese officials to visit Mr. Guillat so that the relationship between Israel and China could move forward. He said it would be difficult, but he would do his best.

A few years later, when we finished our final negotiation and sold back our interest in the hotel project to the Chinese, we were invited to the Israeli consul in Beijing. By then, China and Israel had diplomatic relations, and we attended a party along with a multitude of Israelis, including several members of the Israeli Parliament. We were happy to have played a role in establishing those relationships.

The ox moves slow, but the earth is patient. We were beginning to understand that.

~21~

Interlude:
The Silk Road to Couture

The silkworms die when the spring silkworms die,
and the wax torch turns into ashes and tears begin to dry.
~Li Shangyin, poet, Tang Dynasty

I TOOK THE DOWNTIME available while the hotel was being constructed to focus on other opportunities in China that were far less stressful and much more enjoyable. Since our early days there, I had been interested in China's silk industry and visited several silk factories, during which the episode with the "ugly Americans," the two brothers from Los Angeles in the garment industry, had occurred. China's woven silk goes back thousands of centuries and was the fabric of choice for Chinese and Roman emperors. Silk also linked the Western world to China. The Silk Road became the ancient trade route between the Roman Empire and China. For centuries, China dominated the silk industry, until the early twentieth century, when Japan became the world's top silk producer.

What I discovered after visiting many silk factories in China was that their technology was still behind the Japanese. Because they were not able to weave silk in a 52- or 60-inch width, couture designers were not able to use Chinese silk, even though it was beautifully woven. I approached the silk ministry and told them I could help them obtain equipment that could be retrofitted into their factories, which would allow them to produce silk fabrics in a wider width. This would open up China's silk manufacturing to more markets. They were very receptive to this idea. By the time the hotel was built, several factories were able to produce the wider widths of silk. Now we just had to get the word out to couture designers.

That's when I had the idea to approach *Vogue*, the top women's fashion magazine, to seek their support. Through a friend of a friend, I was introduced to Alexandra Shulman, the editor-in-chief of *British Vogue* at that time. I explained my idea to showcase new silk designs and the fashion that would be coming out of China. Alexandra, who was from England and Hong Kong, loved the idea. The Ministry of Silk was very excited too.

We asked the editor of each magazine (*Vogue* has seven different editions globally, published in different languages) to select two designers to come to China, where we would take them to the silk factories that we had remodeled so they could create new designs using the woven silk. Once the designs were completed, I knew we needed a memorable way to present them and introduce China silk to the world's fashion elite.

It was now 1990, and the hotel was open. Holding the event there would showcase the hotel and China's silk fashions. I happened to remember when Queen Elizabeth II visited China and Hong Kong in the fall of 1986 to acknowledge the Sino-British pact to return Hong Kong to China in 1997. She had given a speech in Hong Kong—while on the waterfront on a beautiful pavilion float that had been built for her—detailing all the years that they had been a part of England.

I talked to the head of the silk ministry, who then contacted Hong Kong, and, lo and behold, they agreed to send the pavilion to our hotel. We set it up in the front of the hotel, where the circular driveway entry was, and that was where we conducted our fashion show. It was a spectacular event covered by all of *Vogue*'s magazines as well as by fashion reporters from every corner of the world.

By the mid-1990s, China once again had resumed its dominance as the world's largest producer of silk. Today, of course, almost everything you put on your body is made in China. Whenever I see something made of China silk, I smile with great pleasure.

~22~

Mr. Wang's Nefarious Businesses

Tension is who you think you should be.
Relaxation is who you are.
~Chinese Proverb

IT WAS THE SPRING of 1990, and the hotel project, now called the Beijing Asia Hotel, had been open for about ten months, but the construction, not yet fully complete, was nearing forty million dollars. The intrigue and tensions with our partners were rising, and at that point, we trusted no one in China. We were constantly getting telexes and phone calls from Mr. Yu telling us that the Chinese side, Mr. Wang (BLIPU), was concerned because the hotel was not making any money, and payments were due to Standard Chartered for the construction financing, among many other debts.

Mr. Wang called an emergency board meeting. With trepidation, Sheldon, Joe, and I traveled to Beijing. We were told this was going to be a showdown, and since we had only sketchy information about the finances of the project, we felt ill-prepared. But we knew it was necessary to attend because of our fiduciary responsibilities to our investors.

The short-term loans from Chongqing (CITIC) were long overdue as were the payments to the Bank of China for the three-million-dollar loan for our joint venture. Mr. Yu informed us that the Bank of China and CITIC would no longer loan the joint venture funds. He also said that the books and records were being kept by five different entities: World China Trade, BLIPU, the City of Chongqing, the Beijing Branch of the Bank of China, and Ramada—who was running the hotel. Each set of financial records for the project was different. We could never get a true number on the escalating costs.

Mr. Yu had moved our offices from the Capital Hotel to the Asia Hotel. Our company, World China Trade, occupied two small offices on the floor that contained snooker tables and a bar and lounge area. Jennie and two other employees worked in one of the offices, and Mr. Yu occupied the other office, which was always locked when he wasn't there. When we asked Jennie for the key, she said only Mr. Yu had it, but from time to time, we would catch her unlocking the door to his office and going in. When Jennie left for the day, she would also lock her office, and when we asked for *that* key, she said there was only one.

The board meeting was held in a closed room on the second floor off of the lobby, which held three ballrooms and a restaurant. The room was designed as a boardroom and contained a large conference table that sat twenty people and chairs and couches along the walls that sat an additional twenty people or so.

At this point, our joint venture was comprised of our company, World China Trade, which owned 50 percent of the joint venture for thirty years; the Beijing Ministry of Public Security (the Chinese counterpart of the KGB), which owned 25 percent; and CITIC (Chongqing International Trust and Investment Corporation), which was the financial arm of the City of Chongqing and owned the other 25 percent. Our original joint venture contract was with the Ministry of Light Industry of Beijing, but, unbeknown to us, the Chinese changed partners in the middle of the joint venture without informing us.

Sitting at the table was the chairman of the joint venture, Mr. Wang; four other directors who were members of the Ministry of Public Security; five directors who were with CITIC; and Mr. Li, the chief spokesperson for the group. He was about seventy years old and had traveled with Mao on his two thousand-mile march through China.

Our group consisted of Sheldon, vice chairman of the joint venture; me as a director, Mr. Yu, president of World China Trade and the first Chinese citizen given the right to participate in a foreign company; and our attorney and partner Joe Brightman. Also present were Mr. Lu, the senior interpreter for the Chinese government (now manager of American affairs for World China Trade); and Richard Chen, vice president of China operations for Occidental Petroleum Corporation. There were also several others in the room taking copious notes.

The board meeting lasted four days and was a circus. All of the accountants from each group were present, including representatives from the Bank of China. Mr. Wang started the meeting and informed everyone that the hotel project was in dire financial straits and that if we were unable to get additional funding, the hotel would have to be closed. This, of course, caused a great deal of agitation among all the board directors, the assorted accountants, and other members attending the board meeting.

The next two days were filled with recriminations, with each side blaming the other. The accountants started to argue with each other. Each side had a different set of financial records, and each argued that their records were the correct ones. There was a large disparity between the different sets of records, which they all blamed on Mr. Wang. He, of course, blamed the City of Chongqing and Mr. Yu. The Bank of China blamed everyone.

Then Mr. Wang, in his very charismatic way, asked the representatives from the Bank of China to fund the project an additional five million dollars. Mr. Li from the City of Chongqing thought that was a very good idea. We thought the representative from the Bank of China, who was the manager of the Beijing branch, would have a fit of apoplexy. His face got very red and flushed, and he started to holler at Mr. Wang, who calmly sat, looked at him, and said that since the City of Chongqing had refused any more short-term loans, the Bank of China was the only source left for funding. The representative from the Bank of China then looked at Mr. Li from Chongqing and asked why they would not loan any more money to the joint venture.

The answer went on for a while. Mr. Li never lost his composure. He had accompanied Chairman Mao on the long march, after all, and was a very patient man. He explained that they had originally put up the guarantee and had yet to receive the guarantee fee. They had made a short-term loan of over twenty million dollars to the joint venture and had not received any payment at all. The loans were seriously overdue, and the costs of the project were continuing to escalate with no end in sight. He stopped just short of calling Mr. Wang a thief.

Then the accountants started to really argue and scream at each other. We didn't get much of the translation as things were really getting out of hand when one Chinese accountant got up, jumped over the table, pushed another accountant against the wall, and started screaming at him nose to nose. Mr. Wang stopped the board meeting, and we all went out to lunch. Everyone calmed down, and lunch, as usual, was a treat. We sat in a private dining room; the excellent food came directly from the kitchen.

After lunch, the meeting resumed, as did the fighting and arguing. Mr. Wang produced a bank statement showing that we had almost no funds in our joint venture account and that all this arguing and bickering would not solve the problem. We needed cash immediately.

The board meeting ended for the day with no resolution, and Sheldon, Joe, and I went back up to our office with Mr. Yu for discussion. Mr. Yu, who had his own set of accountants, for the joint venture, had no answers, except that he also suspected Mr. Wang of misdoing—though we suspected that explanation was only for our benefit.

Mr. Yu left the hotel for an unknown appointment. Shortly after, we received a call from Mr. Xue, now an ex-employee and the man who had helped us find the secret documents. He said he understood there was difficulty with the joint venture. He also said, rather mysteriously, that you never know what people might throw away. That was when we realized he was trying to tell us something. So, Sheldon and I contrived a plan to get Jennie out of the office.

As luck would have it, we noticed an American movie playing on the TV in the lounge that day. Jennie was very interested in the United States, so Sheldon asked her if she wanted to watch the movie with him. That was my chance. I hurried into the office and started to look through the desk while Sheldon took Jennie aside and proceeded to talk nonstop about life in the United States. I knew I had to work quickly, before she might suspect that we were up to something.

Within twenty minutes, I found something in particular that really disturbed me. I took it and returned to the lounge, where I gestured to Sheldon that we had to talk. After Jennie went back to the office, I quietly told Sheldon we had to find Joe. I had something to tell them both—but not here in the hotel. We found Joe in his room, and through hand gestures, motioned for him to follow us. Our rooms were always bugged with microphones, and we were also concerned about conducting conversations in public areas. There were always spotters around who would "casually" listen in. We decided to leave the hotel and go out on the street to talk.

And that was where I showed them both what I had found: copies of two money transfers amounting to over two million dollars from our joint venture account. Most of the documentation was in Chinese, but we were able to make out the number of our joint venture account, the dollar amount, and the words "Toronto, Canada."

Our first thought was to fax a copy of the money transfers back to Los Angeles—then we realized that the fax machine in our office had to be bugged as well. We grew very concerned and apprehensive over what Mr. Wang might do if he discovered that we knew about the money transfers after he had told everyone at the board meeting that the joint venture account was depleted—the same day he had transferred over two million dollars out of the country.

That I had found the copies of these fund transfers in the wastepaper basket in Jennie's office struck me as quite unusual. Money transfers and other financial dealings were always taken care of in the accounting office. Why Jennie would be privy to that was a mystery, and why anyone would make copies of the illegal fund transfers and then leave them next to the top of the wastepaper basket was indeed strange.

The Chinese had more than one agenda. We later found out that there was another strong Chinese faction involved. They were trying to bring Mr. Wang down and were using us as the bait and leverage to do it.

We had made some friends within a large international public relations firm, Hill and Knowlton, who had offices in Beijing. We decided to ask their advice and see if they were willing to expose what was going on. We met with them and told them who our joint venture partners were and about the money transfers. The manager of the office, with a very panicky look, told us that if he was in our position, he would leave Beijing immediately. He advised and pleaded with us to take his car and driver, go immediately to the airport, and do whatever we could to get out of China. He said our lives were in danger, we were involved with very dangerous people, and that he would have nothing to do with this at all.

We were all frightened at that point but decided that we had to go back to the board meeting as we could not leave the country even if we wanted to, not without permission. So, off we went back to the hotel just as the board meeting had resumed. Mr. Wang had copies made of the bank statement, which, of course, we knew were phony since it showed no money transfers. Thus, the arguments continued. We thought of asking Mr. Yu about the transfers but decided against it as we realized that he had to be in league with Mr. Wang.

After much thought, we agreed that Joe, who was leaving the next day, would put a copy of the money transfers in his shoe. When he got back to the United States, he would have the documents translated and then call the bank in Canada for an explanation. Sheldon and I carried copies of the documents with us in our shoes as well.

The board meeting continued, and the arguing went on for another day. Periodically, one group or another would get very upset and walk out of the meeting, returning at a later time. Then Sheldon suggested that we call in the Ramada manager and question him as to the finances of the hotel since Ramada was managing the property. There was a lot of discussion, and it grew obvious that Mr. Wang did not want the Ramada manager reporting to the board.

Sheldon told Mr. Yu that it was very necessary. Begrudgingly, he agreed, and after more discussion, so did Mr. Wang. We had told the Ramada manager to be prepared with a report just in case he was allowed to join the meeting. His report was much different than Mr. Wang's. His sales figures were much higher, and he looked confused as to why we had no funds in the joint venture account since, according to him, a large fund of money should be available.

Mr. Wang said that it was obvious that the Ramada analysis was incorrect. Interestingly, there was not much comment from any of the Chinese at this point. The Ramada manager left the meeting, and the arguing started again, almost as if the Ramada manager had never made the report at all.

The meeting continued until, finally, the Bank of China agreed to lend the joint venture additional funding. The meeting was then adjourned.

The accountants all agreed that they would get together, try to compare notes, and create a set of books and records that everyone would agree upon. That, of course, was never done.

When Joe returned to the United States, he investigated the money transfers and found out that the funds had been transferred into an account in Toronto, Canada. The account listed a business owned by Mr. Wang—a real estate company purchasing, for cash, office buildings and condominiums. Joe also uncovered activity of funds being funneled into other areas that we had no knowledge of.

Joe turned everything over to FBI Agent Messemer who concluded that these funds were being used for illegal criminal activities, including the possible purchase of nuclear secrets.

~23~

Interlude: The Briefcase

What you hear about may be false, what you see is true.
~Chinese Proverb

A T THE SAME TENSION-FILLED emergency board meeting where Mr. Wang had informed the board that the joint venture had no money and more funding was required to complete the hotel construction, Sheldon's briefcase, containing highly confidential and secretive information, disappeared.

A great deal of intrigue was ensuing all around us. Each joint venture partner had its own agenda. Mr. Yu, being a Chinese citizen, was walking a tightrope as he was president of an American corporation and a high-level Chinese citizen. Sheldon was in a similar position as the chairman of an American company doing business in China while secretly reporting to U.S. government intelligence agencies.

Sheldon carried a slim leather briefcase with him everywhere, which contained, among the several documents supposedly kept secret from our other partners, highly confidential correspondences from the American intelligence service. We were so paranoid, he even put it under the mattress at night.

At one point, he excused himself from the board meeting and

went out into the lobby to clear his head, as most of the discussion was in Chinese, and we had to deal with our interpreter, which was very difficult, to say the least. On each hotel floor was a desk, manned by hotel employees who not only reported to management but also to the Ministry of Public Security. Sheldon sat on one of the couches for about ten minutes, and Mr. Yu came out of the boardroom. They had a heated discussion and then returned to the boardroom.

A few seconds after they returned, Sheldon realized he had left the briefcase on the couch in the lobby. He rushed out to the lobby and to the couch, and, lo and behold, the briefcase was gone. It could not have been more than one or two minutes at the most. He immediately went to the Chinese at the desk and asked where the briefcase was. They motioned that they did not understand English, but of course, they actually did in some fashion. Sheldon gestured with his hands and by then was frantic, growing worried over what the consequences would be if the Chinese side got hold of that briefcase.

The desk boys just kept denying any knowledge of anything, until finally, Sheldon returned to the boardroom and told Mr. Yu about the disappearance. Mr. Yu now grew very agitated. At the time, China was controlled, to some extent, by the Ministry of Public Security. There was no telling what might have happened to Mr. Yu or his family if the contents of that briefcase were exposed.

Mr. Yu immediately went out with Sheldon to question the desk boys who kept repeating that they had no knowledge of the briefcase and had seen no one take it. Mr. Yu got very angry, and a great deal of shouting and threatening ensued. He finally made a call from the desk. In less than ten minutes, two very serious-looking Chinese showed up and started interrogating the desk boys.

It wasn't long before all three desk boys looked very frightened. One started to cry and then just burst out in a torrent of Chinese. He then pulled up a chair, stood on it, and pulled a ceiling tile out. He stuck his hand in and pulled out Sheldon's briefcase, wrapped in plastic. Sheldon was relieved but also angry at being treated that way in a hotel our company owned.

Somehow, the story circulated all through Beijing, and Sheldon received calls from several news agencies asking for a story. He declined, not wanting to stir up any problems with our joint-venture relationships. The next day, the following story was circulated by Chinese officials:

"When Mr. Krechman came and sat down at the couch, the desk boys observed him and were concerned, as he was an honored guest, and a partner in the hotel project. When Mr. Yu came out to join him and they got into a heated discussion, the desk boys were concerned and took a special interest. When Mr. Krechman and Mr. Yu went back to the board meeting, the desk boys noticed immediately that Mr. Krechman left his briefcase on the couch. They instinctively realized that the briefcase must be important, therefore they decided to protect it in a plastic case and put it in a safe place, and the safest place they could think of was in the ceiling. They didn't understand Mr. Krechman when he asked them because they did not speak English. They were trying to protect Mr. Krechman and his briefcase and therefore were entitled to commendation."

The U.S. Embassy and the non-Chinese news agencies just laughed at that version, but in China, one must always expect the unexpected. We were just relieved that the contents of the briefcase had not been exposed.

~24~

Mr. Yu, LA, and the FBI

It's the oldest question of all, George.
Who can spy on the spies?
~John le Carré

AFTER OUR INITIAL MEETING with Agent Messemer, during which he told us of Mr. Yu's suspected espionage, he and Sheldon would meet several more times. We wanted to give our government all the assistance we could—and we were concerned over our own involvement, having never before dealt with an investigative agency.

Sheldon called his friend Ford Hart Jr., employed at that time at the White House. We had met him at the U.S. consul in Beijing and, though never quite sure what his job was, we knew that he was involved in the intelligence business. We later discovered that he was part of the White House intelligence agency that reported directly to the president. Sheldon told him of our meetings with Agent Messemer and what had transpired. He said he was unaware of the FBI investigation but told us to cooperate and continue to report to him at the White House on all events concerning Mr. Yu and the FBI.

The very next day, Agent Messemer called Sheldon, requesting another meeting. When Sheldon arrived, Messemer asked if he had spoken to the White House intelligence agency. When Sheldon confirmed he had, Messemer asked why. Sheldon replied that our group had no secrets and that for our protection, we wanted everyone to know what was happening.

Messemer got a very funny look on his face and seemed far more subdued than he'd been in previous conversations. He told Sheldon that the FBI director in Washington had called him and asked for all the details after he had received a call directly from the White House regarding this issue.

That put Sheldon on even footing with Agent Messemer. Messemer commented that we must have friends at a very high level in the White House since the FBI director in Washington was directly involved. Messemer would be under scrutiny from not only the FBI office in Los Angeles but also the national FBI office in Washington. The case had been given a high priority on the FBI's agenda. In fact, Messemer himself considered it to be the most serious case of espionage ever uncovered in the United States. Agent Messemer spoke fairly fluent Chinese and had uncovered another Chinese espionage plot based in Chicago a few years earlier.

At this time, Mr. Yu was trying to acquire a visa to come to the United States. The U.S. government's quota only allowed so many Chinese citizens into the country. They had to apply at the U.S. consul in Beijing, wait in long lines, offer a good explanation for their trip, and be prepared to be rejected most of the time.

Every time Mr. Yu wanted to come to America, we would write a letter to the U.S. visa bureau in Beijing requesting that Mr. Yu be allowed to enter for a pre-determined length of time for purposes of the business of World China Trade. Mr. Yu also requested on several occasions that we write a letter to the visa bureau for different groups of Chinese, all of whom he said would be visiting for reasons important to our business. Agent Messemer told Sheldon that the visa letters we had written were for many Chinese involved in the alleged espionage business.

When Sheldon told Agent Messemer that Mr. Yu wanted us to write another visa letter for him as he was anxious to come to the U.S. to pursue his green card application, Messemer said we should just play along with Yu as if nothing had happened.

We followed the agent's advice. Mr. Yu's visa was ultimately approved, and Sheldon went to the International Terminal at Los Angeles' LAX Airport to wait for his arrival. Sheldon, only allowed to approach to a certain point (airport regulations) and look down at the ramp that the passengers came up after going through customs, stood and stared in disbelief as Mr. Yu ascended the ramp with Agent Messemer. Sheldon grew uncomfortable as they approached, but Messemer, without acknowledging Sheldon, casually said goodbye to Mr. Yu and went on his way. When Sheldon asked Mr. Yu who that was, he replied that the man was a fellow traveler he just met at customs and then quickly changed the conversation.

After Sheldon dropped off Mr. Yu at his hotel, he received a call from Agent Messemer. Sheldon mentioned how surprised he'd been to see him with Mr. Yu. Messenger explained that when Mr. Yu was last in the United States, he had interviewed him, but Yu had denied everything, insisting that he was just a businessman and had nothing to do with politics.

Agent Messemer then informed Sheldon that Mr. Yu was under twenty-four-hour surveillance and was being followed wherever he went. The agent gave Sheldon his cell phone number and said to keep him constantly apprised as to our whereabouts. Our safety was of paramount importance, the agent insisted, and the FBI would be watching. He clearly seemed under the impression that we might be in physical danger. We never thought so. The Chinese were always cordial, especially during our meals together. I have to admit, though, that this double life Sheldon and I now lived was getting pretty exciting.

Our relationship with Mr. Yu had cooled somewhat over time. We were not made aware of all his meetings during his visit to the United States. But about a week after he arrived, we arranged to have dinner at a local Chinese restaurant with him and Ms. Zhang. At that time, she was attending graduate school at the University of Southern California in a special MBA program I had helped her get into for non-residents. It's important to note that our relationship with Mr. Yu and Ms. Zhang was very family-like. We had spent years together, shared hundreds of meals, and our whole family knew them and treated them like one of our own.

Mr. Yu, at this point, was very frustrated with Sheldon who had promised to help him obtain his green card. Yu even accused him of hindering the process. (Sheldon later found out that meant things would have gone much smoother if he'd agreed to falsify Yu's application document, a request Sheldon had refused.) In fact, during our last trip to Beijing, Mr. Yu had been told that his green card had been approved and that he would receive the final documents in Guangzhou. When he arrived at the U.S. visa office in Guangzhou, however, they interrogated him for three hours and then refused to grant him green card status.

He flew back to Beijing and accused Sheldon of stopping the process. Sheldon denied that he had anything to do with it, but the reality, of course, was that Sheldon and I were both involved.

Mr. Yu had a weakness of character that caused him a lot of problems. He had an affair with his senior office assistant, Ms. Zhang, and then with Jennie. His wife, Lily, whom we knew, suspected her husband of infidelity. He told us not to make any waves. Once Ms. Zhang relocated to the United States to attend school, Mr. Yu took up with Jennie in the office in Beijing. Ms. Zhang knew what was going on— and she was not happy about it.

Mr. Yu had requested that we not mention Jennie in front of Ms. Zhang when we met for dinner. But being the pot-stirrer that my husband was, Sheldon causally asked Yu how Jennie was doing at Ms. Zhang's old job. A very strong bond connected Mr. Yu and Ms. Zhang; it went far beyond an affair or a business relationship. We in the United States cannot understand what a person had to do to survive the Cultural Revolution, and those two had met during those times, forming a very strong connection through their suffering.

During the dinner, Ms. Zhang looked at Mr. Yu and casually mentioned that she had heard that Jennie was a spy. Mr. Yu stared at her and went totally crazy. He jumped up in the crowded restaurant and started screaming (very unlike a Chinese man), "Spy, spy, spy! It isn't true!" He then ran out of the restaurant, still screaming. Ms.

Zhang just sat there calmly eating her dinner and smiling. People all around us were staring, and at a table next to us, two men in suits and ties smiled at us and nodded.

Concerned about Mr. Yu, Sheldon exited the restaurant and found him outside, pacing and muttering. Sheldon convinced him to come back in, which he eventually did. He gave Ms. Zhang a dark look. She very sweetly looked at him and asked, "How is Jennie the spy doing?" He totally flipped out. We thought he would punch her, but he just ran out of the restaurant again. At some point, he somehow found a bus that took him back to his hotel.

When we returned home later that night, Sheldon got a call from Agent Messemer, who laughed and said, "It must have been quite a scene in the restaurant." The two men at the other table were FBI agents.

~25~

Oxy becomes a shareholder in World China Trade

Tough times pass. Tough people last.
~Plaque on Dr. Hammer's desk

AFTER THE TIANANMEN SQUARE incident, all the bank credit lines from outside China were closed to the Chinese government, and our hotel project, for lack of funding, was moving very slowly. The original budget of twenty-five million dollars had ballooned to over sixty million. The Chinese were requesting funds from World China Trade to cover half the deficit.

We rejected each request. We had already invested what all parties had agreed upon into the joint venture, and we simply did not have any additional funds to offer. Our position was that if the Chinese wanted to make the project larger or grander, it would be their responsibility to provide the funding. This, of course, did not sit well with Mr. Wang.

He repeatedly requested more funding, and we repeatedly refused. He threatened to close down the project. Our response was "Go ahead." We were in the midst of construction, and closing it down seemed an unlikely scenario—at least, so we hoped.

Union Bank in Los Angeles, our equity lender for the project, was getting very nervous. The project was far behind schedule, and the interest on the loan was growing daily. We had several meetings with the bank, who threatened to call the loan and take the collateral we had put up as a guarantee. That collateral consisted of a combination of letters of credit, CD deposits, and personal guarantees from friends and investors.

Standard Chartered in Hong Kong was also pressuring us because they had already lent the joint venture over twenty-five million dollars and had grown very concerned after Mr. Wang threatened to stop the project.

We met with the bankers in Hong Kong, who told us that it was our responsibility as joint venture partners to share fifty/fifty in whatever the overruns were at the hotel. Furthermore, they would not lend one more penny to the joint venture, and, if the payments were not made on a timely basis, they would foreclose. That was an idle threat. Standard Chartered would never foreclose on a China project, realizing that if they did, there would be no future for them in China. Bankers always threaten, but we took the matter seriously.

We went back to Beijing and met with Mr. Wang to tell him the funds were frozen and that he could expect no more money from outside of China or from World China Trade. After much negotiation, which involved sitting in a room for ten hours with ten other people, nine of whom were chain-smoking Chinese cigarettes (the smoke was so thick, you could hardly see across the table), Mr. Wang told us that it would be possible to arrange a series of short-term loans inside of China. But he warned that these short-term loans would have to be paid back on the date that they were due, or else there would be dire consequences.

Of course, Mr. Wang said as long as the Chinese side would be financing the balance of the construction, World China Trade would need to give up some future rights in exchange for the Chinese shouldering the financing load. We argued about this point for a long while but finally agreed to give the Chinese side some small advantage when, and if, profits came from the project.

We called a board meeting, and Mr. Li and his group came down from Chongqing to attend. The purpose of the meeting was to determine where the joint venture would get the funds to complete the project. As far as Mr. Wang was concerned, however, the purpose of the meeting was to get the City of Chongqing to agree to loan these short-term funds. Mr. Li was very upset and started the meeting off by asking Mr. Wang why the guaranteed fee of one hundred thousand dollars, which should have been paid prior to the start of the hotel's construction, had still not been paid to CITIC. He demanded the payment be made.

Mr. Wang, in his inimitable way, started a dialog that lasted hours. He went through the whole history of the joint venture and somehow never got to the point. Of course, we only heard what was interpreted for us, so the true meaning might not have been what we were told. This went on for about three days, and then Mr. Wang told the officials from Chongqing that the joint venture needed more funds to complete the project. The Hong Kong bank and World China Trade refused to add any more funds. If the City of Chongqing didn't lend the joint venture more money, the hotel project would be stopped.

Mr. Li got very red in the face and started shouting at Mr. Wang. He accused Mr. Wang of suckering him into putting up the whole Chinese side of the investment, even though Chongqing only had a twenty-five percent share in the project. They had also put up a twenty-five-million-dollar guarantee and yet had not received their guaranteed fee. To make matters worse, the project was 50 percent over budget. And now Mr. Wang wanted the City of Chongqing to loan more money to the joint venture?

Mr. Wang, in his very political way, just kept on talking—a strategy that apparently worked. The City of Chongqing finally started funding more money toward the project. The loans were to be paid back in 60-, 90-, and 120-day increments. As far as we know, they never got that money.

Meanwhile, Union Bank in Los Angeles started pressing us to either sell the joint venture back to the Chinese or come up with the money owed to them. The Chinese, seeing an advantage, offered to purchase our share, but since the joint venture was not complete, the amount they offered was minuscule, and all the investors would have lost most, if not all, of their money.

And, of course, there was the issue of World China Trade's stock. Sheldon and I owned 23 percent. Mr. Yu, Richard Chen, and Dean Lee each had 12 percent. The remaining stock was held by our investors, which totaled about twenty different people.

At that time, Occidental Petroleum Corporation had no legal interest in the joint venture. The only connection, as far as the public was concerned, were our two stockholders, Richard Chen and Dean Lee, who were also Chinese employees of Oxy. The Chinese, on the other hand, came to the conclusion that Occidental Petroleum was a partner. It didn't help that Richard Chen and Dean Lee acted as if that were the case toward the Chinese officials when they came to Beijing.

Union Bank finally got its lawyers involved and made a formal demand for payment. We owed them 3.75 million dollars, plus accrued interest totaling at several hundred thousand dollars. The demands started coming in on a frequent basis. Our legal counsel was involved at that point, but things looked very bleak. We felt like the ball in a ping-pong match—both sides were coming at us all the time. We were constantly writing telexes, arguing with Mr. Wang, and fielding telephone calls from our investors, who were upset, to say the least.

The hotel project was more than a year overdue, and the original budget was a joke; we were already past forty-five million dollars and climbing. The Tiananmen Square incident rattled our investors, and the banks were ready to grab all the collateral and put us out of business.

On a Monday morning, we received a call from Richard Chen who requested that we meet immediately. He rushed to our house, and, after we had some tea, he told us that Dr. Hammer had made him an offer he could not refuse for his stock in World China Trade. The Oxy lawyers were drawing up the papers; they wanted the transaction completed within a few days.

The next day, we were contacted by Ray Gill, Oxy's in-house lawyer, requesting a meeting. He told us that Oxy had also purchased Dean Lee's stock and was willing to purchase our shares too. The price he quoted was far too low; we realized that it was just a legal gesture.

Within four days, Occidental Petroleum Corporation had become a 24-percent owner of the stock in World China Trade. Ray Gill and Jack Dorgan—chief financial officer for Occidental Petroleum—were now on our board of directors, replacing Richard Chen and Dean Lee.

The next day, we received a written offer from Occidental Petroleum Corporation to purchase all the shares in World China Trade at a price that would pay off Union Bank and return to the investors their original investment with no profit. It was an open offer to be taken at any time, with no time limit.

The Oxy lawyers sent a copy of this offer to Union Bank, informing them that they now owned a significant share of World China Trade. Union Bank stopped their demands immediately and left us alone to deal with the Chinese.

Once Oxy became a shareholder, everything became much more formal. We had several meetings with Jack Dorgan and Ray Gill and, of course, continued our secret meetings with Dr. Hammer.

The construction went on, and the Chinese side stopped their demands for funding. The intrigue continued, but that, of course, is part of the story.

≈≈≈≈≈

The rapport we thought we had established with our Chinese partners changed considerably at the joint-venture board meetings now that two Oxy executives were present. Everything became less familiar and more formal.

Oxy continued to have severe difficulties in their coal joint venture in Shanxi Province, leading Dr. Hammer to realize that dealing with the Chinese was very different than dealing with the Russians.

Our first board meeting in Beijing with the Oxy executives present was very tense. Jack Dorgan and Ray Gill asked many pointed questions as to Mr. Wang's activities regarding the joint venture. It was obvious that Mr. Wang was irritated but did his best not to show it. He realized that, with Occidental Petroleum involved, he was now dealing with a multinational corporation with influence that reached to the highest levels of both the Chinese and U.S. governments.

The hotel construction was nearing completion, the overruns were horrendous, and the graft was obvious. Sheldon and I, Richard Chen, Mr. Yu, Jack Dorgan, and Ray Gil decided that, prior to the first board meeting we were scheduled to attend in Beijing, we would tour the construction site. Mr. Dorgan asked about the three-story energy center constructed by the joint venture on the backside of the hotel property. We were told originally that the energy center was necessary because the hotel would require its own power source instead of depending on that of the City of Beijing. The electrical power produced by the Beijing City Authority was very erratic; there were always dark hours in some part of the city.

I had always questioned the size of the energy plant and the cost of constructing it. The Chinese engineers consistently said it was necessary. After we toured the project, I decided to visit the relevant city authority that dealt with the plans and specifications for all the new construction in Beijing.

Through an interpreter, I made friends with one of the female Beijing City clerks. Using my knowledge of architecture, design, and construction, I went through all the plans and specifications. I soon discovered that the energy plant was not only supplying electrical energy to our hotel project but also to twenty other new apartment buildings and Mr. Wang's personal office building, which was under construction. The joint venture was also paying for the maintenance, upkeep, and all expenses related to the center, including payroll.

Our directors from Oxy were not at all pleased when they heard this information, along with a multitude of other issues that had come to light regarding Mr. Wang's and Mr. Yu's activities with the joint venture. Finally, the Oxy people requested that the next board of directors meeting be held in Los Angeles, not in Beijing, so they could unveil several issues they had discovered with the Chinese there.

At first, Mr. Wang refused to have the board meeting in the United States. He said this was a China project, and all business that had to do with it should be held in Beijing. We argued that point and told Mr. Yu and Mr. Wang that we had traveled to Beijing for eight board meetings. We always had to pay for our own airfare and hotel accommodations. It was time for Mr. Wang and the Chinese to shoulder those inconveniences.

Mr. Wang finally agreed, and, of course, the joint venture had to pay for all the expenses. Mr. Li and the Chinese directors from Chongqing also came. We arranged for them to stay at a hotel in Westwood close to the Oxy offices, and Dr. Hammer graciously offered to have the board meeting in the Oxy boardroom, on the sixteenth floor of the Oxy building and the same floor that Dr. Hammer's office was located.

We took the whole Chinese contingency to Las Vegas for a visit and then returned to Los Angeles for the board meeting. It was a pleasant time in Las Vegas. We, of course, had to play the part of tour guides, which had always been our role with the Chinese outside of the PRC.

When we returned from Las Vegas, the Chinese contingency, which consisted of fifteen people, asked me to take them shopping. They complained to me that when they had traveled to New York and asked to go shopping, they were taken to Fifth Avenue and all the upscale trendy shops. When large U.S. corporations invited mainland Chinese to the United States, they would always treat them to the finest restaurants and the best stores.

The Chinese would always be polite, but what they wanted was a local Chinese restaurant and a department store where they could purchase items for their families at reasonable prices. I brought the group to a local Montgomery Ward department store in a mixed-ethnic neighborhood, which they all enjoyed. Every time I would host a group of Chinese from then on, they always asked to shop at that store. We created a routine: we would all get ice cream cones in the Thrifty Drug Store and then head over to Montgomery Ward. The Chinese would purchase a variety of clothes and small appliances and would always be very grateful to me.

Just prior to the board meeting at the Oxy offices, Sheldon and I met with Dr. Hammer at his house. We told him everything that was going on, and he was clearly not pleased. He told us that whatever transpired at the board meeting, we were to remain calm.

The meeting lasted three days. The boardroom was spectacular. Pieces from Dr. Hammer's priceless art collection adorned the hallway walls just outside the room. The boardroom itself was very large, with high-tech electronics and a conference table large enough to comfortably sit thirty to forty people. We decided that we would give the chairman's seat, typically reserved for Dr. Hammer, to Mr. Wang, as he was the chairman of the joint venture.

The American side sat on one side of the table and the Chinese contingency settled on the other so that we faced each other. Sheldon and I sat on Mr. Wang's immediate right, with Mr. Yu seated on Mr. Wang's immediate left.

Aside from the normal board of directors, two attorneys from the Oxy office also attended. Dr. Hammer made a brief visit and said that he hoped the meeting would go smoothly and that the project would be a success.

It was up to me to tell the Chinese contingency, almost all of whom were chain-smokers, that the Oxy building was a designated no-smoking, high-rise office building. I explained the situation to Mr. Wang and told him that because Oxy wanted everyone to feel comfortable, they had designated a room on the same floor as the boardroom where the Chinese could go and smoke if they wanted.

Mr. Wang said that this was very inconvenient and that he and the others would not be comfortable sitting in a board meeting without being able to smoke. I explained to him that not only was smoking in public places illegal in the state of California but also that Dr. Hammer had graciously allowed us to use his personal board of directors room—where no one had ever smoked. If they did light up in that room, it would be very insulting and discourteous and would reflect badly on the Chinese government. Mr. Wang just looked at me and walked away.

Mr. Wang started the meeting, the minutes from the prior board meeting were read, and within a few minutes, the meeting turned very argumentative. A lot of blaming from both sides ensued, and there were plenty of issues to blame someone for, including the overruns, the obvious corruption (which, of course, was never admitted to), the amount of money we owed on the short-term loans we borrowed, the ongoing manipulation of the joint venture for the benefit of the Chinese by Mr. Wang, and several other issues that needed explanation and closure.

Two times, Mr. Wang stormed out of the room in anger and, I suspect, frustration. At first, the Chinese would leave the room, go to the designated smoking room for a time, and then return. They kept this up for the first day. By the second day of the board meeting, enmity seethed between the Chinese side and Oxy. It appeared that we had been somewhat naïve in our dealings with Mr. Wang, and the Oxy lawyers were dealing with those issues in a very stern corporate way. Since Sheldon was the chairman of World China Trade, it was his responsibility to bring those issues up at the meeting, after which, the Oxy lawyers would jump in.

Every morning at the start of the board meeting, waiters would bring in carts of fresh fruit, rolls, sweet rolls, and a large variety of breakfast items. These would be replaced during the day with other foods. All this was served on a special bone China that Dr. Hammer had ordered from China. It was very elegant, unlike the rest of the meeting. If looks were daggers, by the end of the second day, we all would have been dead. It was by far the most difficult board of directors meeting we ever had up to that point.

Dr. Hammer came to the meeting at the end of the second day and spoke to everyone about Sino-American relations. He said that the future of their country depended on the foreign companies that wanted to do business with China and share their modern technology so that China could grow and become a major player in the world community. He also told the Chinese that he appreciated their not smoking in the boardroom as he realized from his many trips to the PRC that the Chinese love to smoke, and that it's difficult for them not to have that freedom.

Things did not improve. In fact, by the third day, everything was rapidly deteriorating. Mr. Wang accused the Oxy people of being obstructionists, of not understanding the Chinese, and of causing trouble. The Oxy people based their conversation on facts that Sheldon and I had uncovered and proceeded to push for explanations in a very stern, direct, and rigorous way.

At one point in the meeting, Mr. Wang looked at everyone, took out a cigarette, lit it up, and started to smoke away. I was a bit stunned, and the Oxy people got very red in the face. One of them said in a very polite way that if Mr. Wang wanted to smoke, they would agree to pause the meeting while he went to the smoking room. Mr. Wang just looked at them and continued to smoke while dropping the ashes on one of the bone China plates in front of him.

Mr. Dorgan got up and said he would leave the meeting if Mr. Wang kept smoking. Mr. Wang smiled at him and crushed out his cigarette on the bone China plate. He then casually lit up another cigarette. I thought there would be a physical showdown, but Mr. Dorgan sat back down, and the meeting ended shortly after that.

As we filed out of the boardroom, Mr. Wang came over to Mr. Dorgan and the Oxy attorneys, and with a smirk, asked if they would all join him for dinner at a local Chinese restaurant. One of the Oxy attorneys looked at Mr. Wang and, with a very straight face, said they could not accept Mr. Wang's offer as they had a much more pleasant evening planned—they were going to have their fingernails pulled out with pliers. With that statement, they all turned and walked out. Mr. Yu then asked Sheldon and me to join Mr. Wang and the group for dinner, but we refused.

It was a bad ending to our board meeting.

~26~

The Beijing Asia Hotel is Open

Elegant and Graceful.
~Beijing Asia Hotel brochure

A FTER YEARS OF INTRIGUE, nefarious activities, and the stress of doing business in China, the completion of the Beijing Asia Hotel in 1990 seemed almost anti-climactic. But our adventure was far from over.

The hotel, still thriving in Beijing, is a golden palace that soars several stories high. At the time it was built, it boasted many amenities such as a spa and health club, neither of which were common at the time. It included three hundred tastefully furnished rooms, each with a comfortable work area, and offered luxury suites as well. The executive floors boasted a reception center, business center, small meeting rooms, a reading room, and a lounge area. Office space was also available. Several restaurants and a state-of-the-art conference center that could accommodate a thousand people were also among the amenities.

Before the doors officially opened, we started looking for a hotel management group that could run it. At that time, the Chinese had little or no knowledge of the operation of a modern tourist hotel.

Our board had interviewed the Sheraton hotel chain, Holiday Inn, the Furama Hong Kong Chain, the Nikko Hotel chain, and several other hotel companies. We decided that an American hotel chain would offer the best management for the joint venture, and Ramada was selected.

Ramada offered more than worldwide network reservation service, expertise in managing a modern hotel, and knowledge of how to deal with foreign tourists. They also supplied protection for World China Trade as they would report to the joint venture on all aspects of the hotel operation instead of harboring secrets. Knowing that Ramada would handle all the money was a relief—we knew we would get an honest count.

The terms of the Ramada contract were far more liberal than any of the other hotel chains we interviewed. The Ramada management in their Hong Kong offices was all Chinese, including the general manager of the whole Asian territory. They came to Beijing several times to make presentations and finally agreed on a fee structure between 30 and 40 percent less than any of the other competing hotel management companies that we interviewed. It was Ramada's second hotel management contract in China, the first one being in Southern China, near Guangzhou. We signed a five-year contract with them.

Ramada had brought in two or three managers for our approval prior to the opening of the hotel, and we had all decided on an Austrian with years of management experience in several hotel chains. He was married to a woman from Thailand, had a lot of experience working in Asia, and his manner was acceptable to the board. The joint venture had also financed a large group of young Chinese and sent them to the first hotel school that had opened in Beijing for training.

Ramada was very concerned that they would only be allowed ten expatriate personnel since the hotel would employ over two hundred people that they would be expected to manage. The Chinese were adamant about only allowing those ten personnel and would not bend. Several other hotel companies we had interviewed requested at least thirty to forty expatriate personnel, indicating they would not even consider managing the hotel with less staff. Ramada anxiously and reluctantly agreed to the contract. And since the general manager of the Asian area was Chinese, Mr. Wang was comfortable.

Unfortunately, the Chinese general manager of the Asian area was not so comfortable. Hong Kong Chinese were always concerned when they traveled into Mainland China. If the PRC wanted, they could detain a Hong Kong Chinese citizen, who would have little or no recourse.

One case I knew of involved a Hong Kong Chinese man who traveled back and forth from Hong Kong to Mainland China since his relatives lived in Guangzhou. He eventually found out that the Guangzhou authorities kept a long dossier on him. Because he was a Hong Kong Chinese, it was not very positive. During one trip, as he was leaving Guangzhou, he was stopped at the airport and detained for about two weeks. His airline ticket from CAAC airlines had his name spelled incorrectly, misplacing only one character. When they detained him, they accused him of using a forged ticket with the wrong name. He later found out that they had purposely misspelled his name so that they could detain him in the future.

Our hotel contained three sets of offices. Ramada used the management office; Mr. Wang's office occupied the second, which was set up to monitor the activities of the Ramada management; and the third set was designated as the Chinese office. That office was set up to deal with all the local Chinese since, in fact, they worked and were paid for by the Chinese government, and the hotel joint venture paid the government bureau for the services of the employees.

Ramada was hemmed in, and their activities were watched and questioned all the time. The Austrian manager could hardly purchase a fountain pen without Mr. Wang's permission. The manager constantly complained to us since he was apprehensive about dealing directly with Mr. Wang. There were always Ministry of Public Security agents around the hotel, and the Ramada offices were bugged with microphones.

The Ramada manager did the best job he could under the circumstances but got little help from his boss in Hong Kong, who was also fearful of Mr. Wang and almost never traveled into China. The exception was when he attended the grand opening of the hotel.

Ramada management overall did their best, considering the restrictions placed upon them by Mr. Wang. Yet, as time passed, Mr. Wang began talking about how ineffective the Ramada management was and that we could save money by having the Chinese manage the hotel themselves. This had, of course, been their plan from the start, but we resisted the idea as we wanted Ramada to continue their management.

We eventually discovered that the rooms on the top floor of the hotel were not being rented out. Whenever we asked about this, we would receive a different answer such as the air conditioning was not working on that floor or the heat was inoperative. We walked the floor and found all the rooms locked. Upon asking for the keys, we were informed that they had been lost but the employees would look for them. Finally, desperate to know what was going on, we knelt and peered through the room's keyholes. To our surprise, we found them filled with air conditioners, refrigerators, mattresses, television sets, and other items. The Chinese side had purchased the items with joint venture funds and was selling them and keeping all the profits for themselves.

When we questioned Mr. Yu, he denied any knowledge and said he would investigate. If he discovered our allegations to be true, he promised to talk to Mr. Wang and straighten out the problem. Of course, this was nonsense as Mr. Yu was in on it and receiving part of the profit from all these nefarious activities.

Ramada managed the hotel for about a year and a half while we constantly worked to convince Mr. Wang not to eliminate them. At each board of directors meeting, the issue would come up, and we'd listen to Mr. Wang recite a long list of complaints. We always countered those complaints, expressing the positive aspects of the Ramada management.

We constantly reminded him that part of the Standard Chartered loan construction agreement expressly stated that the joint venture must have a foreign, experienced hotel management company, and if we made the change that Mr. Wang kept requesting, it would be a violation of our loan agreement and the bank could theoretically call the loan.

Mr. Wang insisted that Standard Chartered would never call the loan. We countered that Mr. Wang was not giving Ramada a fair chance and that he could not just break their contract. Mr. Wang's position was that this was Beijing, China; that he was part of the most powerful agency in the country; and that he could do anything he wanted. It was said in a much more subtle way than that, of course, but we certainly got the gist.

Our manager worked in constant turmoil, fearing what new embarrassment or difficulty he might encounter with each passing day. He repeatedly spoke to the Ramada Hong Kong office about his problems and was told that he, in essence, needed to solve them himself.

Ramada management in Hong Kong invited Mr. Wang and our group to come to Hong Kong. We accepted and stayed at the Ramada Renaissance, a new, plush four-star hotel, where we were given suites and wined and dined for three days. Mr. Wang was honored and received several gifts from Ramada, all of which he graciously accepted. He even told the Ramada Hong Kong management that he was satisfied with the Ramada management at our hotel and was in the middle of developing a new hotel in Hainan Island, which he would give them the opportunity to manage also.

When we returned to Beijing, he reverted right back to his insistence that we eliminate our Ramada management. The Ramada manager of our hotel had invited his mother-in-law to visit his wife, and their two children in Beijing. She stayed with his family for about three weeks, then decided to go back to Thailand.

When you enter China, you are required to fill out an identity card, which gathers information regarding who you are, your passport and county, and so on. These cards are either collected at the airport or by the hotel you stay in. The cards are then sent to a division of the Ministry of Public Security and filed.

The manager's mother-in-law and his wife had both filled out these cards when they entered China and assumed they were filed with the Ministry of Public Security. When his mother-in-law was scheduled to leave the next morning, and she and his wife were having tea in one of the restaurants in the hotel, two Public Security people approached and politely asked if they had filled out identity cards when they arrived in China. It was a ludicrous question since the Chinese would not allow anyone in the country without these cards.

Both ladies said that they had indeed filled out the identity cards. They were then told by the security people that their cards must have been misplaced because they could not be located. They requested that the two women fill out new cards so they could have them on file. The women agreed and then filled them out at the table and gave them to the Public Security people—who looked at the cards and then told the two women they were under arrest and to come with them immediately.

The women were whisked away in a van and brought to the Ministry of Public Security, where they were put in a locked room. The room had couches, and the two women were served tea to make them as comfortable as possible under the circumstances. Meanwhile, the manager went looking for his wife and mother-in-law, only to be told by the manager of the restaurant that they had been taken away by Public Security officials.

The poor man frantically ran to Mr. Wang to ask what had happened. Mr. Wang told him that he did not know what was going on, but he would try and find out. Two or three hours went by. The manager was beside himself and called his boss in the Ramada office in Hong Kong and requested that he come to Beijing immediately to help him with the situation. His boss refused and said that under those circumstances, he would not enter the PRC because he was fearful they would not let him out of China.

When we heard what happened, we went to Mr. Yu and told him that this was simply intolerable. He needed to immediately find out what was going on. Mr. Yu then visited Mr. Wang and came back about half an hour later. He informed us that since the wife and the mother-in-law filled out new identity cards, it was essentially an emission on their part that they never filled out identity cards when they entered the country and therefore had violated Chinese law and were being held for prosecution.

Furious, we told Mr. Yu that was ludicrous and that anyone with any sense would see right through this obvious attempt to extort the Ramada manager. He told me there was nothing he could do about it as they had violated Chinese law.

The Ramada manager got in touch with an international law firm with offices in Beijing, and we all met for a conference. The Ramada manager's wife and mother-in-law had been held in the Ministry of Public Security overnight. They were treated very well and respectfully but were not allowed to leave. After a lengthy conversation with the lawyer and manager, the lawyer finally said the Chinese could do whatever they wanted, and there was very little anyone could do about it.

We then met with Mr. Wang and several other directors of the joint venture. We told them we knew that Mr. Wang was part of the Ministry of Public Security and that we were convinced he set this whole thing up to intimidate the manager. We told them that this was a foreign joint venture, the hotel was for foreign guests, and if this was the way foreigners would be treated, the hotel would be a failure.

Mr. Wang said he had once been part of the Ministry of Public Security but insisted that was no longer the case. He told us that the two women had obviously violated Chinese law, and there was nothing he could do about it. We told him we did not believe that, that we knew he was pulling those strings, and that he immediately needed to order those women to be released. He then asked us if we would be more amenable to discussing a change in management if he fixed the situation. We were furious and told him we would not make any decisions based on extortion.

The manager, meanwhile, told Mr. Wang that if he were to arrange the release of his family members, he would resign from his position as manager and leave the country. Mr. Wang said he would do what he could. Two hours later, the women were released. The next day, the manager, his wife, his mother-in-law, and the children left China.

Mr. Wang Comes to LA

Be careful who you call your friends.
~Al Capone

MR. YU'S PHANTOM BUSINESSES, as we would eventually confirm, included arms trading, petroleum deals, kickbacks from suppliers to the joint venture, and most likely other illegal activities. Mr. Yu became the subject of much interest on the part of U.S. authorities both in China and the United States. We continued our relationship with Special FBI Agent Messemer as his and the FBI's investigation into Mr. Yu and Ms. Zhang were still ongoing. However, it was Mr. Wang who really captured the attention of U.S. law enforcement.

Mr. Wang's long-standing relationship with the Chinese espionage community was of considerable concern to the FBI, who believed he was using World China Trade as a front for illegal activities in North America, including the purchase of nuclear secrets. The LA office was responsible for monitoring U.S. security interests in China and all throughout the Pacific Rim. Messemer, who spoke fluent Mandarin and possessed an in-depth understanding of Chinese espionage and criminal activities in the U.S., referred to Mr. Wang as a "Mafia boss" and was very interested in having him visit the U.S. He repeatedly asked if we could arrange for Mr. Wang to come to Los Angeles. Mr. Wang, no doubt aware of the FBI's interest, steadfastly refused every invitation.

One day, Mr. Yu called us from Beijing and mentioned that Mr. Wang and some of his associates were in Toronto, Canada. We suggested that since he had come that far, he ought to fly down to LA and visit us. It would provide an opportunity for us to discuss some of the current problems with our joint venture and finally award us the opportunity to reciprocate Mr. Wang's hospitality.

Mr. Yu said that Mr. Wang had his daughter with him (actually, she was his mistress) and he might come if they could visit Las Vegas too. We told him all things were possible, and Mr. Wang should definitely come. Mr. Yu made the arrangements and called back to say Mr. Wang would arrive in two weeks and that he was coming as well. Sheldon called Agent Messemer with the news. He was pleased and told Sheldon that Mr. Wang would be thoroughly watched every minute he was in the United States.

Mr. Wang arrived in Los Angeles with great fanfare. The first night, we all met for dinner at a local Chinese restaurant in the Los Angeles Chinatown area. Agent Messemer told us that FBI agents would be following us closely. He gave Sheldon a cell phone with a private number and asked him to convey our whereabouts each time we changed our location. He also told us that part of this very intense surveillance was to ensure our safety, which he thought could be in question if Mr. Wang found out about our cooperation with the FBI.

The FBI agents took the hotel rooms above and below Mr. Wang's room and hid microphones and video cameras in his room. The next morning, Mr. Wang was expected at our house for some tea and a meeting. Our son, Robert, who was living with us at that time, remarked that there was a green van parked across the street from our house with very dark tinted windows and several antennas. Sheldon immediately called Agent Messemer and told him about the van. He denied any knowledge of it, but Sheldon insisted that whatever was going on, it was much too obvious. Mr. Wang could be suspicious.

A short time later, Mr. Wang called. Something had come up,

he told us, and he couldn't make it over to our house. Instead, he offered dinner that night at a Chinese restaurant in Monterey Park, a community southeast of Los Angeles that had become almost entirely Chinese. So, we all dined that night at a small, out-of-the-way restaurant called Dumpling Master whose owners were from Beijing.

Sheldon called Agent Messemer and told him where we were having dinner, and wouldn't you know—the green van disappeared, at least for the moment. We always wondered whether Mr. Wang came to our house, saw the van, and drove off because it was so obvious. Before Mr. Wang became chairman of our joint venture, he had worked as a high-level policeman with the Ministry of Public Security.

The restaurant was not crowded, and Mr. Yu, after some negotiation with the waiter, ordered for us. Dumpling Master is well known for the large variety of dumplings they have to offer and a very special Chinese-baked garlic. As we ate the delicious meal, Sheldon and I noticed two Chinese at a table not far from us and later discovered that they were FBI.

Mr. Wang asked us to go to Las Vegas with him and his daughter, three other people in his party, and Mr. Yu and Ms. Zhang. We, of course, agreed and rented a large van for our guests so the ride would be comfortable. Agent Messemer told us that FBI surveillance vehicles would be on the road with us, driving both in front and back of the van—and that just in case we lost their surveillance, they had placed a tracking device on our vehicle.

He kept telling us that we should be concerned for our safety and to be very careful. All Sheldon would have to do was press one button on the cell phone the agent had given him, and it would automatically connect to the surveillance team. Agent Messemer was convinced that there would be a drop contact for Mr. Wang in Las Vegas, and highly sensitive documents pertaining to military intelligence would be passed on. When we loaded the luggage in the van, Mr. Wang kept his briefcase separate and carried it in his lap. Maybe Messemer was right. We left for Vegas in the late morning and headed east on Interstate 15, into the Mojave Desert.

It was quite a ride to Las Vegas, during which a lot of Chinese was spoken. When we reached Barstow, Mr. Yu mentioned that he wanted to stop at a friend's Chinese restaurant. We drove into the city, arriving at a small Chinese restaurant in a shopping center. Mr. Wang and Mr. Yu got out of the van and told the rest of us to wait since they would only be a few minutes. Mr. Wang took his briefcase. They returned in about fifteen minutes, at which point Mr. Wang put his briefcase in the back of the van with the luggage. They said nothing about the visit, and we continued our trip to Las Vegas.

We arrived at about 6:00 p.m. and went directly to the Desert Inn, where we had reservations. We all went to the buffet—an experience our Chinese guests loved. They piled everything they could onto their plates and then shared everything. Sheldon excused himself. While he was in the restaurant bathroom washing his hands, a man moved up next to him and told him not to be concerned—the bureau was on the case. He asked Sheldon to take Mr. Wang to a local casino in downtown Las Vegas.

When Sheldon returned to the table, he glanced at me and then suggested to Mr. Wang that we try the casinos in downtown Las Vegas, where the betting limits would be much lower and we would have more fun. Wang agreed and we all piled into the van.

We arrived at the casino, which was much smaller than the casinos on the strip and very crowded. We stayed and gambled for about an hour. As we were leaving, a very boisterous group of people, who looked like they had a bit too much to drink, pushed their way through us and jostled us, especially Mr. Wang, as they made their exit. He grew upset at being pushed and commented on the bad manners of some Americans.

When we got back to our hotel, Sheldon and I went directly to our room. It had been a long day. As we were preparing for bed, the phone rang. Ms. Zhang, in a very agitated voice, informed us over the line that Mr. Wang had lost his purse at the casino. He was frantic since all his travel documents were inside. She asked Sheldon to drive her back to the casino to see if someone had found it. He explained that it would be an exercise in futility. This was Las Vegas; pickpockets were common. But Ms. Zhang persisted, and Sheldon agreed to drive her back. When they asked the manager if anyone had turned in a lost purse, he, of course, said "No."

When they returned to the hotel, Sheldon asked Mr. Wang's "daughter" what was in the purse. She said it contained more than $20,000 in cash. Sheldon told Ms. Zhang that Mr. Wang should not carry such large sums of money. She later told us that the figure she'd given us had just been a misunderstanding. There had been only $2,000.

Wearily, Sheldon returned to our room. A moment later, the phone rang again. It was Agent Messemer. He said it was a shame Mr. Wang had lost his purse—which, of course, no one had told him about. Sheldon said that it reputedly contained $20,000. Messemer replied that it had contained substantially more. When Sheldon asked the agent if he intended to return it, his reply was that he knew nothing about a purse or who might have taken it.

The ride back to Los Angeles was peaceful and without much conversation, other than the private conversation that Mr. Wang and Mr. Yu carried out in the back of the van.

Mr. Wang stayed in Los Angeles for a few more days, and we held a meeting at our offices in West Los Angeles. We, of course, had allowed Agent Messemer to place microphones and a video camera in the office. So, everything was recorded. We wanted to have a conversation with Mr. Wang regarding the money transfer documents we had uncovered that showed transfers from the joint venture account to a bank in Toronto. Agent Messemer had asked us not to mention it to Mr. Wang, but we decided otherwise.

We showed Mr. Wang copies of the transfers and asked for an explanation. He demanded to know where we had gotten copies of those documents, to which we answered that we could not disclose that to him. He turned and gave Mr. Yu a very dark look. We again asked him for an explanation. Wang then told us a long story.

It seemed that another entity that he was involved with had several million dollars of excess cash and wanted to use it to finance the purchase of some businesses and condominiums in Canada. The relevant Chinese law at that time prohibited the transfer of those funds outside of China. Since he was a partner in the joint venture, he asked Mr. Yu if he could deposit the funds in our joint venture account and then wire those funds to Canada. He said that Mr. Yu told him that since he was a joint venture partner and that it was not costing the joint venture anything, it was okay. We then asked Mr. Yu why he never told us, and Mr. Yu said that it was such a small matter, he didn't feel it was necessary to bring it to our attention.

We then told Mr. Wang that what he had done, with Mr. Yu's approval, was a crime in the United States. It was called money laundering. We also told him that if it was against Chinese law to send those funds outside of China, he had committed an illegal act in China as well, and he had put our joint venture in jeopardy. He replied that we should not be at all concerned with any violation of Chinese law. He would take care of any problems that might emerge.

We then asked him for proof that the funds were not part of the joint venture account and were indeed separate funds. He gave us some wrinkled-up pieces of paper with Chinese writing on it and said that was the proof. It was ludicrous. Mr. Wang, with the help of Mr. Yu, obviously had stolen funds belonging to the joint venture.

Then Sheldon paused for effect, and with great seriousness, told Mr. Wang that the FBI was aware of the transfers and had already contacted us to discuss them. Mr. Wang sat up straight in his chair and asked for the name of the agent. Sheldon told Mr. Wang, who was now paying rapt attention to his every word, that Special Agent Robert Messemer had contacted us. Sheldon added that we were very uncomfortable with the situation and didn't want to make excuses for Mr. Wang or have the joint venture investigated because of his actions.

Sheldon reminded him that the FBI was a very serious intelligence organization, something Wang already well knew. Then he leaned across the table and quietly asked Mr. Wang what exactly his relationship was with the Ministry of State Security. Wang made no reply but gathered up his things, said the meeting was over, and left. Mr. Yu and Ms. Zhang, who had been translating, followed him out. Two days later, Mr. Wang and Mr. Yu were back in Beijing.

Agent Messemer called Sheldon after the meeting and said he was upset that he had disclosed to Mr. Wang our knowledge of the money transfers. Sheldon told Agent Messemer that he, I, and our investors had a lot at stake, and we wanted Mr. Wang to realize that we had knowledge of his illegal actions and that we were cooperating with our government, not his.

~28~

A Visit to the Ministry of Security

Only two U.S. citizens had ever been in the building, and both were taken to the ministry unwillingly and under guard. They're thugs.
~Denny Barnes, commercial attaché, U.S. consul, Beijing

WE RETURNED TO BEIJING a month later, determined to do something about Mr. Wang. He was taking advantage of the joint venture in ways that were becoming increasingly shameless. The man now wore a gold Rolex with a diamond bezel and enjoyed being chauffeured around town in a late-model, long-body BMW. In addition to the illegal funds transfer from the joint venture account, Wang had turned the top floor of the hotel into a personal warehouse, selling the items we had previously noticed when we had peeped through the rooms' keyholes on the black market. He was making a fortune at our expense.

We decided to drop by the U.S. Embassy and visit Denny Barnes. He listened to our story, then told us that we were not the only American joint venture that was full of corruption. Ours was very blatant, however, and the U.S. government was interested in making it an issue with the Chinese government. Most foreign corporations in China were large, multinational companies that knew they were being exploited but didn't care enough to do anything about it. They were betting on the future and were willing to put up with the present.

Mr. Yu had been cheating us too. We weren't sure what the relationship between him and Mr. Wang was, but it seemed they were both collaborators and competitors at the same time. When we confronted Mr. Yu, he denied having any knowledge of the corruption but agreed that Mr. Wang was probably doing some things that were not legal. Mr. Yu told us that the Minister of Public Security was a friend of his and would certainly want to know of any misdeeds by Chinese members of the joint venture team. If Mr. Wang had committed crimes, he would be punished, Yu added. We didn't know whether to believe him, but he was still the president of our company and conducted all our business in the PRC. Unfortunately, we had no one else to rely on.

We decided to meet with one of our other joint venture partners and flew to Chongqing. The city was a 25-percent partner, and we were to meet with the mayor, Mr. Li, and all the other officials involved in the joint venture. Chongqing, the largest city in China, housed over eighteen million people at that time. The huge city, which sits on the banks of the Yangtze River in central China, has earned the nickname, "the furnace of China" because of its searing-hot temperatures. No one seemed able to understand why Chongqing would agree to be a partner in a hotel project located 1,500 miles away in Beijing.

We had never been to Chongqing and thought the trip would be interesting. We also wanted to inform our partners as to Mr. Wang's usage of our joint venture funds. We were fortunate—instead of the old Russian jets CAAC flew around China, we were put on a new 737, recently introduced by the Chinese into their flight system. After we were seated, the Chinese stewardess (as they were called in those days) came out and told everyone to stay in their seats through take-off and landing. The aircraft took off, and immediately, everybody got up and started looking out the windows. Sheldon and I were astounded at how everyone just ignored the stewardess, though she didn't seem to mind. A few live chickens also happened to occupy the seat across the aisle from us.

We arrived and were met by members of the mayor's office. From there, we were taken in a Red Flag limousine to the Holiday Inn on the banks of the river—a very spectacular experience. We checked into the hotel, along with Mr. Yu and Jennie, who had accompanied us. They had taken separate rooms, though only one of them was ever used.

Mr. Yu suggested we go to a special restaurant he had visited before and thought we might enjoy. The mayor had provided us with a car and driver, so off we went. Somewhere deep in the heart of the city, we were dropped off, and we walked up the stairs of a very crowded place and headed into the restaurant. Each table had a large steel pot heated by live coals. The pot was divided into two compartments, each of which was filled with bubbling liquid. One side was a brownish-red; the other was almost a bright red. All the tables were filled with people who were sweating profusely.

It was hot outside, and, of course, the restaurant had no air-conditioning. We sat down and the waiter brought us platefuls of raw food, meat, fish, poultry, vegetables, and some other food items that were unrecognizable. We were instructed to take whatever pieces of food we wanted and then dip them into either side of the pot. After they cooked, which happened very quickly, we would eat that food. Chongqing is known for the hottest, spiciest food anywhere. The first piece of food Sheldon tasted almost took his head off, it was so spicy. He coughed and sputtered and could hardly catch his breath for a while. That was when I put my food in the brownish-red side, which proved much more mildly spiced than the bright-red side. Sheldon did the same with his next pieces of food. Mr. Yu put his food in the bright-red side and ate with relish. He must have had a cast-iron stomach.

We then headed to a meeting at the mayor's office and were ushered into a very large room, with couches and chairs facing the front doors and maybe thirty chairs on each side. As per Chinese custom with foreigners, we sat on one side of the mayor, and Mr. Yu took a chair on the other side. Tea was served, and then Sheldon made a speech about how we admired China, how appreciative we were to the Chinese for giving us the opportunity to join in the hotel project, and how thankful we were that CITIC had so graciously put up the guarantee for the construction financing. That, of course, brought up the issue of the guarantee fee.

The mayor told us he was very upset that they had not received their fee. He told us that this guarantee was the first one they'd made for a hotel project and asked why their fee had been left unpaid for five years. That led to a discussion regarding Mr. Wang and the Ministry of Public Security in Beijing. Sheldon told the mayor that we suspected some very serious misdoings and that since he was a partner, he should be aware of what was going on.

Just about that time, one of the mayor's assistants started to shake his head, and, seconds later, appeared to be having an epileptic fit. He fell to the floor with froth coming from his mouth and thrashed around for a few seconds. Everyone stopped talking and just looked at him. Then two other men from the group jumped up. One took his head and inserted something in his mouth; the other started to massage him at pressure points located at various places along his body.

Meanwhile, everyone just stared silently. After a few minutes, the shaking stopped. They wiped his head, and then he sat back up, looked at everyone, and smiled. The mayor continued talking right where he had left off, without missing a beat. The meeting continued. No one said a word or offered us an explanation about what had just transpired, but we realized we had once again witnessed the miracle of Chinese medicine.

The meeting finally ended with the mayor's assurances that he would support us in any way that he could. He also suggested that Sheldon personally meet with the Minister of Public Security in Beijing to detail the corruption within the hotel project and request an immediate investigation by Chinese authorities. We realized we were being used, though once again we didn't know why. Now, Sheldon was even more determined to meet with the minister.

When we returned from Chongqing, Sheldon dropped by for another visit with Denny Barnes to bring him up to speed on everything. Denny didn't think much of the idea of Sheldon meeting with the Minister of Public security. He explained that U.S. citizens were not allowed in the ministry building and were prohibited by Chinese law from having any direct contact with public security personnel.

Barnes said that to his knowledge, only two U.S. citizens had ever been in the building, and both were taken to the ministry unwillingly and under guard. "They're thugs," he said. According to Sheldon, those aforementioned Ministry of State Security thugs were our partners in the joint venture, and he fully intended to have his meeting. He wished Sheldon luck and assured him that if he were detained, the embassy would lodge a formal complaint. Barnes no doubt meant that to be comforting.

When Sheldon returned to our office, he asked Mr. Yu to set up the appointment. Mr. Yu said it would be very difficult to do as only a few foreigners were ever in that ministry, and since Sheldon was an American citizen, it was a very sticky issue. This discussion went on for several days. It seemed we were getting no closer to the meeting. Everyone in our office was very nervous. One day, Jennie received a phone call. All of a sudden, she started to shake and cry. Finally, she put the phone down. Mr. Yu came out, and they had a long conversation in Chinese. It was obvious, she was very upset.

We had to repeatedly ask Mr. Yu what was going on before he finally told us. Jennie had received a threatening call from someone in the Ministry of Public Security. They warned her that she was too close to the Americans, and she should remember that she was a Chinese citizen living in China, she had a family, and if she was not careful, she and her family could disappear or worse.

Sheldon finally told Mr. Yu that if he did not arrange this meeting, we would call a press conference and tell the world what was going on. One hour later, a meeting was set up for the next day. Mr. Yu always played both sides. This time, he told Sheldon he should tell the minister what was on his mind. When Sheldon asked if he would accompany him to the meeting, Yu had an excuse ready and told us that Mr. Ming, a translator and one of our office staff, would go instead.

Mr. Ming, clearly not happy about joining us in this meeting, told Sheldon to be very careful about what he chose to say—that he did not grasp the power that the Ministry of Public Security wielded and what they were capable of. Sheldon told him not to worry, but Mr. Ming was thoroughly frightened. To be honest, Sheldon and I were both anxious the next day when he kissed me goodbye and he and Mr. Ming headed off for the meeting.

The Ministry of Public Security, located next to Tiananmen Square in a location that communicated to everyone its importance, is headquartered in a large, drab, cement-colored building, more reminiscent of post-revolutionary Russia than anything Chinese. If architecture is language, this building bespoke machine-like, anonymous power—all efficiency and no ornamentation. It was the only building with armed guards in front, along with large iron gates topped with barbed wire. As the two men drove in, Sheldon was sure he saw Mr. Wang's BMW ahead of them.

They were greeted at the door of the car and escorted into the building by armed guards. Sheldon admitted later to developing a very queasy feeling in the pit of his stomach, though he tried to act as calmly as possible. They were taken to a meeting room, where four people awaited them, each one dressed differently. The minister, dressed in a blue Mao outfit, was a small man of about sixty-five years. Another larger, heavyset man occupied the room, dressed in a gray Mao outfit and seeming about the same age as the minister. The other men were younger. One wore thick glasses and an ill-fitting Western-style suit, and the other looked like a thug. He had on casual clothes and was obviously armed.

Sheldon was introduced to the minister and his secretary/interpreter, the young man with the glasses. The thug just glanced at Sheldon and nodded, and the older man in the gray outfit didn't say a word. Sheldon asked Mr. Ming the identity of the older man in the gray suit. Mr. Ming looked at him and whispered that he should not ask that question. Things seemed off to a bad start. They hadn't even begun to discuss Mr. Wang and were already arguing.

When Sheldon persisted, Ming started to shake and said he was afraid. Sheldon insisted. So, finally, in a very shaky voice, Ming asked the question. The answer was, "It is not necessary for Mr. Krechman to know the identity of this gentleman." Sheldon requested that Ming tell them that if they did not identify this man, he would leave since he had no desire to remain in a meeting with someone he had not been introduced to.

Mr. Ming, clearly panicking at that point, pleaded with Sheldon to forget the matter and continue with the meeting. Sheldon simply insisted again. Choking out the words, Mr. Ming complied. From the back, the thug glared and then took a step forward. After a few seconds of resounding silence and a nod from the minister, the translator introduced the other man.

The mystery man turned out to be in charge of all the Ministry of Public Security's business affairs—and was Mr. Wang's father-in-law.

With the tension somewhat relieved, the men sat down and drank some tea. Sheldon sat next to the minister, and the thug sat across from him. No business cards were exchanged, which was very unusual for a Chinese meeting.

Sheldon told the minister of his and my suspicions, and the minister took notes on the back of an envelope Sheldon had given to him with an enclosed copy of a very strong letter we planned to send to the Chinese central government. Sheldon explained that we had put all our assets on the line for this project. We had taken investment dollars from many of our friends and neighbors, and we had worked diligently to make this project a success, with little or no financial rewards. We had been told that the Chinese were honorable people, and that before we would allow ourselves and our friends to have such a financial setback, we would expose this story to the world.

Sheldon told him that, if necessary, we would go before the U.S. Congress and report this story, which could hurt, if not eliminate, China's most favored nation's status, which was just coming up for renewal. (Denny Barnes had told him to say that.) Sheldon added that we were Jews, and if they pushed our backs to the wall, we would never stop talking about this miscarriage of justice.

Mr. Ming nearly fainted from fear after Sheldon had him deliver this verbal threat to the Minister of Public Security in the Ministry of Public Security. Sheldon spoke every word in a very respectful way, but he wanted to make it absolutely clear that we would not stop. The minister looked at him, and in a very gracious way, said there was nothing we could do to harm Sino-U.S. relations. He also said that he would look into the allegations and pursue an investigation. He assured Sheldon that if Mr. Wang or any parties were guilty, they would be ferreted out and prosecuted. Sheldon thanked him.

As they drove out of the building, Mr. Ming started to cry and told Sheldon that he had made a serious mistake and feared that his life was now in danger. The next day, he disappeared. We later learned that he escaped from China. We also found out that the minister Sheldon had met with had a condominium in Vancouver, purchased with funds from our joint venture project.

~29~

Threatened in Beijing

Get out of China or great harm will come to you.
~Ministry of Security Thug

AFTER THE HOTEL PROJECT was completed, our Chinese partners mounted a campaign to eliminate World China Trade from the joint venture. It was a process at times subtle and at others crass. We were being cheated by Mr. Yu and Mr. Wang—and perhaps others; of that, we were sure. But it was difficult to pin anything down, and since the Chinese authorities were fully complicit, we had no one to appeal to.

After holding several meetings at the U.S. Embassy with Denny Barnes to complain about the situation, we were told that seemingly every American business in China was being similarly cheated, but no one else seemed particularly interested in putting a stop to it. The embassy wanted to cooperate with us in bringing the situation to light, but the political pressures from Washington put a finite limit on their zeal.

The state department was engaged in a tense dialog with the Chinese following the Tiananmen Square democracy protests, and powerful American corporate interests considered corruption a price of doing business in China. There was little political support for a crackdown. The only people who were worried were those within the embassy who monitored Chinese organized crime and espionage. They knew that Americans were being used as fronts for Chinese officials' illicit businesses and for the benefit of the Chinese espionage agencies.

The Chinese security agencies' actions mirrored that of organized crime in the United States. Double-dealing, embezzlement, and intimidation were the norm. Our joint venture partners kept four sets of books, each different, and most of the written records were in Chinese. It was impossible to figure out where the money went and to whom. The Chinese were masters of ambiguity. Direct questions were answered with exquisitely vague replies. By the time our project was completed, three different banks held notes on it, none of which were ever paid on time or given a straight answer to the simple question: Where is the money being spent?

Standard Chartered, our original lender, threatened to throw us into default several times but never did. The bank knew that it had little recourse within the Chinese judicial system, particularly against partners who were themselves instruments of the Chinese government. Mr. Wang always insisted we needed more money, and the banks, especially the Bank of China, would grumble for a while and then come up with the funds.

We suspected that officials at the Bank of China were being paid off. If so, it was a slick deal. They would lend the money, and then our partners would kickback a portion of the proceeds and siphon off the rest for themselves. We soon found ourselves in a situation where the Chinese side stole every new loan dollar that came in, by whatever means, while expecting World China Trade to pay the debt. Our joint venture agreement, loan agreements, corporate bylaws, and subsidiary contracts of every kind were honored only when convenient or necessary to save face.

Now, when we traveled to Beijing, a complete lack of trust existed between Mr. Yu and us. We rarely had dinner at his house any longer, and he kept his office door locked when away. Jennie was standoffish and distant. We were treated like dissident strangers instead of as part of the company. Of course, we took as much control as we could, and we questioned many things—the answers to which were mostly evasive.

Mr. Wang was more antagonistic than ever since Sheldon's meeting with the Minister of Public Security and consequently more dangerous. Denny Barnes made it clear to us that Mr. Wang was no better than a common criminal, and we'd better watch our backs.

On this particular trip, as the situation worsened, one of our American investors, Joe Massie, a director of our corporation, came to Beijing to attend a board meeting. We were expecting a showdown and felt we might need outside assistance. Sheldon asked Denny Barnes, who spoke Chinese, to attend the board meeting. He had never attended before, and with relations currently strained between China and the United States, he had to get permission from Ambassador Lily. Denny got the okay, and we decided that we would not tell the Chinese or Mr. Yu prior to the meeting. We wanted to make the point to Mr. Wang and his cohorts that our government was standing up for us.

Denny met us at the hotel entrance just prior to the meeting, and we all walked in together. Mr. Wang looked at us, and Sheldon introduced Denny. He then explained that we had invited him to the board meeting because we were concerned that the American side of the joint venture was being swindled, and we wanted a representative from the U.S. government present so that our government would have firsthand knowledge of the actions of Mr. Wang and the Chinese.

Mr. Wang grew very reserved and asked for Denny's credentials. Denny produced them and surprised Mr. Wang by having a conversation with him in Mandarin. Mr. Wang finally said that it was his understanding that the Chinese side should have been given notice that we were bringing a representative from the United States government to the board meeting, and that if they had been notified, they could have also brought a representative from the Chinese government.

After about ten minutes of arguing and discussion, we all agreed that Denny Barnes would have to leave the meeting, but our point was made. Denny asked us for an immediate briefing after the meeting's conclusion.

Mr. Yu told us we had made an egregious mistake, and that the Chinese side now knew that the American side did not trust them. That would have been laughable had he not said it in all seriousness. We explained to Mr. Yu, that was indeed the case, and we did not trust the Chinese side. We also voiced our concerns about Mr. Yu's business loyalty. While we realized he was a Chinese citizen, he was also the president of our company and had a fiduciary responsibility to all the shareholders.

The board meeting ended after three very frustrating and contentious days and with several issues unresolved, including the Ramada management situation. It left everyone with a bitter aftertaste.

That night, Sheldon, Joe, and I had dinner with Denny Barnes and discussed what had occurred at the meeting. Denny told us what we had already heard from other sources: that the Chinese were taking advantage of all the American companies that were trying to do business in China, and ours was one of the most blatant. He said he also suspected that the Chinese had other purposes for this joint venture because of the way it was being conducted and because our partners included Mr. Wang and the Ministry of Public Security.

Denny was pushing us to hold a press conference. Exposure to the foreign media was one of the few things feared by the Chinese. It was possible, he thought, that the government could be forced into arresting Mr. Wang to save face. Ostensibly, the punishment in China for graft was execution by firing squad. Public executions were held right down the street from our hotel in the Workers Stadium. It was a public spectacle in which the family of the executed person was charged for the bullet. Execution in this manner represented the ultimate loss of face.

If we exposed Mr. Wang and forced a trial, the press conference would be interpreted as nothing less than a death threat. It would be a high-stakes gamble. We decided to decline. On the one hand, we didn't want Mr. Wang to die for his sins, and on the other, we weren't convinced he'd ever be charged. If every Chinese official involved in graft were arrested, the government would fall overnight. Corruption was endemic in China.

As we were leaving the restaurant, which was in our hotel, two men (obviously security people), bumped into Denny and knocked him forcefully against the wall. They grunted out what was supposed to be an apology, but you could feel the hostility emanating from them. Denny left and went back to the U.S. consul, and we retired to our rooms, which were next to each other on the fifteenth floor of the hotel.

We were sound asleep when the phone rang at 11:30 p.m. Sheldon answered, and a man asked in broken English if he was Mr. Krechman. When Sheldon asked what he wanted, he started threatening him in a very antagonistic, angry voice, saying the Chinese wanted Ramada out and that we were no longer welcome in China. He added that we'd better leave the country immediately or we would be in physical danger, and they would get us. Sheldon asked him who he was and offered to meet him immediately to discuss just what he wanted. He refused and said we'd better heed his warnings and hung up.

About five minutes later, Joe started pounding on our door. When Sheldon opened it, Joe told us he had just received a threatening phone call too. There was nothing we could do but try to go back to sleep. We put a chair under the doorknob of our room but realized it was just an exercise in futility. We were in Beijing, China, in a hotel owned by the Ministry of Public Security, which, in reality, could do anything it wanted. Still, it gave us a psychological measure of comfort, and we finally went to sleep.

We were awoken again at about 3:00 a.m. by more door-pounding. Sheldon, in a bathrobe and slippers, opened it to find two public security men standing there, demanding that he turn over his passport. He refused and told them to go away. They said they were sent to get his passport and would not leave until they had it. Sheldon told them that if they continued to pressure him for the passport, he would immediately go to the phone, call the American Embassy, and report that he was being harassed by the Ministry of Public Security.

They told him to try the phone, which he did—it was dead. Sheldon told them the only way they would get his passport would be to physically take it from him, and he was willing to put up a fight. He then slammed the door shut and slid over the skimpy little chain that prevented anyone from breaking in. We were shaken but tried to go back to sleep. They pounded on the door for another half an hour and then finally stopped.

Obviously, we got little if any sleep that night. In the morning, we met Joe and went down to the Western restaurant in our hotel for breakfast as per our normal routine. They served a buffet every morning that included eggs, bacon, fruit, ham, Chinese bread, and cheeses. Joe ordered his usual coffee to start, and Sheldon and I had some tea.

When Joe took his first sip of coffee, he spat it out all over the floor and started to cough heavily. I immediately started pounding him on the back. When he finally stopped gasping, he said the coffee was laced with some evil-smelling liquid that was almost unbearable. We looked around and saw what looked like some of the kitchen help staring at us with malevolent, dark looks.

We decided that we should immediately go to the U.S. consul and ask for advice. We got into one of the hotel cars with a driver to take us there. When we arrived, we met with Denny Barnes and the chief intelligence officer of the consul. They took us into the courtyard because they suspected that all the rooms in the embassy were bugged. There, we related the events of the prior night.

The chief intelligence officer looked at us in a very serious manner and said that we were dealing with thugs. He said that it was known for these people, if they wanted to get to someone, to take away that person's children if necessary. He also told us that based on our circumstances, and the people we were dealing with, we should take the threats very seriously and immediately take refuge in the U.S. Embassy. He said that the United States government could not protect us unless we were in the embassy and that if we left, we would, in his opinion, be taking our lives in our hands.

Joe, Sheldon, and I talked about what our next course of action should be. Joe thought we should take the advice of the intelligence agent and take refuge in the embassy. Sheldon and I rejected that thought. Maybe we were naïve, but we did not want to be prisoners in the U.S. Embassy. At that point, we had spent over 1,200 days in China dealing with the Chinese and their children and had developed the hotel complex, which was obviously successful. We had personal guarantees and all our investors' capital at stake. We talked the situation over for a few minutes and made the decision that Joe, who still had his passport, would leave the country right away while we would stay and try to hold things together.

Joe returned to the hotel with us to get his things but cautioned Sheldon to be very polite with Mr. Wang. Sheldon told us not to worry, but I knew Sheldon was really angry and that was not the course of action my husband would take.

Mr. Wang had been made aware of our presence the moment we entered the hotel. We found Mr. Wang in his office, and Sheldon requested an immediate meeting. He told us that he and other directors would meet with us in the boardroom in one hour. When we entered the boardroom, Mr. Wang was there with the two security people who had pounded on our hotel room door and three of the other board directors.

He asked Sheldon the purpose of the meeting. That's when Sheldon, from the perspective of the Chinese, went berserk. He started pounding his fists on the table and shouting at the top of his lungs that Mr. Wang and the Ministry of Public Security were no better, and in fact, far worse than Hitler's Nazi Gestapo. His face was blood-red, the veins were popping out on his forehead, and he was shaking with anger.

He screamed out, "How dare you threaten us? Carole and I have put our hearts and souls into dealing with China and the development of the hotel project. If this is the payback that we are receiving, being threatened and intimidated, then the Ministry of Public Security is filled with nothing but thugs and hoodlums who have no respect for their joint venture partners, human dignity, or humanity and are obviously the dregs of society." He added that Mr. Wang was the worst of the lot since he was in charge.

Mr. Wang jumped back from his chair, and the two Public Security men that had pounded on the door of our room jumped up and started toward Sheldon with menacing looks. Mr. Wang waved them back to their chairs, and in a very calm voice (through an interpreter) asked Sheldon why he was so upset and if he could explain to him just what a Nazi and the Gestapo were.

Sheldon calmed down and did his best to explain what Nazi Germany was like. Sheldon told him of the telephone threat the night before and about the two Chinese men who had pounded on our door and demanded his passport. Mr. Wang insisted it was all a mistake, that it would never happen again, and that he would personally guarantee our safety.

Then he invited us to dinner that night in a small room off the kitchen of the hotel, where the food was always the best. As usual, we didn't talk business at meals. We shared food, talked amiably, and toasted each other. Our problems were far from over, but something had happened. The threats suddenly stopped. Mr. Wang, an agent of the Ministry of State Security, had never had anyone stand up to him before. We had not solved our business problems, but we had gained respect. It was a quintessential moment. In China, they would steal you blind, threaten you, and then take you to dinner.

~30~

The Final Negotiation

*Armand Hammer, the financial entrepreneur whose extraordinary
career spanned seven decades and half a dozen different businesses
and whose avocation as a collector of art added to an already controversial life, died Monday at his home in Westwood.*
~LA Times, *December 11, 1990*

AFTER A BRIEF ILLNESS, Dr. Hammer died on December 10, 1990, at
the age of ninety-two. He had still been at the helm of Oxy, although in February of that year, he finally named Ray Irani, Oxy's
president and COO, as his successor.

Sadly, the doctor passed away the day before he had planned to
celebrate his own belated bar mitzvah. Hammer, raised in a non-ob-
servant family, had brought in two rabbis in Beverly Hills to perform
the ceremony. The bar mitzvah would have included a fundraising
dinner at the Beverly Hilton Hotel to benefit two organizations: the
Pacific Jewish Center and the Jerusalem College of Technology. The
ceremony was changed to a private memorial service, which was attended by two hundred people, including celebrities and titans of industry who celebrated his accomplishments in business, art, diplo-
macy, and philanthropy.

We were deeply saddened by the loss of our mentor who had
guided us into China and thus, the adventure of a lifetime, and we
were soon to discover the nearly devastating impact his death would

Within days of his passing, everything dramatically changed for World China Trade. The two Oxy employees on our board of directors resigned immediately, and Oxy revoked their standing offer to purchase World China Trade's shares that same day.

Union Bank went into attack mode and employed outside legal counsel. Occidental Petroleum also employed outside legal counsel, as did Standard Chartered. In response, World China Trade investors employed their own legal counsel. And there we were, in the middle of it all, with lawsuits flying. A constant legal barrage on a daily basis from all sides ensued.

With so many large corporations and banks involved, no one knew quite what to do. The judge who was trying the case in superior court, a well-known woman and the wife of the district attorney of the City of Los Angeles, remarked that this was the most complicated case she had ever been involved with as a judge.

The Chinese, knowing all too well what was transpiring, realized our weakened position and tried to negotiate with us to purchase our shares. At this point, Mr. Yu had been in the United States for several months. He was having his own troubles with the FBI and his green card status and did not want to leave the country out of the fear that he would never be able to obtain a visa to return.

Negotiations raged on via phone and fax between Mr. Wang in Beijing, and Sheldon, Joe, and me in Los Angeles. The pressure mounted. We had refused any offer that would not pay back the banks and our investors. The bank, of course, was only concerned about the repayment of their loan.

Finally, we agreed on a value with Mr. Wang and negotiated an agreement, which was faxed over and signed by Sheldon and me and the Chinese side. Mr. Wang requested that the three of us (Sheldon, Joe, and me) travel to Beijing to sign the final papers. We said yes, but only after Mr. Wang agreed that the joint venture would pay for all our expenses, including business-class air travel.

The night we arrived, we were given rooms on either side of the elevators on the fourteenth floor, no doubt to remind us of who was in control. We anticipated that the final meeting would be held the day after we arrived, but of course, we wound up waiting for three days without any notice.

We met with Mr. Tian, the Chinese lawyer representing Mr. Wang and his company BLIPU. He told us that he had reviewed the agreement and was looking forward to consummating the transaction. We asked Mr. Tian when the meeting would be, and he told us, "Shortly."

So, we wandered through the hotel, feeling proud of what we had created. We tried each of the seven restaurants in the building, including a Korean barbecue. Our hotel also offered the first fast food-type diner, located on the street at the end of the office building.

We wanted to go back to our company offices, which Mr. Yu had moved to the hotel, but found ourselves barred from even entering them. Jennie and Mr. Yu's wife locked themselves in and refused to open the door for us. We found Mr. Wang and asked him to open the door with a passkey, which he said he didn't have. We then asked him to forcibly open the door. He refused. We argued for a while and then gave up the idea.

On the third day, as we were leaving the Western restaurant after lunch, a young man approached and asked us to follow him, as the meeting was about to begin. We had received no advance notice whatsoever. We accompanied him to our boardroom, and as we entered, we realized that sitting at the table were several Chinese individuals we had never met before. Mr. Wang was not even seated at the table but in a chair at the side of the room. His demeanor was very different than we'd ever seen it. Instead of blustering and taking charge, he was quiet and very respectful.

After being positioned in the middle of the table, through an interpreter, we were introduced to Mr. Jin Li Zhou, seated directly across from us. He was the head of the Ministry of State Security, a much more powerful and influential body than even the Ministry of Public Security. The company that was purchasing our shares was a Hong Kong front company owned and controlled by the Ministry of State Security. The FBI later told us that they had known about

Mr. Jin for years but had never had the opportunity to speak to an American who'd met him. Jin's reputation was infamous.

Mr. Jin made the first statement. "Mr. Krechman, Mr. Wang and I have been friends for over thirty years." Sheldon tried to remain nonplused since, over the past several months, he had been sending letters to many top Chinese officials accusing Mr. Wang of theft, mismanagement of funds, and a variety of other charges that, if proven correct, would entitle Mr. Wang to an execution.

Sheldon thought for a while, having learned the valuable lesson to think before speaking in China, and then replied, "Mr. Wang has done a wonderful job in the development of the project, and we should thank him, for, without him, the project would never have happened."

Mr. Wang looked at Sheldon, smiled, and gave him a thumbs-up.

Mr. Jin smiled as well, looked at Sheldon in a very pleasant way, and said, "Mr. Krechman, you don't really expect me to pay this amount of money for your shares. The hotel is a losing proposition, and as a good businessman, I am sure that you will agree with me that the value of your shares is considerably less than what is stated in this agreement."

Sheldon told him that this had been negotiated by Mr. Wang. Mr. Jin replied that Mr. Wang was not the buyer, he was. We all looked at him, and even though we were surprised, we understood after years of doing business in China that the unexpected was considered normal.

Sheldon told Mr. Jin that as far as we were concerned, the meeting was over and that we were going to go directly to the United States Embassy and file an international complaint. Mr. Jin replied that we were welcome to use a hotel car and driver. That was the beginning of a negotiation that lasted three weeks.

After the initial meeting, we went off to the U.S. Embassy and spoke to Denny Barnes, even though we understood that there was really nothing that the embassy could do since it was a commercial transaction.

We returned to the hotel and met with Mr. Tian, Mr. Wang's

lawyer, and asked him for help. He explained to us that Mr. Jin was a very important and powerful personage, and it was all his decision.

Over the next two weeks, we held several meetings with the Chinese, yet the time went by without any resolution. Mr. Jin seemed to have disappeared, and all our negotiations reverted to Mr. Wang who was friendly but stubborn. He said that the real price for our shares would have to be half of what we had listed. We told him that was unacceptable and that we could only accept the number we agreed upon.

Every night, at about 11:00 p.m., the second elevator, which was next to the door to our room, would stop and open continually. Sheldon would go out and wedge one of the plastic slippers that came with our hotel room into the elevator door track to hold it closed. (The maintenance department was never to be found). At about midnight, someone would pull out the slipper, and the door would open and close all night long until about 8:00 a.m. when it would start functioning properly again, somehow miraculously repaired. We eventually almost got used to the noise of the opening and closing of the elevator doors.

Several impromptu meetings were held in which someone would come up and find us, and we would then meet in small groups for endless rounds of discussion. We were getting weary but knew the Chinese were trying to wear us down to their advantage.

But the food was great, and we had a chance to enjoy the hotel project that we had worked on tirelessly over the years. We ate in all the restaurants and examined every inch of the hotel from the inside out. I even made several lists of items to be repaired, replaced, or changed. We met all the employees and were treated like the owners. All our expenses were paid for by the joint venture, including our car and driver. The only expense we argued about was the overseas telephone charges. It remained a point of contention up to the day we left.

Frequent telephone conversations took place with Marty, our lawyer in Los Angeles. The three or four law firms involved, the judge, the banks, and, of course, Oxy were all very interested in settling this issue.

Things changed daily. Finally, we agreed on a value of $7.5 million dollars—close to our original agreement. However, when we sat down with Mr. Jin after negotiating this new agreement, he informed us that the Chinese government would deduct the relevant Chinese income tax from the payment. What that tax was and how it was to be calculated, no one quite knew.

We told him that the agreed-upon payment was to be paid in full, with no deductions. Mr. Jin said that he was not responsible as this was a PRC government tax issue. We informed Mr. Jin that he could do anything he wanted and that we would not agree with the settlement if there were any Chinese taxes deducted.

We negotiated for another week. Mr. Jin then suggested a new idea: If we worded the agreement in a specific way, we could avoid the taxes. The wording he wanted had no material change in the agreement. It was just a face-saving tactic.

After three weeks of stomach aches, headaches, and confusion, everything was agreed upon—at least, so we thought.

We then arranged a board of directors meeting to agree and ratify the sale agreement. Ms. Zhang flew in from Los Angeles to attend the meeting as she was a director and represented Mr. Yu's interest.

At the board meeting, she introduced a letter from Mr. Yu complaining that we had asked for a resolution whereby the funds would be put into a joint account and whereby none could be released without the signatures of both Sheldon and Mr. Yu. The new quasi-buyer, Mr. Jin, suggested stopping the process since there were apparently difficulties among the World China Trade directors. Sheldon, Joe, and I held an emergency board meeting in the next room.

Since collectively we owned more than 50 percent of the stock in World China Trade, we removed Ms. Zhang and Mr. Yu from the board. Ms. Zhang refused to vacate, and the Chinese, for the first time, did not seem to know what to do. We argued in the boardroom for two more days until finally convincing Ms. Zhang that our intention was not to take advantage of anyone and that she would get her rightful share. She then voted our way, and we re-instated her to the board.

Two hours before the signing ceremony, we met with Mr. Wang and told him that we had some unpaid expenses that were due and reminded him that we were also entitled to a director's fee for all the board meetings we had attended. He, of course, refused. We told him that we would not sign the agreement without getting paid our reimbursables and our fees.

Mr. Wang started screaming, "Now you want this, then you want that." I replied that it was in our contract, and we hadn't seen a dime of that money. Mr. Wang walked out in a huff and headed to his office upstairs. I took the contracts off the table, rolled them up, and went after him, yelling, "This isn't right. We've always been promised our board fees. We paid our own way here for years to have meeting after meeting to get this thing done, and we don't have a deal until we get paid." With that, Sheldon and I stormed up to our room.

About half an hour later, the doorbell rang. When I opened it, a man handed me a suitcase and left. I put the suitcase on the bed and opened it—it was filled with money—lots of it. Sheldon and I laughed and had a great time playing with the money and throwing it around on the bed. I finally put it in a bag and then back into the suitcase it had all arrived in. Then we went in to sign the documents.

Minutes before the signing ceremony, I produced some additional invoices for more reimbursables. Mr. Wang ran out of the room saying it was finished, no more, it was finished, as I followed out after him, waving the bills in my hand. Those were also paid.

Prior to the signing ceremony, the documents had to be translated and printed in both Chinese and English. We told Mr. Wang that we wanted an independent translator, having learned this lesson the hard way, to ensure that the documents said the same thing in both Chinese and English.

We requested Mr. Fan Shi Long, a friend unconnected to our joint venture partners. He was the editor of the magazine *China Reconstruct*, printed in six languages and distributed throughout the world. Mr. Fan did not have a private phone, so Mr. Wang sent a car and some public security officials to get him. Mr. Fan arrived, commanded respect, and did a very good job on the documents.

Mr. Jin took Sheldon aside—with an interpreter—and said, "Mr. Krechman, I want you to know that I have seen all the letters you have written about Mr. Wang to our government, and when we had our first meeting, you said such nice positive things about him, and I wonder why."

Sheldon looked at Mr. Jin and, after a few moments of thought, replied, "Mr. Jin, you are a master, and I would like to become your pupil, as I could learn much from you." Mr. Jin smiled, put his arm around Sheldon's shoulders, gave him a small hug, and walked away.

We expected a formal banquet, which we were not looking forward to. Much to our surprise, Mr. Jin had the special private room prepared for us, and only twelve people attended. It was very intimate. Mr. Wang was not invited.

Mr. Jin ordered the food and then ordered a very special rare (150 proof) Moutai wine. We started toasting. Mr. Jin would give a toast to me, and then Joe would give a toast to Mr. Jin, and then so forth around the table. By the time the first course of food was served, we were all blasted and didn't eat a thing. We just kept toasting.

Mr. Jin told Sheldon that I was a very smart person and very forceful and that he was henpecked. Sheldon agreed and told him they could share me. He laughed, and we all continued toasting for over two hours. Poor Joe was really gone, and we had to take him up to his room. We left him sitting on his bed. When we returned three hours later, he was still sitting stiffly on the bed. We laughed and a lot of the tension was released from all of us.

The final moment came with Sheldon, me, and Mr. Jin in the lobby of our hotel, all hugging goodbye in front of a multitude of Chinese people.

We then went off to visit the Israel Embassy in Beijing. We had been invited to a party with seven members of the Knesset, and a group of Israelis wanting to do business in China. At the party, we were asked by the group to help them understand how to do business with the Chinese. We told them to treat the Chinese like they were Israelis, but to also remember, "The journey of a thousand miles begins with the first step, and the ox moves slow, but the earth is patient."

The next day, our friends at the U.S. Embassy, including Denny Barnes and Agent Messemer—who was now assigned to the embassy—took us to the airport. We were flying to Hong Kong and, from there, back home. I carried the suitcase full of cash as we headed to the airport. The only flight we could get that day to Hong Kong was on China Airlines, which we rarely flew. We got onto the plane, which had a very strange configuration. We sat in first class, with the galley right behind us in the middle of the plane. Everyone from the embassy stood on the boarding bridges, waving goodbye to us, happy that we had safely made it on our flight.

Then they took the bridge down, and we rolled out to the tarmac, where we just sat, not moving at all, for quite some time. I began to get pretty nervous, and then, all of a sudden, right where I was sitting, the carpet on the floor of the plane rolled back to reveal a trapdoor. I watched two men in black overalls coming up the ladder beneath the door, my heart pounding so fast I could hear it beating in my ears. I was sure they were going to take us off the plane, take our money, and we would just disappear. That's what went through my mind in the five seconds it took them to get to the top of the ladder.

Well, as it thankfully turned out, they were mechanics, there to fix something in the galley behind us. We arrived safely in Hong Kong and turned the money over to our banker at Standard Chartered who, in turn, wired it to our bank in America.

When we returned to the United States, all the lawyers and the banks told us that we had failed—the Chinese would never send the funds as we agreed.

The day the agreement specified for the funds to be in our bank account in Los Angeles, Mr. Jin wired the total amount we had agreed upon.

About Face

~31~

The Deportation of
Mr. Yu Xue Wen

Fool me once, shame on you; fool me twice, shame on me.
~Anthony Weldon, 1651

IN THE SUMMER OF 1992, Agent Messemer called us from the federal prison in Terminal Island, in Wilmington which is in the Harbor area of Los Angeles. He stated that Mr. Yu was on trial, and a deportation hearing was scheduled for 1:00 p.m. that day. He was concerned that without our testimony, the court might not be able to find sufficient reason to deport Yu back to China, and, if left on his own recognizance, he might disappear in the United States. Messemer was frustrated. He had previously told us the political powers in Washington were against the FBI prosecuting Mr. Yu for his alleged espionage activities here in the United States. He needed our help.

At one point in the past, while Mr. Yu had been under heavy FBI surveillance, he told Messemer that if the agent traveled to Hong Kong to meet him, he would reveal all the details of the espionage activities that had gone on in the United States. Messemer received permission from his superiors in the Justice Department and headed to Hong Kong for the meeting.

When he arrived, he contacted Mr. Yu and asked to meet him

at a local restaurant. Mr. Yu said he was prepared to tell all to Agent Messemer but asked him to travel with him in an automobile to an undisclosed location. Messemer discussed this with the security personnel at the United States Embassy and was told he would be putting his life on the line. Mr. Yu's intentions might be devious.

Messemer took the advice of the security personnel and declined to go. Mr. Yu then refused to give Agent Messemer any information, and he returned to the United States.

After Agent Messemer's call, we immediately contacted our attorney who had worked with us in China. The three of us then got into our cars and drove down to the Terminal Island federal prison. The guard at the gate refused to allow us entry as we had no papers or credentials—only the name of Agent Messemer. Finally, the guard made a call to the prison officials, and Agent Messemer came down to the entry gate. The guard then opened the gate and allowed us into the prison compound.

Agent Messemer wore a special name tag; we, on the other hand, came in looking every bit like the civilians that we were. Prison officials questioned the agent regarding our identities and status. He explained that we were critical witnesses in the upcoming deportation hearing.

The agent ushered us into a room with a conference table and several chairs. We sat down as the deputy who was present closed the door to the room, which had a small window encased in steel mesh. I remarked to Agent Messemer about the lack of doorknobs and the fact that we were effectively locked in a room obviously meant for interrogation purposes. Agent Messemer seemed surprised and clearly uncomfortable over being locked in a room with no access out except for pounding on the door for a prison guard to unlock it.

Agent Messemer explained his concern over Mr. Yu potentially being released and reiterated how critical it was that we and our lawyer testify to Mr. Yu's activities and the history of our joint venture. Agent Messemer then went to the door and knocked very loudly. It took ten minutes before a prison staff member came to open the door and release us. The prison staff person questioned Agent Messemer as if we were in custody and told us we could not leave the room. Messemer countered that we were civilians there to testify in the up-coming deportation hearing.

We were then ushered into another room, this one with inside doorknobs, and left alone. On the desk sat a brief detailing what had transpired since the arrest of Mr. Yu three days earlier. The brief stated that Mr. Yu had been arrested and detained upon arrival at the Los Angeles office of immigration, where he had gone to supposedly receive his green card status.

Mr. Yu was being sponsored by a local California businessman who had falsified Yu's green card application. When the California businessman learned that Mr. Yu was under heavy surveillance and investigation by the FBI and that Mr. Yu had been less than truthful with him, he wrote to the immigration bureau and canceled the application and sponsorship. When the bureau received these documents, they concluded that Mr. Yu was in this country illegally, and, after consultation with Agent Messemer, they decided to detain him and keep him manacled and held incommunicado until the deportation hearing could be convened.

The immigration bureau and Agent Messemer decided that it was in the best interests of our country that Mr. Yu not be allowed to see anyone prior to the hearing, so they moved him in manacles from jail to jail until finally transporting to the federal prison in Terminal Island for the hearing the same morning we arrived. Agent Messemer brought in the federal immigration prosecutor to meet with us. She was obviously not fully prepared and did not have all the pertinent facts regarding this case. We briefly discussed some of the facts and then entered the courtroom for the hearing.

The immigration judge, like the prosecutor, was a woman, as was Mr. Yu's attorney. I could see the strain on Agent Messemer's face, as he had spent many years investigating Mr. Yu and was very concerned that the hearing would go in Mr. Yu's favor.

We all assembled in the courtroom. If looks could kill, we would have been eliminated by the dark daggers Mr. Yu sent our way.

The hearing began with the prosecuting attorney's opening

statement. She then called each of us to the stand to testify regarding Mr. Yu and his past activities. Our lawyer then took the stand and produced several documents that were most damaging to Mr. Yu.

Mr. Yu became very agitated and started stomping his feet on the floor and shouting that he was innocent and was being persecuted by Agent Messemer and the United States government. The judge warned him to be quiet, and after a short while, Mr. Yu calmed down.

Mr. Yu then took the stand, denying all the allegations against him. He reiterated his statement of being unfairly persecuted and declared that he was a Chinese citizen in good standing and not related to any political party. The prosecutor asked him why his passport stamp indicated that he was a member of the communist party. He replied that an error must have been made when his passport was issued to him.

The judge finally called a recess and told the court and Mr. Yu that she would not make any decision in this matter for at least six weeks. During that time, Mr. Yu would remain incommunicado. His lawyer objected and requested that Mr. Yu be allowed to at least go to his apartment to collect his clothes and other possessions. The judge refused and said that after hearing the testimony, she believed that Mr. Yu posed a potential threat to our government and its national security.

She then offered Mr. Yu and his attorney the choice of immediate deportation, with the stipulation that Mr. Yu and his immediate family would never again be allowed into the United States for any reason whatsoever, and that copies of these proceedings would be sent to immigration authorities in other countries having the same sympathies as the United States. Mr. Yu's attorney asked the judge for a recess so that she could discuss this choice with Mr. Yu.

The court reconvened an hour later. Mr. Yu's attorney stated to the judge that Yu would agree to be deported immediately if he could spend a few days saying goodbye to all his friends and collect his personal belongings. Mr. Yu also requested that he be allowed to take a regularly scheduled airline back to China.

The judge listened to the request and then stated that this was not acceptable at all. If Mr. Yu accepted what the judge suggested, the court would notify the Chinese government that Mr. Yu was being deported, and he would then be taken in handcuffs by a federal U.S. Marshal to San Francisco, then handed over to CAAC for transportation back to Beijing.

Mr. Yu, having no other choice, accepted the proposal. After his transport to the airport that same day, he traveled, accompanied by the marshal, to San Francisco. CAAC refused to take Mr. Yu on orders from their superiors. The federal marshal then arranged to fly Mr. Yu to Tokyo, where he was handed over to the Tokyo authorities, who then sent him back to China in disgrace.

Epilogue

Let China sleep, for when she wakes,
she will shake the world.
~Napoleon Bonaparte

AFTER WE SOLD THE hotel back to the Chinese and Mr. Yu had been deported, Sheldon and Bob Messemer continued to meet on a regular basis for many years. He always asked when we planned on writing a book about our experiences. Bob continually told Sheldon that if we really knew the whole story, it would surprise us, and that this investigation was the pinnacle of his career.

Finally, in 1998, Sheldon started to put down on paper some of our experiences. When he told Bob we had decided to write the book, he was very encouraging, and over the next several months, they emailed each other and met for lunch frequently.

He told Sheldon to be prepared: there would be some very unhappy people in China when this book surfaced—we might be the target of retaliation. He suggested hiring a bodyguard after the book got published, a suggestion he reiterated several times in subsequent conversations.

Every time they met, Sheldon kept asking about whatever files the FBI kept on World China Trade and us. Messemer kept mentioning

283

voluminous amounts of material, all classified. So, it would be difficult if not impossible to acquire the files. At one lunch, he suggested going through FOIA (Freedom of Information Act) to see if we could obtain them.

Sheldon secured the proper form and sent it to the FBI FOIA office in Washington D.C. Three weeks later, they acknowledged receipt of our request but said it was necessary to send them a notarized statement indicating that Sheldon was the person who was requesting the information. He sent it off; four weeks later, he received a form reply that they had searched their databases back twenty-plus years but found no files corresponding either to World China Trade or Sheldon Krechman or Carole Krechman. Sheldon then posted an appeal. Another four weeks passed, and he received a sheet of paper—that was obviously not a form letter—that stated they had again searched all the files and that they were closing this issue. They suggested that he contact the FBI office in LA.

Very frustrated at that point, we traveled to Washington D.C., where we met with Senator John Kerry's chief of staff, explained our situation, and asked for help. She, in turn, introduced us to John Kerry's intelligence aid, who met with us, asked a lot of questions, such as, "Do you still have those papers that you found?" (referring to the two million dollars transferred from our joint venture account by Mr. Wang), and said that he would investigate the matter.

We also met with the state department's liaison to the White House, who also promised to investigate. He assured us that he would keep our documents in a safe. Later, he shared with us that intelligence told him, "Not to touch this with a ten-foot pole."

Sheldon then wrote to the FBI office in Los Angeles and waited for several weeks. We finally received a letter stating that they had found the files, but Sheldon had to go through the process of notarization again, which he did.

After several more weeks, he then called the FBI legal counsel, who was the signatory to the letter we received, and asked about the files. He complained that their office was understaffed and overworked and that he had no idea at all when we could expect the files.

He explained that every word in every document would have to be gone over to see if any of the content was classified, and if so, it would be stricken from the file.

We waited several more weeks and received a letter from the Los Angles FBI office saying that the request had been sent back to the head office in Washington D.C., and we had been assigned a file in their system.

Finally, after several weeks, we received the thousands of pages of highly anticipated documents, but to our immense disappointment, they provided absolutely no insights into what the FBI and the CIA had uncovered. Why? Because nearly every single page was redacted with huge, blacked-out boxes covering the information. Would we ever know if any of the two million dollars Mr. Wang had transferred from our joint venture into various banks in Canada and the U.S. was used to buy nuclear secrets?

Coincidently, in 1999, not long after we received the redacted documents, a federal court hearing in Albuquerque made national news when *The New York Times* reported that China, working with nuclear secrets stolen from the United States, had taken the lead in the development of miniature nuclear warheads. The investigation centered on a Los Alamos nuclear scientist, Wen Ho Lee, who was accused of fifty-nine counts of mishandling classified information by downloading nuclear secrets—"weapons codes" used for computer simulations of nuclear weapons tests—to data tapes and removing them from the lab. He was suspected of having shared U.S. nuclear secrets with China.

The investigation was led by none other than FBI Agent Robert Messemer who testified at Lee's arraignment that he effectively had declassified the equivalent of more than four hundred thousand printed pages of highly classified computer data.

Investigators were never able to establish what Lee did with the downloaded data, and a huge public outcry ensued that he had been made a scapegoat. After ten months in jail, Lee pleaded guilty to a single count, and the other fifty-eight charges were dismissed with an apology from U.S. District Judge James Parker for his incarceration.

In 2021, as this book was underway, I once again reached out to the Los Angeles FBI department under the Freedom of Information Act to see if I could get the FBI documents on World China Trade. Since nearly thirty years had passed, I thought perhaps some of the classified information might now be declassified, and we might discover the long-awaited answers to our questions. After several phone calls, I was told there were no records of World China Trade, and the files did not go back that far.

≈ ≈ ≈ ≈ ≈

Throughout the years, during our trips home from China, we would occasionally visit Dr. Hammer, usually at his home. Richard Chen kept him up to date on our business activities, and often, we would talk about his art or other interests of his. He once gave me a beautiful poster signed by the artist Chin Yiffi Fey from his gallery. We were like family, and he was excited and proud of what we had accomplished.

Our experience in China, including all the drama, intrigue, and frustrations, became the adventure of a lifetime, and none of it would have happened if Dr. Hammer had not facilitated our entry into this land of mystery, ambiguity, incredible culture, and history, and given us a chance to meet the real Chinese people in the People's Republic of China. I am often asked if Sheldon and I thought Dr. Hammer had an agenda for us, and if we were just pawns in a bigger game. Looking back, I think he truly believed the roller rinks had potential in China, and he also came to realize that our presence there was good PR for him during his difficult negotiations with the Chinese for the coal mines. Over the years, he made many wonderful connections for us, and up until his death, he did his best to protect our financial interests there as well.

≈ ≈ ≈ ≈ ≈

After we sold the hotel back to the Chinese, Sheldon returned to China once with our son. (That's a story for another book.) I have not been back, but I look forward to returning one day. The Asia Hotel is still thriving in Beijing—a world-class hotel that was ahead of its time in many ways, and one that has stood the test of time. It's an accomplishment I will always be proud of.

≈≈≈≈≈

We live in very uncertain and perilous times. China makes no secret of its desire to dominate the world. We can continue to ignore the very real threat that China presents to a free world and our global economy, or we can take charge of our destiny.

Let's not forgot Napoleon's prophecy.

Acknowledgements

MY HUSBAND SHELDON WOULD have been so thrilled to see this book come to fruition. It had been a dream of his to tell our story for many years. I'm grateful for all the memories and stories of our years in China that he put down on paper over the years. They helped to jog my memories of key events and many other experiences during our time there, that have come together to make this book a reality.

I know Sheldon would also want me to acknowledge FBI Agent Robert Messemer, who became a good friend and confidant of Sheldon's long after we returned from China, and who encouraged Sheldon to tell our story.

There would of course be no story, without Dr. Armand Hammer who encouraged us to explore opportunities in China. He was a wonderful mentor who helped to make important business connections for us over the years and did his best to protect our interests in China.

I am grateful for the support of dear friends who have been there for me over the past two years since Sheldon's death and urged me to write this book. It helped to ease this sad and painful time for me.

I especially thank Suzanne Harvey and Carol Contes, for reading the book as it evolved and cheering me on to the finish line.

Special thanks to Simone Montavlo for the beautiful cover design and for helping with the images in the book.

And to Cheryl Benton, my editor and publisher, thank you for your enthusiastic response to my story, for your unparalleled editing skills, patience, and your knowledge and professionalism as publisher which resulted in a beautifully produced book.

Every book needs a good PR team, and I thank Devon Blaine and her group for getting the word out.

About the Author

I̲T'S NOT UNUSUAL FOR someone trained as an architect to have extraordinary vision. It's what they do. And Carole Sumner Krechman has brought this vision to all areas of her business, philanthropic and personal life alike. She's also a thought leader. In technology, international business and peacemaking.

A serial international entrepreneur, architect by education and training, Carole built a successful design company that spanned the globe. In the 1980s operating out of Beijing, thanks to her benefactor, Dr. Armand Hammer, late chairman of Oxy Petroleum, Sheldon and Carole Sumner Krechman spent eight more years doing business in China and completing the project. The team found investors and lenders, built their vision into the Beijing Asia Hotel, created the design team with Chinese, Japanese, Hong Kong, and Thailand natives joining her as the first American woman to design and develop a modern,

Western hotel, apartments and office building in downtown Beijing.

Krechman is likely the only 80-year-old woman to be awarded a technology patent from the US government. This patent creates a foundational change in how we communicate, delivering video to any cell phone on demand. Additionally, Carole is concurrently the Chairman, Founder and President of the Peacemaker Corps Association, a non-profit dedicated to teaching children around the world how to make "Peace in the Streets." PCA is a United Nations NGO with ESCSOC status. www.peacemakerscorps.org (www.PSGFF.com).

As a life-long activist/volunteer and former Chairman of the Board of Friends of the United Nations, with 30 years of volunteer service to the UN, she was honored for her years of philanthropy and innovation by receiving the 2008 Purpose Prize Fellowship. This award is similar to a Nobel Peace Prize just for seniors.

Made in the USA
Columbia, SC
19 August 2023

21772179R00178